DEALING WITH SATAN

By the same author

Nine Suitcases by Béla Zsolt (translation)

DEALING WITH SATAN

Rezső Kasztner's Daring Rescue Mission

Ladislaus Löb

A SURVIVOR'S TALE

JONATHAN CAPE
LONDON

Published by Jonathan Cape 2008

2 4 6 8 10 9 7 5 3 1

First published in Great Britain in 2008 by
Jonathan Cape
Random House, 20 Vauxhall Bridge Road,
London SW1V 2SA

www.rbooks.co.uk

Addresses for companies within The Random House Group Limited can be found at:
www.randomhouse.co.uk/offices.htm

The Random House Group Limited Reg. No. 954009

A CIP catalogue record for this book
is available from the British Library

ISBN 9780224077927

The Random House Group Limited makes every effort to ensure that the papers used in
its books are made from trees that have been legally sourced from well-managed and
credibly certified forests. Our paper procurement policy can be found at:
www.rbooks.co.uk/environment

Mixed Sources
Product group from well-managed
forests and other controlled sources
www.fsc.org Cert no. TT-COC-2139
FSC © 1996 Forest Stewardship Council

Typeset by Palimpsest Book Production Ltd, Grangemouth, Stirlingshire
Printed and bound in Great Britain by Mackays of Chatham plc, Chatham, Kent

For Egon Mayer

CONTENTS

Acknowledgements

This book, like most, could not have been written without the help of many people. I am profoundly grateful to the following:

To Zsuzsi Kasztner, for so unstintingly sharing her intimate knowledge of her father with me; to Zsuzsi's daughters Merav, Michal and Keren, for making me feel welcome during my work on the story of their grandfather; and to Zsuzsi's cousin Yitzhak Katsir, for improving my understanding of his uncle's life and work by many judicious comments.

To Egon Mayer, of New York, an unborn child in Bergen-Belsen, for strengthening my resolve to do Kasztner justice, as he would have done in a book left unfinished when he died aged fifty-nine; and to Egon's daughter Daphne and his widow Marcia, for their continuing interest in my project.

To Israeli academics Yehuda Bauer, Shlomo Aronson, Yechiam Weitz and Aryeh Barnea, for their precious time and expert advice.

To Thomas Rahe, Klaus Tätzler, Bernd Horstmann, Karin Theile, Stefanie Billib at the Bergen-Belsen Memorial, for so readily providing me with documentation and information; to Rainer Schulze of the University of Essex and Winfried Wiedemann of the Foundation for Memorials in Lower Saxony, for giving me access to the Memorial's resources; to Axel Brandt and Bertram von Boxberg, for allowing me to quote from interviews held at the Memorial.

To Yad Vashem, the Shoah Foundation, the Memorial Museum of Hungarian Speaking Jewry, the YIVO Institute for Jewish Research, the Center for Oral History at the University of Connecticut, and the Imperial War Museum, for supplying me with important archival material.

To fellow-survivors Shoshana Hasson, Peretz and Nonika Revesz, Tamar Abraham, Judit Makai, Ariela Mayer, Naomi Herskovitz, Lea Fürst, Margit Fendrich and Miryam Sommerfeld, for meeting me in Israel to exchange memories of life in the concentration camp.

To my step-brother David Kohn in Haifa, for many thoughtful suggestions.

To Victor and Miki Harnik in Haifa, for going out of their way to give me all the practical and moral support I needed.

To Gaylen Ross in New York, for responding so generously to all my queries while filming her own documentary on Kasztner.

To Ellah Allfrey and Will Sulkin at Random House, for guiding the book safely from proposal to publication, and to Vanessa Mitchell, for her thorough and sensitive copy editing.

To Sheila, my long-suffering wife, for persevering with her criticisms of my manuscript despite my protests.

To all of them my warmest thanks for their help and my apologies where I have failed to make the best use of it.

Ladislaus Löb
Brighton, 2007

Illustrations

1 Ladislaus Löb, aged five with parents Izsó and Jolán Löb
2 Ladslaus Löb, aged nine 3 Jolán Löb, 1940 4 Löb family
5 Rezső Kasztner, 1947 6 Rezső Kasztner with wife and child
(by kind permission of Kasztner family) 7 Zionist Leaders (from
Szaboles Szita: *Trading in Lives? Operations of the Jewish Relief
and Rescue Committee in Budapest, 1944–1945*) 8 Shmuel Tamir
(photograph by David Rubinger) 9 Joel Brand (from Szita:
Trading in Lives?) 10 Hansi Brand (from Szita: *Trading in Lives?*)
11 Judge Halevi (© Yad Vashem, the Holocaust Martyrs' and
Heroes' Remembrance Authority) 12 Adolf Eichmann (© Yad
Vashem, the Holocaust Martyrs' and Heroes' Remembrance
Authority) 13 Kurt Becher 14 Dieter Wisliceny 15 Hermann
Krumey (© Yad Vashem, the Holocaust Martyrs' and Heroes'
Remembrance Authority) 16 Irma Grese and Josef Kramer
(© Yad Vashem, the Holocaust Martyrs' and Remembrance
Authority) 17 Bunk beds cartoon (© Irsai) 18 Loaves of bread
cartoon (© Irsai) 19 Béla Zsolt 20 Leopold Szondi (© The
Szondi Institute) 21 Joel Teitelbaum (© exclusive publishing
rights by Trainer Studios) 22 Dezső Ernster (© The Metropolitan
Archives) 23 Bergen-Belsen (© Yad Vashem, the Holocaust
Martyrs' and Heroes' Remembrance Authority) 24 Bergen-
Belsen deserted (© Bergen-Belsen archives) 25 Ladislaus Löb
as a child refugee, aged eleven 26 Löb Senior 27 Rezső Kasztner
with daughter (by kind permission of Kasztner family)

Key Persons

Vaada and associates
Barlas, Chaim, Jewish Agency representative
Biss, Endre, Vaada member
Brand, Hansi, Vaada member
Brand, Joel, Vaada member
Dobkin, Eliahu, Jewish Agency member
Fischer, József, leader of Bergen-Belsen group
Fleischmann, Gizi, Zionist activist
Goldstein, Peretz, parachutist
Kasztner, Rezső, Vaada executive vice-chairman
Komoly, Otto, Vaada chairman
Krausz, Moshe, head of Budapest Palestine Office
Mayer, Saly, Swiss Joint representative
McClelland, Roswell, US War Refugee Board representative
Offenbach, Shulem, Vaada member
Palgi, Joel, parachutist
Schweiger, Moshe, Vaada member
Sharett, Moshe, Jewish Agency member
Springmann, Samu, Vaada member
Szenes, Hanna, parachutist
Weissmandel, Michael Dov, rabbi

Germans
Becher, Kurt, SS Obersturmbannführer (lieutenant-colonel)
Eichmann, Adolf, SS Obersturmbannführer (lieutenant-colonel)

Grüson, Max, SS Hauptsturmführer (captain)

Himmler, Heinrich, Reichsführer-SS (SS supreme commander)

Hunsche, Otto, Hauptsturmführer (captain)

Kaltenbrunner, Ernst, SS Oberführer (head of SS security)

Kettlitz, Herbert, SS Sturmbannführer (major)

Klages, Otto, SS Obersturmbannführer (lieutenant-colonel)

Krell, Erich, SS Hauptsturmführer (captain)

Krumey, Hermann, SS Obersturmbannführer (lieutenant-colonel)

Müller, Heinrich, SS Gruppenführer (squad leader)

Veesenmayer, Edmund, SS Brigadeführer (brigadier-general, ambassador to Hungary)

Wisliceny, Dieter, SS Hauptsturmführer (captain)

Hungarians

Horthy, Miklós, Regent

Szálasi, Ferenc, Arrow Cross leader

Sztójay, Döme, Prime Minister

Israelis

Agranat, Shimon, Supreme Court judge

Gruenwald, Malkiel, defendant

Halevi, Benjamin, District Court judge

Silberg, Moshe, Supreme Court judge

Tamir, Shmuel, attorney

Foreword

Two months and a day after my eleventh birthday the gates of Bergen-Belsen concentration camp closed behind me. It was 9 July 1944. Five months later, with the Second World War set to last another half-year, I crossed the border into neutral Switzerland. As the Allies were closing in on Nazi Germany, and the camp I had left was turning into the hell commonly known as 'Belsen', I was looking down on Lake Geneva with its peaceful backdrop of snow-covered mountains, stunned but alive and safe. I was not alone, but one of 1,670 Jewish men, women and children from Hungary who had been released from Belsen thanks to a unique deal between another Hungarian Jew, Rezső Kasztner, and Adolf Eichmann, the chief architect of the Holocaust. In fact Kasztner saved many more, but ten years on he was accused of collaborating with the SS. In a law court in Israel, a modern, democratic country in the twentieth century, a judge ruled that Kasztner had 'sold his soul to Satan'. Eventually the highest court in the land reversed the judgement, but by that time Kasztner was dead. The Jew who had saved more Jews from the Holocaust than any other Jew had been gunned down in a street in Tel Aviv by a Jewish gang.

The repercussions went far beyond the private sphere. The issues were deeply rooted in Israeli politics and the violent arguments surrounding the case rocked the young state to its foundations. The trial marked the beginning of Israel's gradual shift to the right, which still determines the course of events in the Middle East.

Kasztner himself remains a controversial figure: a traitor to some, a hero to others. This book is based on the belief that the second assessment is nearer the truth. It tells the story of a man who had the courage and resourcefulness to stand up to the Nazi mass murderers and save thousands of lives before being assassinated for his pains. It tells the story of how 1,670 people survived in Bergen-Belsen until he rescued them at the last moment before hell broke loose. Finally, it tells the story of one child who, thanks to him, lived to grow up after the Holocaust.

This book brings the three stories together in a detailed and comprehensive narrative. Accordingly, it concentrates on three main topics: Kasztner's negotiations with the SS in Hungary, Germany and Switzerland; the everyday life of the 'Kasztner group' in Bergen-Belsen; and the trial and assassination of Kasztner in Israel. The events are no longer completely unknown. They are discussed, from one point of view or another, in greater or lesser depth, in a number of books, chapters and articles, mostly by Israeli academics. They also appear in many newspaper and internet commentaries, ranging from the serious and responsible to the unscrupulously tendentious and scurrilous. I have tried to steer clear of both the academic and the journalistic extremes. My aim is to be as accurate and as objective as possible, and at the same time to appeal to the general reader rather than to the historian, lawyer or political scientist. While most existing publications are primarily concerned either with Kasztner's negotiations or with his trial and assassination, I have placed equal emphasis on our own everyday experiences in Bergen-Belsen while we were waiting to be saved by him.

As a child of eleven I was of course too young to understand all that was happening to us in Bergen-Belsen, but old enough to notice many things and to acquire what are now patchy memories. To fill the gaps, and to add a more mature perspective to my juvenile recollections, I have drawn on many conversations with fellow-survivors and a wealth of unpublished reminiscences, memoirs and interviews from archives in Israel, the USA and Germany.

For Kasztner's negotiations my prime source was a report written by the man himself soon after the war, which was eventually published in German under the title *Der Kasztner-Bericht*. While Kasztner is clearly trying to present his own case in the most favourable light, the report, used with some caution, is an indispensable account of his work with – or rather against – the SS.

A few words about the structure of the book. The first chapter is about my own childhood memories of life in a small, anti-Semitic town in Transylvania. The next chapter locates these particular memories in the wider context of the Holocaust in Hungary. The subsequent chapters move to and fro between two parallel stories. My stay in the ghetto of Kolozsvár is followed by the beginnings of Kasztner's 'relief and rescue committee' and the first phase of his negotiations with Eichmann, leading up to our departure from Budapest to Bergen-Belsen. Kasztner's continuing encounters with the SS alternate with scenes from our daily round in captivity, ending with our release to Switzerland. The narrative then shifts to Geneva and Nuremberg, where Kasztner spent most of the first three years after the war. It ends with Kasztner's ill-fated trial and his assassination in Israel.

Kasztner had to face terrible situations and resolve appalling dilemmas. He had neither the time nor the temperament to engage in lengthy reflections about the ethical implications of what he was doing. He saw that lives were at risk and he acted as quickly and as decisively as he could to save them. Without ignoring the excruciating moral issues raised by his dealings with some of the most evil men ever known, I believe that what he did was right. I hope that this account will assist the recognition that is due to his astonishing achievement.

CHAPTER 1
A Jewish Child among Jew-haters

A small town in Transylvania

I was about six years old when I had my first conscious experience of anti-Semitism. A Hungarian lout, probably in his late teens, was sauntering along the main street of our small town in Northern Transylvania, bawling a scurrilous song to the tune of 'Hatikvah' – the anthem of Zionism then and the national anthem of Israel today. I did not catch the text as a whole, but I still remember the refrain: 'Bloody Jews, stinking Jews, go to Palestine'. I also remember wondering whether the singer was mad and whether somebody would come to arrest him. Nobody did.

That was in 1939. Northern Transylvania, previously part of the Austro-Hungarian Empire, had belonged to Romania since the Trianon Treaty of 1920, which was meant to tidy things up after the First World War. They were not tidy enough for some, and in 1940, one year into the Second World War, Hitler forced the Romanians to return the region to his Hungarian allies as a reward for services rendered. The red-yellow-and-blue Romanian flags on public buildings and private houses were swiftly replaced with red-white-and-green Hungarian ones, and the Hungarian army came marching in as if it had won a famous victory. On 19 March 1944

the Germans occupied Hungary, and the two countries, which nevertheless continued to be allies, jointly lost the Second World War. In
1945 it was the Soviet Union's turn to be generous with other people's
territories and Northern Transylvania was once again apportioned
to Romania.

Between 1920 and 1940 the majority of the inhabitants had been
Hungarians who bitterly resented the Romanian rule. From 1940 the
Romanians, still a minority, were equally hostile to the Hungarian
regime. Today there is a growing Romanian majority and the two
communities are said to be developing a kind of peaceful coexistence.
Perhaps it will work, but I cannot help thinking that the only time I
have seen Hungarians and Romanians forgetting to hate each other
was when they were busy hating the Jews. For the Jews themselves,
life in Transylvania under the Romanians had been uncomfortable
but bearable. After the Hungarian takeover it became much harder.
The German occupation of Hungary, including Transylvania, brought
the final disaster, when the two allies promptly joined forces to complete
the last stage of the Holocaust. The few Jewish survivors who subsequently returned to the region were not made to feel welcome.

I was born on 8 May 1933 in the capital of Transylvania – Kolozsvár
in Hungarian, Cluj in Romanian. I was the only child of Izsó Löb
and Jolán Löb, née Rosenberg. We lived in a small town, or rather
an overgrown village, called Margitta (or Marghita), about 150 km
north-west of what I will continue to call Kolozsvár.[1] Before March
1944 Margitta had about 8,600 inhabitants, of whom 2,600 were
Jews. By mid-May 1944 it had about 6,000, of whom none were
Jews. After the Holocaust some 400 of the 2,600 Jews were still alive,
but very few of them went back to live among neighbours who had
proved so unneighbourly.

Since the Second World War Margitta has seen the development
of some new industries and part of its original village architecture
has been replaced by jerry-built concrete blocks in the notorious
communist style. In the nineteen-thirties and forties it was an

agricultural town, surrounded by wheat fields, orchards, pastures and vineyards. The streets were unpaved, unlit at night, thick with dust in dry weather and in wet weather covered in mud so deep that the carts drawn by oxen or horses often got hopelessly stuck. Our own street was called 'Sáros utca', Muddy Street. Lined by acacia and mulberry trees, it led out to the vineyards and the Jewish cemetery on the hillside beyond. That was where my mother was buried at the age of thirty-six, when I was nine.

Each morning the town's cows were driven through the streets to the pastures and each evening back to their stables. I was fascinated by the way their udders had swollen during the day. Many of these cows were infected with TB, the disease that killed my mother, although she may have picked it up not from the cows but rather from her dressmaker, who was said to have TB and who used to spread her customers' clothes on her bed. For a while my father had a special licence to sell salt, both wholesale and retail. The salt trade was a state monopoly and such licences were awarded to veterans of the First World War decorated in compensation for their wounds. His store was in the main street and he kept a large block of salt in front of the door, where the passing cows regularly stopped for a lick before continuing their walk.

Most of the buildings in Margitta were single-storey, some with storks' nests on their chimneys, and hen-coops, pigsties, stables, water wells and other paraphernalia of rural life in their back yards. We rented the ground floor of a rare two-storey villa, whose owner lived in a hut at the bottom of the garden. We were a relatively well-off, more or less middle-class family, but still had to get water from a well and use an outdoor privy. We had (somewhat erratic) electricity, but no phone or radio. Every noon a town crier would walk the streets, beating his drum and reading out the news when people had gathered from the houses nearby. If a plane flew over the village all the children – and some adults – would run outside, craning their necks to stare at it. I remember my excitement when a small single-propeller machine flew so low that I could see the face of the pilot in his leather helmet and thick goggles. Cars were rarer than carts and had to be started with a crank. Train or bus connections to the world outside, although they existed, were infrequent. On the buses children shorter than a metre, as measured against a rule drawn near the door, paid half fare. When the trains were slowed down by track repairs, passengers would leap off into the fields and then clamber back on, loaded with potatoes and onions, before the engine regathered speed. Later there were trains which people could not jump off because they were sealed and guarded by armed gendarmes.

Jews lived in every part of the town, but were concentrated in and around Main Street, which was also called Petri Street as it ran on towards the village of that name. The half-hour hike to Petri through the wheat fields lined with poppies and cornflowers was one of the earliest explorations I remember. While the markets and stockyards were at the other end of the town, most of the shops and offices were in the Petri Street area, as were the premises of the Jewish institutions. There was an impressive Great Synagogue for the mainstream Jewish community, built in the 1860s and extended in 1910, and a smaller one for the Chassidic congregation. Apart from their official purpose, the synagogues were ideal places for exchanging the latest news and discussing business during prayers, while copiously spitting on the bare wooden floor. There was a *mikveh* where the faithful took their weekly ritual bath, a *matzot* bakery that supplied the unleavened bread for Passover, and a *cheder* where the Orthodox children received their religious training. When the Jews were deported, the Great Synagogue became a warehouse and the Chassidic synagogue a stable.

There were three Christian churches. The Catholic and the Reformed were built in the eighteenth century, painted in warm ochre and topped by the onion spires typical of the region; the Eastern Orthodox hailed from the nineteenth century and supported a mass of silvery domes. When I visited Margitta after the war the three

Christian churches were still standing and showed signs of careful maintenance. There was no Great Synagogue, no Chassidic synagogue and no ritual bath. When I asked people in the street what had happened to them, nobody seemed to know. Eventually I discovered that the Great Synagogue had been pulled down in 1977. Not that it mattered. There was nobody left to use it anyway.

The 2,600 or so Jews of Margitta represented all segments of Hungarian Jewry. There were some socialists or communists. There were Zionists, ranging from the far right to the far left. There were Chassidim with dangling sidelocks, dressed in black kaftans and wide fur hats, whose wives, as prescribed, were shaved bald under their wigs. But the majority were moderately religious and fairly well-educated Neologues, who identified with traditional Hungarian society and culture but still considered themselves Jewish and more or less assiduously observed the important festivals. This last group comprised most of the professional and business people in the town. My own father and mother mixed mainly with them, and their children were my friends. With the Gentiles we had little social contact. For all our assimilation we were different from the Hungarians and unwanted by them. To us they were a vaguely hostile presence, to be avoided whenever possible. To some extent I was the stereotype of the sheltered middle-class Jewish boy whose education in good manners, politeness and sensitivity did not exactly make life easy when confronted with rough Hungarian peasant kids. But I would not refuse the occasional chance to join a chaotic game of football in the street.

On Saturdays most of the shops were closed and the streets were full of Jews going to the synagogues. At midday Jewish housewives appeared everywhere, bearing home the earthenware pots in which the traditional *cholent*, beans with smoked goose breast, had been simmering since Friday in the Jewish baker's oven and beating the law that forbids any work, including the pressing of a switch or the striking of a match, on the Sabbath. Another regular feature was the Saturday afternoon promenade. The young Jewish men and women, in their smartest clothes, would converge on the town centre. Strolling up and down Main Street in small groups, the sexes strictly segregated, they seemed to be absorbed in their conversations, but were in fact observing each other intently out of the corners of their eyes. Personally, I thought this game boring and usually tried to track down my friends and do something interesting.

True to form, Jews played a leading part in the commercial and professional life of Margitta, although there were no Jewish civil servants. Three of the town's six lawyers were Jewish, as were both pharmacists and all four medical practitioners. Dr Emil Goldberger was one of the best-known characters. He acted as his own receptionist, secretary and lab technician, and was constantly seen dashing to his patients' bedsides in a carriage and pair – often forgetting to charge the poorer ones for these home visits. On a less happy note, I can still taste the cod liver oil he used to prescribe for me as a tonic. Jews in business included a landowner, two wine-growers, four wholesale merchants, two bankers, two tobacconists, a grocer, a hairdresser, a haberdasher and a wine-seller. There were also rabbis, teachers and circumcisers employed by the religious communities; several self-employed Jewish joiners, tailors and cobblers; and labourers, odd-job men, and others of uncertain occupation and income. One of the richest men was József Wollner, who owned a small shoe factory. Most of the buildings around the small passageway between Petri Street and Körtvélyes Street belonged to him. I do not know the official name of the passageway, if indeed it had one. Everyone called it 'Wollner sikátor', Wollner Lane. An outstanding Jewish institution was the 'Kóser' run by József Klein and his three sons, Ferenc, Miklós and László. This kosher restaurant, bar, café and hotel was the favourite meeting place in town, even for many Gentiles, who enjoyed the excellent Jewish food and the cosy atmosphere.

In short, Margitta was a *shtetl* like many others in Hungary up to the Second World War. Like the others, it owed much of its prosperity and culture to its Jews, and like the others, it sent them to their deaths when the opportunity presented itself.

My family

I was four years old when my mother caught TB. Streptomycin was still unknown and we had neither the money nor the opportunity to send her to a sanatorium in Switzerland, where she might or might not have been cured. So she spent five years in bed in Hungary and died when I was nine. All that time I had to keep at a safe distance from her for fear that I might become infected. When I wanted to talk to her I had to stop in the doorway, and there was no question of even the slightest physical contact. I can imagine how painful this must have been for both of us, but I cannot recapture any feelings. I must have been good at blotting out unpleasant things. Ironically, it was discovered many years later that my lungs were scarred. I had in fact had TB and recovered without anybody realising that it was more than a bad cold or flu. I do not know whether this happened during my stay in Bergen-Belsen or at some other time. In any case, all the misery of being kept at more than arm's length from my mother had been quite unnecessary.

Towards the end of my mother's illness I was sent to stay with my grandfather and aunt in Kolozsvár. My father and my grandmother were in Margitta, looking after my mother. One morning I was overcome by a restlessness I had never felt before. In the afternoon a telegram arrived and my aunt told me to get ready to travel to Margitta because my mother was getting worse. The only train available that night stopped a few stations short of Margitta. Everything was closed, except for a cold and dusty waiting room that seemed to be darkened rather than lit by a bare bulb. I stretched out on one of the benches, but was too tense to sleep. It was then that my aunt explained to me that my mother had actually died in the morning. I spent the next hours alternating between crying and dozing. At daybreak an enterprising drayman turned up on the off-chance of picking up a

fare before the train to Margitta was due. Wrapped in coarse blankets, we completed the last leg of our journey on a horse-drawn
sledge. It was January 1942.

When we arrived in Margitta in the middle of the morning, my
father was waiting for us in our cold apartment, unshaven, red-eyed,
with a deep cut in his lapel, as prescribed for Jewish mourners. 'We're
alone now,' he said, and when he kissed me his bristle felt damp and
scratchy against my face. He was weeping again as he recalled my
mother's last words. 'I'm all right now,' she had said, 'but for the rest
of you there are hard times ahead.' A little later she had cried out 'I
can't see any more,' and died. The TB saved her from the hard times,
but without the TB she might well have survived them, as did her
husband and son. All too soon we had reason to remember her
prophecy – or was it simply sober foresight?

According to Jewish custom, my mother was buried as soon as we
had arrived, and I recited the *Kaddish*, for the first of many times,
at her grave. I don't remember what everybody else did afterwards,
but I spent the rest of the day on my own, tobogganing on the
hillside next to the cemetery.

I have been told that, for many years after my mother's death, I
refused to talk about her. In fact I would not have known what to
say because I had never really known her: having to stop on the
threshold of her bedroom had taken its toll. One of the few things I
remember is that her two favourite tunes were 'The stars were shining'
from *Tosca* and 'Solveig's Song' from *Peer Gynt*. Perhaps she was at
heart a melancholy person, but my father often praised her quick
wit and composure. Two incidents bear witness to this.

At one time during her illness she had a particularly bad coughing
fit. One of the two doctors by her bedside said to the other: 'This
could be the exitus.' When she had regained her breath she remarked:
'Well, doctor, it wasn't the exitus, was it?' I understand that this was
the last time the doctor risked such bedside predictions, whether in
Latin or Hungarian.

At another time my mother was woken by an intruder climbing in through the window that she kept wide open in all weathers – a recommended treatment for TB. She always had a syphon beside her, and in best slapstick fashion she squirted a jet of soda water straight into the intruder's face. He uttered a few words that were definitely not Latin and retreated through the window faster than he had entered. But no amount of composure was a match for the TB bacillus.

While my mother was ill, our housework was done by local peasant maids, but my mother's younger sister, my little aunt Sári, often came to stay with us and became something between an elder sister and a second mother to me. I remember her taking me to the river where she taught me to swim and to the local fleapit where we watched Tarzan, Laurel and Hardy, Bette Davis and Errol Flynn in *Elizabeth and Essex* (translated into Hungarian as 'Love and the Scaffold'), and a Spanish Civil War epic glorifying the defence of the Alcazar of Toledo by heroic Falangists against dastardly Republicans. Popeye gave me an enduring love of spinach. As we watched the film, we would nibble sunflower seeds, and I was very proud of being able to open them in my mouth and spit the shell out without using my hands. What I did not know then was that my young aunt was a member of the communist youth movement and had been arrested and tortured several times by both Romanian and Hungarian police, but had refused to give away any secrets. Later she was to pass up a chance of surviving the Holocaust out of loyalty to her parents.

My father was thirty-seven years old when I was born. He had left secondary school after four years, and at nineteen, soon after the outbreak of the First World War, volunteered for the Austro-Hungarian army. Some of his friends had persuaded him that he had every prospect of being slightly wounded and returning with his arm in a sling to Vienna or Budapest, where all the girls would run after such a dashing soldier. In reality he was hit in the knee by a Russian dum-dum bullet – banned by international law – and spent several days lying in a swamp before being picked up and taken to a military hospital in Vienna. Rather than strutting up and down the Ring with his arm in a sling and the girls running after him, he lost his knee cap and walked with a stiff leg and a stick for the rest of his life. Thirty years later that dum-dum bullet would prove to be a great asset.

When my father had recovered from becoming a war hero he began to make a living by buying and selling, exporting and importing things. If I ever knew exactly what those things were I certainly do not remember now, but I do remember that he travelled a lot – sometimes with a Romanian prince, bribed up to the hilt, whom he employed to open doors normally closed to Jewish traders. Bribery and corruption were integral parts of the East European economies and my father knew well how to use them. But he also knew how to put honesty to good use. Once he was travelling by train from Hungary to Romania, or possibly from Romania to Hungary, with a suitcase full of silk, hoping to make a big profit, especially if he could avoid paying duty. He hoisted the suitcase into the luggage rack and waited, passport in hand and an innocent expression on his face. The customs officer duly arrived and demanded to know what was in the suitcase. Looking even more innocent, my father said: 'It's full of silk.' The customs officer laughed and walked on to the next compartment. On a later occasion, again involving a train and an official, my father's shrewdness and presence of mind actually saved his – and my – life, as we shall see. In Hungary, for much of the twentieth century, a Jew needed more than his fair share of such qualities in order to survive, but the stress gradually wore down even the strongest constitution. My father's physical and emotional health was in tatters long before he died at eighty-five.

My paternal grandfather had died young, leaving behind my father, his younger brother Lázár and four sisters. Three of the sisters – my aunts Bella, Szidi and Janka – were married with several children;

the fourth – Szeréna – was said to be 'not quite there'. My father's brother, like his father, died young. He had three daughters and a son, and for a long time my father supported them as well as his widowed mother. One of the daughters – Boris, short for Borbála or Barbara – had the good fortune to move to Bucharest and be spared the Holocaust, which bypassed Romania. The two other daughters – Helén and Goldi – survived Auschwitz and Bergen-Belsen, and the son – Sanyi – the slave-labour service. My maternal grandparents, Sándor and Ida Rosenberg, had four children: in addition to my mother and my aunt Sári there were two sons – Mityu and Lajcsi – who emigrated to France before the war, fell out with each other and were rarely heard of. All my other relatives, who were living in or near Kolozsvár, died in Auschwitz. There is not much point in trying to count exactly how many.

None of my extended family had stayed at school beyond their mid-teens, but they spoke Hungarian, Romanian and Yiddish, and were hard-working, literate, and good at arithmetic. Some of the men were artisans, while others made their living as small dealers in whatever goods they could find to deal in. The women looked after their homes and their children, and occasionally helped their husbands with their businesses. They generally took their Jewishness for granted without thinking too much about it. They tended to eat kosher food, to avoid work on the Sabbath, and to go to the synagogue on the important festivals, but as far as I can tell they followed the religious practices as reassuringly familiar customs rather than intense spiritual exercises. My father and mother were less observant, but we too were fully aware of our Jewish identity. And just in case we ever forgot, there were enough others around to remind us.

My own Jewish education was like that of most assimilated children. While the Orthodox received a thorough grounding in the Torah, Talmud and all the learned commentaries, I was only taught to read aloud the words of Hebrew prayers and biblical passages, without the slightest idea of what they meant. My teacher was a young man studying to be a rabbi at the local *yeshiva*. When I read well, sweets would drop on the table from on high. I cannot remember whether I really believed that they were sent from heaven or realised that they came from the same source as the nail clippings my teacher kept producing with a pen knife while I was struggling with the Hebrew letters. By the time my mother died I was able to recite the *Kaddish* in the synagogue three times a day for a year without any difficulty. I still did not understand the words, which were in any case Aramaic rather than Hebrew, but somehow it did not seem to matter.

I had two famous relatives, although we could have done without their fame in both cases. In 1924 in Chicago two rich, brilliant and bored young men murdered a young boy for the thrill of committing the perfect crime. It was not quite perfect, because they were caught, but they became the defendants in one of the most celebrated criminal trials of their time. The victim was Bobby Franks, aged fourteen. The murderers were Nathan Leopold and Richard Loeb, aged nineteen and eighteen respectively. They were sentenced to life imprisonment. Leopold was released in 1958, while Loeb was murdered in prison in 1936. The case inspired many novels, plays and films, including Alfred Hitchcock's *Rope*. Early in the twentieth century an uncle of my father had emigrated to America. He never reported back to the family, but some travellers claimed that he had become a rich businessman in Chicago. In which case it is more than likely that Richard Loeb was my American second cousin.

Very much later, another second cousin acquired a sadder fame. His name was Emil Grünzweig. He was the son of my cousin Goldi, who had survived Auschwitz, and her husband Smile, who had survived slave labour. They had returned to Transylvania after the Holocaust and emigrated to Israel a few years later with their two sons, Emil and Lulu. By 1983 Emil, a teacher and former paratrooper aged thirty-five, had become one of the leaders of the Israeli 'Peace Now' movement. On 10 February a demonstration was held in Jerusalem against the war in Lebanon and the massacre of Palestinian refugees in the camps of Sabra and Shatila. When a right-wing extremist threw a hand grenade at the demonstrators six people were injured and one of them died. The one who died because he had tried to make peace was Emil. The annual Emil Grünzweig Human Rights Award of the Association of Civil Rights in Israel honours his memory.

But I have jumped almost half a century. I must return to my own childhood and explain how my path came to cross Rezső Kasztner's. To a large extent the history of every Hungarian Jewish child in the mid-twentieth century is a history of anti-Semitism. The chapter that follows recalls what it was like for one particular young boy.

Encounters with anti-Semitism

I suffered infinitely less than most Jews in Europe under the Nazis. In comparison with that of millions, my experience of the Holocaust, both metaphorically and literally, was child's play. I cannot tell why I was granted such an easy passage. Perhaps I was just lucky. Or perhaps it was not quite as easy as I remember and I have repressed more of the pain and the fear than I realise. What is certain is that even in the ghetto, in the cattle truck and in the concentration camp I felt protected by my father, however illusory that idea may have been. Afterwards my father and I never really talked about what we had been through. This reticence on both sides has cost me a great deal of insight and, possibly, catharsis. But juvenile and patchy as my memories are, I trust that they will contribute to an understanding of the anti-Semitism that was rampant in fascist Hungary and that reached its monstrous consummation in the last phase of the German-led Holocaust.

The Hungarian troops arrived in Margitta on 6 September 1940. They were greeted in Main Square by veterans of the First World War. These included about a hundred Jews, who were wearing their medals and welcomed the Hungarians with open arms. The leader of the Hungarian troops, a Colonel Szőnyi, ordered the Jewish veterans to leave before he allowed the celebrations to continue. One of our neighbours was overheard saying to the Hungarian soldiers: 'Thank God you're here. We didn't know what to do with these Jews any more.' On the next day the arrests of so-called communists or collaborators with the Romanians began. Most of those arrested were Jews, and most of the charges were false. Such harassments were to continue until there were no Jews left in Margitta.

I had joined the local 'elementary school' at the age of six in September 1939 under the Romanian regime. Before I finished my first year, Margitta was Hungarian. For some time the Jewish children were taught together with the Gentiles. Like many Jews, my parents strongly believed in education, and I could read and write long before I started school. As a result I constantly got top marks. It may also have helped that my teacher was a kind woman who treated everybody in the class with equal fairness. At some point during the four years I spent at that school the Jewish children were separated from the rest and put in a class of our own under a new teacher. He was a fierce man with knee-high black boots, piercing black eyes, a bushy black moustache of the kind favoured by army sergeants, and a lapel badge in the red-white-and-green Hungarian national colours. He took every opportunity to tell us what he thought of us dirty Jewish brats and our whole filthy race. He also had a habit of pointing to the map on the wall which showed the newly recovered part of Transylvania as a bulge protruding east of central Hungary and bounded on three sides by Romanian territory. Romania, he kept informing us, was a big open mouth waiting to swallow Hungary. In all the reports I got from this teacher my marks were near the bottom. Perhaps I was so afraid of him that my work had suddenly plummeted. But I rather suspect that I was the object of a deliberate strategy, either on his part or on that of the authorities. He may also have been unhappy teaching stinking Jews. If he was, he did not have to suffer long. Soon there were no stinking Jews left for him to teach.

Anti-Semitism often went hand in hand with nationalism, not a happy mixture for those at the receiving end. At short intervals every household was obliged to hang out the red-white-and-green Hungarian flag, probably to celebrate some war Hungary had once joined and lost. On this occasion the flag at our house was hanging just at the right height for a little boy to keep jumping up and down trying to reach it. I do not remember whether I succeeded, but somebody must have reported the incident, because suddenly two armed gendarmes burst into my mother's bedroom, shouting 'Where's the Jew Löb?' My mother did not know where my father was at that particular moment, but eventually he was found, put on trial and sentenced to a hefty fine because his son had 'insulted the Hungarian nation'.

On another occasion it was my mother who served as the culprit. She had always been an extremely tidy person with the highest standards in cleanliness and hygiene. Not least with my health in mind, she took the greatest care to ensure that all the personal effects she used were regularly disinfected and the sputum she coughed up burnt. Nevertheless, somebody – perhaps that same guardian of the Hungarian flag – informed the authorities that the 'Jewess Löb', with her 'devilish intelligence', was deliberately spreading germs all over the neighbourhood. Once again my father, as the head of the household, was put on trial and ordered to pay another hefty fine because his wife had been trying 'to poison the Hungarian nation'.

While we were living on the ground floor of the villa in 'Muddy Street' a Hungarian civil servant and his family moved into the flat on the top floor. My mother used to feel particularly low in the early afternoons. It seems hard to believe, but far from telling his children to be quiet, the civil servant encouraged them to make as much noise as possible above my mother's head, although they did not need a lot of encouragement. When the deportation came, we had to leave our furniture and personal possessions behind. After the war one of my cousins who had survived Auschwitz travelled to Margitta to collect them for us. She found the civil servant and his family still living on the top floor, with all our belongings around them. At first they claimed that everything was theirs. When my cousin threatened them with the police they admitted the truth, but explained that they had regarded it as their 'humanitarian duty' to 'protect' our possessions.

In 1943, when I was ten, I went to live permanently – or so it seemed – with my grandparents in Kolozsvár, as my father was often away from home on what the anti-Jewish government had left him of his business. Kolozsvár was a big city with smart shops and restaurants, a choice of theatres and cinemas, many churches, several synagogues, a cathedral, a university and a number of secondary schools. There was neither dust nor mud in the streets which, unlike those of Margitta, were not frequented by cows. I would roam alone for hours, imagining that I was an intrepid explorer. Unfortunately my explorations often came to a sudden end, when gangs of yobs, deciding that I looked Jewish, let loose volleys of abuse that would have been followed by rocks if I had not escaped to less rough neighbourhoods as fast as I could.

In Kolozsvár I became a pupil in the local Jewish *gymnasium*. Ironically, it was the Hungarians who had allowed the Jewish school to reopen in 1940, thirteen years after it had been closed by the Romanians. They might as well not have bothered. By the summer of 1944 there was no Jewish *gymnasium* and there were no Jewish children or teachers in Kolozsvár. They had gone to Auschwitz and the gas chambers. As in Margitta, a flourishing Jewish community was destroyed within a few weeks. When the Germans arrived on 19 March 1944 the city had a population of 115,000, including 16,700 Jews. After the Holocaust fewer than 1,000 Jews were still alive. In a sense I lost two home towns.

My encounters with anti-Semitism as a young child in Transylvania before the German occupation of Hungary were neither particularly dramatic nor particularly painful, but each time they brought me up against a hostile world that I tried to forget as soon as possible. With constant anti-Semitic abuse echoing around me, I did not easily forget. It is astonishing how much venom a simple word like 'zsidó' (Jew) could carry in the mouths of our Hungarian fellow-countrymen, and to this day, when I hear it, I have to stop myself thinking also of the epithet 'büdös' (stinking) that usually accompanied it. 'Stinking Jew' was the phrase that awaited us whenever we ventured out of our houses. 'Stinking Jew' was the phrase that turned us into disgusting sub-humans in the eyes of the Gentiles. 'Stinking Jew' was the phrase that silenced any qualms our enemies might have felt about humiliating, robbing and finally delivering us to murder.

My experiences of anti-Semitism before that 19 March did not prepare me for the Holocaust. Nothing could. But, as I have said, when the Holocaust came I suffered less than the vast majority of Europe's Jews and I have lived to tell the tale. I – and many others – owe that to Rezső Kasztner. To show what he saved us from, and what impossible odds he had to overcome in order to do it, I will briefly outline the specifically Hungarian variant of the Holocaust.

CHAPTER 2

The Holocaust in Hungary

The Golden Age

Millions of words have been written about the Holocaust and there is no need for me to recall the terrible events even in the broadest of outlines. What made the Holocaust in Hungary different was the accidental but decisive fact of its timing: the murderers came late, and they were in a hurry.

By the fifth year of the Second World War the Nazis had destroyed all the Jewish communities in occupied Europe. The Hungarian Jews were still surviving thanks to the special alliance between Hungary and Hitler's Germany, but were now, in the last few months of the dying Third Reich, about to become the victims of the swiftest and most brutal operation of the Holocaust. Ironically, this was happening only a few decades after the happiest period in our whole history.

The period between 1867 and 1918 was the 'Golden Era' of Hungarian Jewry, as Randolph Braham, the outstanding historian of the Hungarian Holocaust, has called it.[1] In 1867 the Jews were granted full civil rights in the newly established Austro-Hungarian Dual Monarchy. In 1918 the First World War ended with the break-up of the Dual Monarchy, and the worst Hungarian Jewish nightmare began.

At the time of the Dual Monarchy, Hungary was a semi-feudal country ruled by a conservative government under the Austrian emperor, who was also the Hungarian king. The top layer of society consisted of the land-owning aristocracy, the bottom layer of the impoverished peasantry. Those at the top, if they needed a job, joined the army or the civil service. Those at the bottom scraped a living as best they could, resentful and envious of their social superiors. Between the two layers there was a gap that had to be filled if Hungary was to survive in the modern world.

The filling was industry, finance, law, education, science, the media, the arts, offering a range of occupations that had become indispensable for a European country by the second half of the nineteenth century. In Hungary, perhaps more than anywhere else, the upper classes looked down on these occupations, while the lower classes regarded them with distrust. Consequently they were ready to be taken up by anybody else who was able or willing to do so.

Many Jews were both able and willing. The result was a prosperous Jewish middle class that came to provide a disproportionately large share of Hungary's leading professionals. They made a very significant contribution not only to the economic modernisation of the country, but also to its social and cultural advancement.

These middle-class Jews regarded themselves as loyal and integrated members of Hungarian society. Some were extremely patriotic, as they were soon to prove by their enthusiastic service during the First World War. In return, they enjoyed equality, justice, freedom from persecution and even, to a degree, the opportunity to join the aristocracy – for a few decades.

At least this applied to the various shades of educated, assimilated and Neologue Jews, who lived in the larger cities, followed liberal religious practices and embraced Hungarian customs. They represented the majority of Hungarian Jewry, but they were not the only ones. There were also, mainly in the villages, the Orthodox, uneducated Yiddish-speaking *Ostjuden* from Eastern Europe: small shopkeepers, tradesmen, hawkers, religious teachers, *Luftmenschen* (drifters) and *Schnorrer* (beggars) who struggled to make a living and who followed strict religious rules, sometimes to the degree of extreme fanaticism, in isolation from their Hungarian surroundings. The tensions between these two segments of the Jewish community did not make life easier for any of us when the disaster came.

I could say that we – or rather my grandparents and great-grandparents – had never had it so good. But even in those halcyon days anti-Semitism was endemic in Hungary. The upper classes never unreservedly accepted Jews as their equals, while the lower classes suspected them of being hand in glove with the rulers. Some anti-Semitic circles directed their hatred against the poor Orthodox 'Eastern' Jews, while others lumped all the Jews together as a convenient target for their poisonous blend of religious, racial, economic, political and personal resentment. It was common practice to blame 'the Jews' for all evils, whether public or private, and any kind of smouldering discontent could easily turn into aggression.

The decline

Having lost every war in its history, Hungary joined the First World War on the German and Austrian side, and lost again. As a result of the Trianon Treaty of 1920 it had to cede two-thirds of its territory to neighbouring countries, and one-third of its original inhabitants became the minority in what had been their homeland. One year earlier the communist Béla Kun had set up a Soviet-style regime, but this had soon been ousted by a right-wing counter-revolutionary movement fuelled by nationalism, fascism and anti-Semitism. In 1920 the counter-revolutionaries' leader, Admiral Miklós Horthy, was declared regent of Hungary. He held that office until 1944.

In the nineteen-twenties and -thirties Hungarian politics, under successive right-wing governments, was dominated by two discrete issues – 'Revisionism' and the 'Jewish question' – which were constantly lumped together by their unscrupulous champions and the confused

masses. 'Revisionism' stood for the aspirations to regain the lost territories. In the absence of an effective opposition on the left, all the
dynamic political forces gathered on the right, straining for such a
restitution. The 'Jewish question' was a catchphrase designed to avoid
an honest confrontation with economic and social ills, projecting them
instead onto the eternal scapegoat, the Jews. The pernicious alliance
of chauvinism and anti-Semitism was soon to prove fatal for the Jews
and, ultimately, not very profitable for the Hungarians either.

Between 1938 and 1941 Hungary recovered many of the territories lost in 1920. But there was a price to pay. The return of the
territories was a gift from Hitler, who had bullied the countries holding
them into compliance. In exchange he expected Hungary to give
more and more active support to the Nazi war effort, and Hungary
obliged, finally sealing its own fate by entering the war on the Axis
side in 1941. Hitler, of course, also expected cooperation in his paramount project, the extermination of the Jews. He did not have to
push very hard. Most of the time the dominant elements in both the
Hungarian leadership and the Hungarian rabble were only too pleased
to assist or even to outdo the Nazis in harming Jews.

Two decades after the end of the First World War anti-Semitic
hysteria, whipped up by relentless agitation, had reached a very high
level. Three major pieces of legislation, modelled on the Nuremberg
racial laws of 1935 in Germany, were enacted in quick succession.
Bad enough in themselves, they laid the foundations for the worst,
which was soon to follow.

The First Anti-Jewish Law was passed in 1938. Supported by the
Christian churches, it reduced the permitted proportion of Jews in
financial, commercial, industrial and cultural enterprises to 20 per
cent. Jewish leaders more or less readily accepted the law in the
mistaken belief that it would take the wind out of the sails of the anti-
Semitic forces.

The Second Anti-Jewish Law was passed in 1939. It was again
supported by the Christian churches, but this time Jewish leaders

campaigned against it, although to no avail. The law defined a Jew as a person who belonged to the Jewish community either before or when the law was announced or who had one parent or two grandparents in the same position. It restricted the Jews' political and civil rights, prohibited them from holding any governmental positions, and set a 6 per-cent quota for their participation in most professions or businesses. Jews were forbidden to edit or publish journals, and to produce plays or films. The permitted number of Jews employed by individual firms was drastically reduced. Some 250,000 Jews lost their regular income and were obliged to find other, often devious, ways of making a living.

The Third Anti-Jewish Law was passed in 1941. Despite its harmless appearance, it had wide implications. It extended the definition of Jew to any person who had at least two Jewish-born grandparents, and banned both marriage and extramarital sexual relations between Jews and non-Jews. The result was a much enlarged pool of victims, not least 100,000 converts, many of whom had so far been protected, to some extent, by the Christian churches.

Every new burst of anti-Jewish legislation was accompanied by more hatred and trumped-up charges. The Jews were capitalists plotting to undermine the Hungarian economy. The Jews were communists scheming to overthrow the Hungarian state. The Jews were rootless cosmopolitans, out to destroy pure Hungarian culture. The Jews were parasites sucking the blood of the poor Hungarian people. The Jews were a fifth column working for the victory of the enemy. Hounded by ferocious propaganda and mass hysteria, the Jews were harassed by the authorities and abused, verbally and sometimes physically, by the rabble. Almost unopposed, the right-wing press and politicians, noisily supported by a mob made up of all classes, demanded harsher and harsher measures against them. Initially the rationale – if there was such a thing behind the mindless violence – was to rob and then drive the Jews out of the country. Before long it became robbery and extermination.

The year of the First Anti-Jewish Law also saw the introduction of an original Hungarian institution called the 'Military Labour Service'. Most Jewish men aged between twenty-one and sixty were drafted into the army, but rather than joining the ranks of 'Miklós Horthy's beautiful soldiers', as a popular marching song of the time had it, they became slave labourers. Wearing civilian clothes with yellow armbands, they were forced to carry out dirty, gruelling or dangerous assignments either at home or, once Hungary had joined the war, on the eastern front. Overworked and underfed, scorched in summer and freezing in winter, lacking basic sanitary and medical facilities, they suffered brutal abuse by sadistic guards and officers. Of more than 100,000 men drafted between 1939 and 1944, some 40,000 died of these hardships.

In August 1941 some 16,000 Austrian, Slovakian and Polish Jews, who had fled to Hungary, were taken by Hungarian and German soldiers to Kamenetz-Podolsk in the Ukraine and machine-gunned together with 7,000 local Jews. In January 1942 in Délvidék (Vojvodina), the Hungarian-occupied part of Yugoslavia, 3,300 men, women and children were either shot or drowned in the frozen rivers by Hungarian paramilitary gendarmes on the pretext of fighting partisans: 700 of these were Jews.

From the summer of 1942, after the infamous Wannsee conference, Hungary came under increasing German pressure to press ahead with the deportation and extermination of its Jews. At the same time various anti-Semitic politicians of the Hungarian extreme right complained to the Germans about their own government's lack of zeal for that cause. Horthy was not a fanatical anti-Semite but an opportunist who tried to walk a tightrope between the German and Hungarian demands for more decisive anti-Jewish action and his fear of international ostracism and Allied retaliation. Unwavering in his zig-zag course, he appointed and dismissed a series of prime ministers and governments. Some were more fervently pro-Nazi and anti-Semitic than others, but none could be accused of loving the Jews.

As the fortunes of the German and Hungarian armies declined, Horthy and his entourage, notably the prime minister, Miklós Kállay, began to contemplate ditching their senior partner and agreeing a separate peace with the Allies. The treatment of the Jews also improved somewhat. Hitler was aware of both developments. He had no intention of giving up his territorial hold on Hungary or abandoning his obsessional project of eliminating all the Jews of Europe. He issued two invitations Horthy could not refuse.

The first meeting took place on 17–18 April 1943 in Klessheim Castle in Austria. Horthy was received by Hitler and his foreign minister Ribbentrop. Hitler demanded the replacement of Kállay and urgent measures against the Jews. When Horthy explained that everything had been done short of killing all the Jews, Ribbentrop replied that they should indeed be killed or deported, and Hitler agreed. For once Horthy stood firm. Kállay was not dismissed and the Jews were neither killed nor deported. At least not for the time being.

The second meeting, again in Klessheim, was held on 18 March 1944. Hitler ordered Horthy to choose one of two options: he could either appoint a new government subject to German approval or face the occupation of Hungary by the German army. Horthy chose the former, but he could just as well have chosen both or neither. In fact Hitler had tricked him. The train taking Horthy back to Hungary was artificially delayed and by the time he reached Budapest German troops had quietly occupied Hungary, encountering no resistance. It was 19 March 1944, one of the darkest dates in the history of Hungarian Jewry.

At this meeting too the question of what to do about the Jews had played a central part. No formal agreement was recorded, but it is generally believed that Horthy consented to Hitler's demand for 100,000 Hungarian Jews to be sent to work in the Reich. Horthy's consent was subsequently used by the Nazis and their Hungarian accomplices as a pretext for the wholesale deportation of 450,000 Hungarian Jews.

Three days after the German occupation of Hungary, on 22 March, Horthy announced a new Nazi-friendly puppet government. From the Jewish point of view, the most pernicious figures were: Döme Sztójay, prime minister and foreign minister; László Endre, state secretary in charge of political (Jewish) matters; László Baky, state secretary in charge of the gendarmerie; László Ferenczy, gendarmerie chief overseeing the apprehension and dispatch of Jews to concentration camps. This quartet, comprising some of the most bloodthirsty anti-Semites that could be found in a fervently anti-Semitic population, was primarily responsible for the Hungarian contribution to the Nazi Holocaust. All four were sentenced to death and executed after the war.

The disaster

From 19 March 1944 the situation of the Jews rapidly became disastrous. The events of the next few months are perfectly summed up by Randolph Braham: 'In no other country was the Final Solution programme – the establishment of the central and local Jewish Councils, the isolation, expropriation, ghettoization, concentration, entrainment and deportation of the Jews – carried out with as much barbarity and speed as in Hungary.'[2] For the sake of clarity, one more word should be added to that list. Extermination.

The invading German troops were immediately followed by Adolf Eichmann and his staff, whose job was to rid Hungary of its Jews, as they had done elsewhere.

In overall charge of the destruction of five to six million Jews was the RSHA (Reichssicherheitshauptamt, Reich Security Main Office). The head of the RSHA was Reichsführer-SS Heinrich Himmler. His immediate subordinate was SS Oberführer Ernst Kaltenbrunner, chief of the SD (Sicherheitsdienst, Security Service), which had intelligence functions, and of the Sipo (Sicherheitspolizei, Security Police), which included the Kripo (Kriminalpolizei, Criminal Police) and the Gestapo (Geheime Staatspolizei, Secret State Police). The chief of the Gestapo was SS Gruppenführer (major-general) Heinrich Müller. The commander of all the security units in Hungary was SS Ober-gruppenführer (lieutenant-general) and Waffen SS General Otto Winkelmann. The head of the SD in Budapest was SS Obersturm-bannführer (lieutenant-colonel) Otto Klages. The most senior diplomat was Edmund Veesenmayer, German ambassador and plenipotentiary for Hungary. The highest SS ranks of Reichsführer and Oberführer had no equivalents in the Allied armies.

Within the RSHA the office directly responsible for Jewish affairs was department IVB4, headed by SS Obersturmbannführer Adolf Eichmann, the logistic mastermind of the Holocaust. The rank and file for the destruction of the Jews came from the SD, the Sipo and the SS Feldgendarmerie. The Sipo in particular contained the 'Sondereinsatzkommandos', special operational units, also known as 'Judenkommandos', who carried out, or supervised, the worst atrocities against the Jews. Eichmann had direct access to Kalten-brunner and the two Heinrichs – Müller and Himmler – which he used when it suited his grand project. His immediate staff included Obersturmbannführer Hermann Krumey, Hauptsturmführer (captain) Otto Hunsche, Hauptsturmführer Siegfried Seidl, Haupt-sturmführer Dieter Wisliceny, Obersturmbannführer Theodor Dannecker, Hauptsturmführer Franz Novak and some others.

If these arrangements look somewhat untidy, it is because they were. Far from being a monolithic structure, the Third Reich was a messy conglomerate of criss-crossing, overlapping and clashing outfits, with their leaders jockeying for position, pursuing private vendettas, and ruthlessly competing for power, influence or profit.

Eichmann's Judenkommando numbered less than 200. Clearly such a small unit would have been unable to deport nearly half a million men, women and children in a matter of a few weeks without the wholehearted support of the Hungarians. Endre, Baky and Ferenczy placed the Hungarian police, gendarmerie and civil service at Eichmann's disposal, and large sections of the Hungarian population enthusiastically joined in the game. In fact, once the floodgates had been opened by the German invasion, the Hungarians often proved even more zealous persecutors than their welcome invaders. They joined in the humiliation, maltreatment, dispossession and deportation of their Jewish neighbours, taking revenge for real or imagined Jewish insults, supposedly cleansing the fatherland of Jewish poison, or simply enjoying the sadistic abuse of their helpless Jewish victims. It was in this climate that the Hungarian officials, policemen and soldiers, under the guidance of their German advisers, carried out the deportations more smoothly and speedily than had ever been seen before.

Within a week of the invasion 300–400 men of the Judenkommando and other German units, ably assisted by Hungarian authorities and informers, arrested about ten thousand individuals all over the country. These included politicians, civil servants, army officers, intellectuals, artists and scientists, who were regarded as potential enemies of the Nazis. The chief purpose of the arrests was to create an atmosphere of uncertainty and fear as a precondition of absolute domination. Of those arrested, 3,000 were Jews. Some were prominent members of the community, others ordinary people picked up at random in the streets. They were dispatched to a number of detention camps in the country.

Over the weeks that followed, the government issued a barrage of decrees designed to isolate, expropriate and finally annihilate the Jews. The most conspicuous was the order for all Jews over six years of age to wear a yellow star of David from 5 April. The star had to be 10 centimetres in height and width, firmly sewn on the left breast of any outer garment, and worn whenever we left our homes. A number of Jews, including some veterans of the First World War, were exempt from wearing it, and this law was to save my own life. Psychologically, the star exacerbated our growing sense of helplessness and inferiority, but it had a more important practical effect: it marked us out as Jews wherever we went. Those who were caught without it were arrested, abused and finally deported. Those with it were ostracised, mocked, abused and finally deported. One could say that the yellow star was our ticket to Auschwitz.

There were many other measures that made our lives very difficult. The Hungarians and Germans, sometimes in cooperation and sometimes in competition, systematically robbed us of everything we had. The few Jewish lawyers, journalists, doctors, pharmacists and artists still working lost their jobs. All Jewish enterprises, shops and workshops were expropriated and assigned to gentiles. Household items, furniture, radios, phones, cars, works of art and any other objects owned by Jews that took an extortionist's fancy were confiscated. We were forbidden to leave our apartments at night and during most of the day, to travel without rare and expensive special permits, to visit parks, public baths and swimming pools, or to enter restaurants, bars, cafés, theatres and cinemas. Restrictions were imposed on the amounts of butter, eggs, rice, sugar, fat, milk and meat that we were allowed to buy. All Jewish organisations, with the exception of the Jewish Councils set up by the Germans, were banned. Books by Jewish writers were removed from bookshops and libraries, and publicly burned. Jewish bank accounts were frozen and Jews were allowed to have only a very limited amount of cash. As air raids multiplied over Budapest the Jewish leadership was ordered to evict thousands of Jews from their homes to make room for bombed-out Hungarians. Other evictions occurred when Nazi officers decided to take up residence in the elegant villas of formerly rich Jews.

For the deportations the country, with the exception of Budapest, was divided into five zones, which were made *judenrein* (cleansed of Jews) in rapid succession. The first consisted roughly of the Carpathian Mountains in the north-east. The second was Transylvania in the east. The third was situated north of Budapest, the fourth and fifth south of Budapest, east and west of the Danube. The Jews were rounded up and herded into ghettos by eager Hungarian gendarmes under the expert guidance of Eichmann's Judenkommando. Their abandoned homes were looted or appropriated by Christians. The ghettos were sometimes closed-off town districts, but more often disused brickyards and other industrial installations, where the captives were held under inadequate shelter or in the open air, with a minimum of food and no sanitation. They were searched – and often tortured – by specially trained detectives for any valuables they might have concealed among the few possessions they had brought to the ghetto or hidden in the world outside: as well confessions and confiscations there were deaths and suicides.

After a few weeks in the ghettos the inmates were rushed by gendarmes to a nearby railway siding and, with curses and blows, made to board the cattle trucks that awaited them. Seventy or more men, women and children were crammed into each truck. There were two buckets, one holding drinking water, the other serving as a toilet, neither of which was big enough. The doors were sealed from outside. Without food, suffocating in the extreme summer heat, heaped on top of each other, they travelled to the Slovakian border, where their Hungarian guards handed them over to German SS soldiers. It took several days until they arrived in Auschwitz. Many died on the way. The others had to undergo the 'selection' process. They were lined up in front of a German doctor, who with a wave of his hand sent those he thought capable of hard labour to the right, and the others – the old, the children, the sick – to the left. Those sent to the left immediately went into the gas chambers. Of those sent to the right, and distributed to camps all over the German-held territories, the strongest or luckiest survived, while the others did not. All this is well-known today thanks to thousands of testimonies by survivors. Millions more left no testimony.

The ghettoisation – to use an ugly word for an ugly thing – started in Zone I on 16 April, and by 3 June the Jews of all five zones were in the ghettos. The deportation started on 15 May with Zone I and was completed on 8 July with Zone V. In less than two months about 150 trains left the Hungarian provinces, carrying some 450,000 Jews to Auschwitz. About 330,000 were gassed on arrival. Including those who died in Budapest, in the forced-labour service, and on the infamous 'death marches', more than 500,000 Hungarian Jews were killed during the German occupation. Some 255,000 survived the war, about half of them in Budapest and half in concentration camps liberated by the Allies.

The Jews of Budapest were due to be ghettoised in July and deported in August, but were given a reprieve when Horthy suspended the deportations on 7 July in response to heavy diplomatic pressure from abroad. Some 200,000 Jews living in the capital were ordered to move into 2,600 'Jewish houses', which carried a large yellow star on their frontage and accommodated on average three persons per room. Tens of thousands preferred to hide elsewhere at the risk of being captured, tortured and killed. Many owed their lives to 'protective passes' and 'protected houses', above all thanks to the efforts of the Swedish diplomat Raoul Wallenberg and his Swiss colleague Charles Lutz.

Horthy's July ban on deportations was followed by a similar order from Himmler on 25 August, but the respite proved to be only temporary. As the Soviet Army advanced deep into Hungary, Horthy finally decided to extricate his country from the war. On 15 October he announced a unilateral ceasefire on the radio. The Germans immediately forced him to resign and appoint as prime minister and head of state Ferenc Szálasi, the leader of the extreme fascist and anti-Semitic Nyilas (Arrow Cross) party. This signalled the last stage of the Hungarian Holocaust.

Within a week, the new regime, to the delight of Eichmann, decided to send large contingents of Jewish men and women to Austria to work on fortifications against the approaching Russians. No transport was provided, and as autumn turned into winter 80,000 Jews were forced to cover the 220 kilometres to the border on foot, without food, drink, shelter or warm clothing, while armed gendarmes submitted them to verbal and physical abuse, killing those who were unable to continue or whose faces they did not like. These 'death marches' claimed many thousands of victims.

In November all those Jews without protection papers were ordered to move into the ghetto, where conditions were even worse than in their previous accommodation. Since Szálasi's coup, gangs of Arrow Cross killers had been constantly on the rampage, grabbing what was left of Jewish property, dragging Jews out of their hiding places or their 'protected' residences, and murdering thousands. As the Red Army closed in on Budapest, their reign of terror became bloodier and bloodier. Their preferred pastime was herding Jews to the Danube embankment and shooting them into the freezing river. About half the Jewish population of Budapest, 100,000 men, women and children, died in this reign of terror, even though they had escaped wholesale deportation.

A sad distinction belongs to a provincial internment camp called Kistarcsa, near Budapest, which was the starting point of both the first and the last deportation. On 28 April, two weeks before the deportations began 'officially' on 15 May, 1,800 inmates were taken to Auschwitz. On 12 July, five days after Horthy's order to stop the deportations, Eichmann put another 1,500 on a train to Auschwitz. Alerted by Jewish leaders, Horthy ordered the train back. On 19 July Eichmann summoned the Jewish leaders to a meeting and kept them in his office until his henchmen had dispatched yet another train with the same contingent of 1,500. By the time the Jewish leaders were able to contact Horthy once more, the train had left Hungarian territory.

The Jewish Councils

One of the most insidious tactics employed by Eichmann throughout the Holocaust was his use of Jewish Councils. In Hungary he acted with unprecedented speed. On 19 March 1944, only hours after the occupation, two of his senior officers, Wisliceny and Krumey, called at the offices of the Jewish Community at 12 Síp Street and left a summons for the leaders of all the Jewish organisations to attend a meeting the next day. Some 500 Jewish representatives turned up, many of them carrying suitcases because they expected to be immediately arrested and taken away. Assuming an air of sincerity, Wisliceny assured them that there was no cause for alarm, as they would be able to continue their work undisturbed under the SS. Krumey, in a similarly polite manner, explained that there would be no arrests, no violation of personal or property rights and no deportations. He demanded that a *Judenrat* (Jewish Council) be set up by the following day as the official body governing all the Jews in Hungary. Wisliceny warned of harsh measures if Jews tried to withdraw their bank deposits, but declared that if any Jew were to be arrested it would not be because he was a Jew, but only because he was personally suspected of some wrongdoing.

This mixture of threats and false promises was typical of the Nazis' cynical but effective technique of playing on the Jews' fears and hopes in order to turn them into willing tools of their own destruction. The Central Council of Hungarian Jews was promptly set up as ordered. It consisted of Orthodox, Neologue and Zionist representatives. Dr Samu Stern – a rich banker with connections to the Hungarian ruling class, president of the Pest Jewish Community and head of the national organisation of Neologue Jews – was appointed its chairman. Essentially, the Council's duties consisted in conveying the Germans' orders to the Jews and ensuring that the Jews did as they were told. To begin with, it had to draw up two lists, one of all the Jewish institutions, the other of all the Jewish property in Budapest.

The first meeting between a delegation of the Council and Eichmann took place on 31 March at Eichmann's headquarters, the Majestic Hotel in Buda. Keeping silent about the impending deportations, Eichmann assumed a businesslike and conciliatory pose. When Stern complained about the harsh anti-Jewish measures that were being announced day by day he assured the delegates that the Jews had nothing to fear from the Germans. They would continue to be treated fairly and well. Any transgressions against them would be punished. The administrative and economic constraints on them would last only until the end of the war. He was, of course, lying.

After the meeting the Central Council instructed the leaders of the Jewish communities in the provinces to follow all the directives that would be passed down from the capital. It also called on the Jewish population to maintain discipline and obey orders. In several large towns Jewish Councils were set up and told to adhere to the policies of the Central Council.

Upright and conventional citizens that they were, the Councils tried to protect their fellow-Jews by appeals, petitions and personal approaches to Hungarians in high places, but to no avail. The Hungarians refused to help, the Germans issued orders, and the Councils obeyed. There was very little else they could have done, but the fact remains that, however reluctantly, they contributed to the smooth running of the Holocaust. It was they who published the newsletters announcing Eichmann's orders, produced and distributed the yellow stars, selected Jewish properties for confiscation, delivered Jewish money and valuables to the Germans, and compiled the lists of Jews for ghettoisation and deportation to the gas chambers. They enjoyed certain privileges, such as exemption from wearing the yellow star and a degree of freedom of movement. Some of them misused these for their personal advantage, but the majority did all they could to alleviate the suffering of their constituents. Sadly, they could not prevent the ultimate disaster and, having been forced to assist the enemy in the destruction of their own people, they usually ended up sharing the same fate.

There is no simple explanation as to why the Councils obeyed the German orders so readily. One reason was that they were simply afraid of what the Germans might do to them if they refused. Another reason was that by being compliant they hoped to induce the Germans either to stop short of extermination or to spare as many lives as possible until the collapse of the Third Reich. Yet another reason was that they could not – or would not – believe that what had happened to the Jews elsewhere could happen in a civilised country like Hungary. They regarded themselves as assimilated and patriotic Hungarians, committed to the existing conservative order and proud of their contribution to the advancement of the fatherland. They naively expected Horthy and the Hungarian elite to appreciate their loyalty and to protect them from the Nazis. Such were the views of the Councils and they were shared by many of their constituents. Unfortunately, the Hungarians had different ideas.

The worst accusation levelled against the Jewish Councils is that they deliberately failed to warn their communities of the approaching Holocaust. It is claimed that they lulled the masses into a false sense of security by keeping silent about the true destination of the deportation trains, by making them believe that they were about to be relocated to work within the Hungarian borders, and by assuring them that all would be well if they did as they were told by the Germans. These deceptions by the Jewish Councils are said to have prevented the Jewish masses trying to resist or escape.

A crucial question is how much the Jewish Councils actually knew about Auschwitz. In the early years of the Holocaust reports of massacres were reaching Hungary through refugees from German-occupied Eastern Europe, but no exact information was available. However, by the spring of 1944 the facts about the death camps were becoming common knowledge both in Hungary and elsewhere.

The most important document detailing the truth about the death camps was the *Auschwitz Protocols* by two young Slovak Jews, Rudolf Vrba (originally Walter Rosenberg) and Alfred Wetzler. Having been in Auschwitz since 1942, Vrba and Wetzler escaped on 7 April 1944 and hid in Slovakia. In less than two weeks they wrote a joint account, giving exact details of the mass murders that had taken place between July 1942 and April 1944 and of the preparations in progress since January 1944 for the arrival of the Hungarian Jews. The report was translated into Hungarian and given to Jewish leaders, church dignitaries and potentially sympathetic politicians. One copy found its way to Switzerland, where it received a great deal of press coverage in July, and to the USA, where it was published by the War Refugee Board in November. But even when the deportations from the provinces were in full flow the Jewish leaders continued to deceive themselves and their communities, rationalising the irrational, closing their eyes to the blatantly obvious, and hoping against hope that by appeasement and submission they could weather the storm.

They were wrong, but even if they had done everything they could to warn their people, there would hardly have been any large-scale resistance or mass escape. The Jewish community was torn by bitter ideological in-fighting. The Neologues, considering themselves enlightened westerners, blamed the Holocaust on the refusal of the Orthodox from East Europe to assimilate to their host nation. The Orthodox in their turn saw the Holocaust as God's punishment for the secularity of both the Hungarophiles and the Zionists, or as the price that had to be paid for redemption by a Messiah who was yet to come. There was no effective central organisation to reconcile these conflicts. The potential for concerted action, limited from the outset, had been reduced to almost nothing by restrictions on travel and communication. The able-bodied men were away in the slave-labour service. There was no hope of obtaining arms. Divided between themselves, demoralised by constant anti-Semitic propaganda, paralysed by economic and social repression, hounded and maltreated by the Hungarians, deceived and terrorised by the Germans, the Jews of Hungary had no means to fight and nowhere to run.

There were some exceptions. Members of the Zionist youth organisations carried out many daring underground rescue operations and tried to deliver warnings about the imminent deportations, albeit with little success. Otto Komoly, the president of the Zionist Association, saved hundreds of children with the assistance of the Red Cross. The head of the Budapest Palestine Office, Moshe Krausz, was instrumental in obtaining protective passes for tens of thousands from foreign diplomats.

The most spectacular venture was that of Rezső Kasztner and an informal committee of Zionists called the Vaada. While the Jewish Councils tried to ward off the worst by accommodating Eichmann and his henchmen, this small group resorted to every trick, bluff and ploy it could muster in order to save lives. Like the Councils, Kasztner was accused after the war of collaborating with the enemy, although he had not done so deliberately or for his own advantage. Ultimately both the Councils and Kasztner turned out to be tragic victims of the Nazis but, unlike the Councils, Kasztner in his own way stood up to them and, at least to a certain extent, achieved what he had set out to do. Faced with one of the most vicious gangs of criminals ever to have exercised power, he refused to give in to despair. With his unique blend of audacity, determination and sheer *chutzpah*, he saved more Jewish lives during the Holocaust than any other Jew.

CHAPTER 3

The Kolozsvár Ghetto

To the brickyard

Just as my first year at the elementary school in Margitta had been cut short by the Hungarian takeover of Transylvania, my first year at the *gymnasium* in Kolozsvár was cut short by the German occupation of Hungary. I remember very little either of the six months I spent at the *gymnasium* or of the ominous 19 March 1944. But I do remember my grandmother carefully cutting six-cornered stars measuring exactly 10 centimetres in every direction out of yellow material and sewing them firmly on our coats and jackets. The order was actually issued on 29 March and by 5 April all the Jews in the streets of Kolozsvár – and everywhere else in Hungary – were wearing them. I wish I could say that I wore mine with pride and defiance, but the truth is that it made me feel exposed, threatened and embarrassed whenever I stepped out of our house, which was precisely what it was intended to do. Occasionally I forgot all about it for a while, but an overheard remark by a passer-by or a reflection in a shop window reminded me with a jolt that I was a stinking Jew.

On 2 May posters went up ordering all the Jews in town to prepare for removal to the ghetto. On 3 May newspapers carried notices to the same effect. The ghettoisation was to take place street by street and we were all to wait at home until the gendarmes came to round us up. The amount of luggage we were allowed to take was strictly limited. On 8 May I celebrated my eleventh birthday, or rather, I did not celebrate it, because the adults were not in the mood to throw a party. But I was given a present that was as good as any party – my first watch. It had 'Doxa' printed on its face and numbers that glowed green in the dark. I drove everybody to distraction by announcing the exact time again and again, until I was silenced by the threat of having the precious gift confiscated.

A few days later my grandparents, my aunt, my father – who had joined us in Kolozsvár – and I were standing in the street with our bundles, guarded by armed Hungarian gendarmes and stared at by our Gentile neighbours, some from behind lace curtains, others openly from the opposite side of the street. Our front door had been sealed and marked 'property of the Hungarian nation'. Eventually a truck arrived and the gendarmes, with loud jeers and curses, ordered us to climb on the back. My elderly grandparents and my father with his stiff leg could not make it on their own and were brutally man-handled onto the truck by one of the gendarmes. Another gendarme spotted my Doxa watch, yanked it off my wrist and slipped it into his pocket.

The watch was not the only treasured possession I lost that day. I also lost the little toy dog my aunt Sári had made for me out of left-over bits of material and two black shirt buttons for eyes. Over the years he had gone somewhat out of shape and become threadbare, but I loved him and carried him with me wherever I went. At night he slept on my pillow, always with the light on, because he was afraid of the dark. Now, as I was about to climb on the truck, the gendarme who had pocketed my Doxa watch grabbed my arm and snatched the dog out of my hand. He then gave me a rough push and walked away whistling, perhaps to collect more trophies from eleven-year-olds.

Eventually the gendarmes decided that they had squeezed enough Jews into the back of one truck. They gave a signal to the driver and turned to the next group in the street, leaving us in the charge of a scruffy, sallow-faced individual in his twenties. He was not wearing a gendarme's uniform but a civilian suit that was suspiciously smart and did not quite fit him. Perched on the tailgate, his face distorted with hatred, he spent the whole journey to the ghetto shouting obscenities at us. What he seemed to enjoy most was repeatedly informing us stinking Jews that we were at last getting what we deserved. I have often wondered since whether he too eventually got what he deserved. He was a gypsy.

Within a fortnight some 18,000 Jews from Kolozsvár and the surrounding small towns and villages were taken to the ghetto.[1] Like many others, this ghetto was a disused brickyard, called the Irisz Estate, on the outskirts of the city, surrounded by barbed-wire and board fences and guarded by paramilitary gendarmes or regular policemen. Brickyards were almost tailor-made temporary homes from home for Jews awaiting deportation. The long roofs resting on wooden posts, which normally protected drying bricks from the rain while letting the wind through in all directions, now gave a semblance of protection to the Jews, who would soon be beyond the need for protection of any kind.

It was summer and we did not have to worry about the cold, but in search of at least an illusion of privacy we cobbled sheets or blankets together to form makeshift walls; those who had enough sheets or blankets could also use them to cover the dusty floors we slept on. The irregular rations provided by the authorities consisted mainly of broad beans, which we cooked in metal bath tubs that had been delivered to the ghetto from plundered Jewish homes. We supplemented this with whatever provisions we had brought with us or could buy from peasant women who lined up on the other side of the fence to do business. Fifteen taps were supposed to supply 18,000 people with water for drinking, cooking and washing. There were no toilets. Some of the men dug ditches to serve as latrines, two for men and two for women. They could be used by twenty persons at a time and were almost completely open, adding humiliation to the discomfort and embarrassment felt by all. The clusters of fat black flies landing on everything, including us, did not improve matters, and neither did my constant fear of falling into the cesspit.

I must have shared some of the physical and emotional stress of the adults, who bore the full burden of the hunger, the dirt, the spreading diseases, the growing number of deaths and suicides, the menace of the vicious guards, the trauma of having been thrown from a civilised existence into a subhuman predicament at hardly a moment's notice. But, for a child of eleven, the ghetto was also an exciting adventure. Living practically in the open between those sheet-and-blanket walls, with the routine of home and the discipline of school receding into the past, was almost like an indefinite camping holiday. The brickyard was criss-crossed by a rusty narrow-gauge railway designed to carry bricks, and we played exotic games pushing each other around in the small open cars for long hours, without being told to have our bath and go to bed when we were having most fun. I missed my Doxa watch and my toy dog, and sometimes wondered how much longer we had to stay there, but life could have been worse. In other words, I did a sterling job of ignoring a reality that was too frightening to face.

But even I was vaguely aware of something sinister going on in one particular building. I have learnt since that this was the 'mint', where men and women were tortured into confessing where they had hidden their valuables. After a while I also began to notice that occasionally large groups of people were marched away somewhere and did not come back. I now know that the whole ghetto of 18,000 people, with a few hundred exceptions, was deported to Auschwitz in six trainloads between 25 May and 10 June.[2] I also have a dim memory of being alone in our makeshift room one afternoon, when a patrol of armed gendarmes came looking for people to take away. I hid in a ditch, where I held my breath until I almost burst and closed my eyes firmly so that the men wouldn't see me. I cannot tell why my grandparents and my aunt had left me on my own but, as for my father, he had slipped out into the city on an important errand.

The escape

On the morning of 2 June British and American planes coming from bases in Italy bombed Kolozsvár for the first and only time during the war. The ghetto was outside the target area, and as we were listening to the distant explosions we were for once safer than the Gentiles. According to a report I have read since,[3] the city was hit quite hard. The raid lasted about 40 minutes: 1,200 bombs were dropped, killing 460 people and injuring nearly 1,000. There was damage to the railway station, the army food stores, the steel works, the match factory and the Dermata shoe factory. The shoe factory was closest to us and I can still see the column of smoke rising from it. In the confusion that followed the raid, my father and I escaped from the ghetto. This seemed quite simple to me at the time, but my father had made careful preparations, as he explained later. I could almost say that our escape started in a trench in the First World War.

When my father had been patched up after having his knee blown to bits by that Russian dum-dum bullet, he received a certificate that declared him 50 per cent disabled, although he had by no means lost half his energy and vitality. According to the anti-Jewish laws, a Jewish veteran who was 75 per cent disabled thanks to being wounded in the War to End All Wars did not count as Jew. He was exempt from the obligation to wear the yellow star, the restrictions on travel, and finally from ghettoisation and deportation. The same applied to his wife and his children. My father scraped the '50' off his certificate and wrote '75' in its place. Naturally he knew that he had no hope of getting away with this, but he also knew all there was to know about corruption in Transylvania. Unlike the gendarmes, who grabbed what they wanted by brute force, the police and civil servants were quite willing to look kindly on backhanders. On the afternoon when I was hiding from the gendarmes in that ditch my father bribed a police guard to let him out of the ghetto. He walked into the city and, following either his instincts or the Jewish grapevine, promptly found a civil servant who, for another bribe, supplied him with an official copy of the certificate. Now the 75 per cent looked as kosher as if Moses himself had written it.

My father returned to the ghetto and waited. In the chaos after the air raid he pulled the yellow stars from our jackets. He took me by the hand and we strolled to the gate. Thanks to yet another bribe, the policeman standing guard opened the gate and we stepped out onto the straight road leading to the city. We were free, at least for the time being. I should add that my father had tried to persuade my aunt Sári to come with us. By pretending to be his wife she would have enjoyed the same precarious immunity as he and I did thanks to the false disability certificate. But her parents had no certificates, true or false, that would have released them from the ghetto, and she refused to leave them. She refused to leave them again a week or two later, as I heard after the war. On arrival in Auschwitz, when those who looked strong enough for slave labour were separated from the old, the children and the ill, she again refused to leave her parents and was immediately gassed together with them.

Against a backdrop of smouldering ruins, my father and I hurried from the ghetto to the railway station and managed to catch a train that was about to leave for Budapest despite the bomb damage to the buildings and tracks. The train was swarming with plain-clothes detectives in search of Jewish fugitives. They demanded to see everybody's identity papers, which they checked with particular thoroughness when they thought that the holders 'looked Jewish'. If they decided that further confirmation was needed, at least for men, they took them to the toilets to see whether they were circumcised. Dozens of frightened Jews, whose documents turned out to have been forged, were ordered off the train to be transported to the nearest ghetto. One of the detectives stopped in front of us. When he saw my father's certificate he asked with a frown: 'This is a copy. Where's the original?' I have already mentioned my father's presence of mind. While I froze with fear, he pulled up his trouser leg. Pointing to the dents and scars where there should have been a kneecap, he said: 'This is the original.' The detective nodded and continued his round.

I do not remember the rest of the journey. My next memory is of staying in a hospital in Budapest, where a Christian doctor had admitted my father as a 'patient' and me as his 'companion'. We stayed in the hospital for a few days, but there were too many spies and informers around and we had to move on before we were found out. I have often thought of that Christian doctor and the appalling risk he took in hiding two Jews he had never seen before. I wish I knew his name so that I could thank him personally and tell the world about one brave and good man among thousands of cowards, opportunists and murderers.

The disability certificate, being a suspicious copy rather than a clean original, was unlikely to protect us long. Even if it had been legitimate it would not have guaranteed our survival in fascist Hungary indefinitely. After Szálasi's coup on 15 October the Arrow Cross gangs often ignored any protective documents and killed Jews whenever they felt like it, but my father saw things clearly enough already in June to realise that he had to find a better way of keeping alive.

When we left the hospital we had two choices. One was offered by a second cousin called Ernő Löb, who had been studying architecture in Budapest before Jews were banned from the universities. He belonged to a group of radical young Zionists and together with his friends was preparing a hiding place in the city. One of the university buildings had been joined to the building next door, and in order to show an even façade to the street, a false storey about one and a half metres in height had been added. This space was closed off from the rest of the building but, not unlike Anne Frank's bunker in Amsterdam, could be reached through a door that had been constructed in one of the lavatories and hidden behind tiles. The young men had bribed a caretaker to allow them to do this. Inside the bunker they laid mattresses on the floor and piled up stocks of tinned food, bottled water and a radio. My cousin offered us a place and my father was tempted to move in. But eventually he decided to go for the other option, and so did my cousin. As the search for Jews intensified, my cousin's friends moved into the bunker. After the war we heard that the building had been hit by an Allied bomb and all the people hiding in it killed.

The other option was to join the 'Kasztner group'. With the false certificate my father could move around Budapest without the Jewish star and in precarious freedom. Always energetic, and now driven by fear of death, he dragged me to and fro between the offices of the various Jewish organisations, asking for information, trying to guess the truth behind the rumours, and searching for advice and help. He had already heard in the Kolozsvár ghetto that we would be sent to work in humane conditions to a town in western Hungary which bore the reassuring name of 'Kenyérmező' ('bread meadow'). This story – invented by the Hungarian authorities, as we now know – was disseminated by the Jewish Council. In fact there was no town of that name large enough to accommodate even part of the masses in the Kolozsvár ghetto, let alone in all the ghettos of Hungary, and I think my father realised that. In Budapest the relatives of people already deported from the provinces suddenly started receiving post-cards bearing the idyllic name of 'Waldsee' ('forest lake'). The senders reported that they had arrived safely at their destination and were being well treated. The truth was, as we found out after the war, that they had been forced to write these cards by the SS before they were gassed. I remember 'Waldsee' coming up quite often when my father was exchanging hearsay with other anxious Jews. Many of them kept assuring each other – or rather, themselves – that there was no cause for alarm if we were going to such nice-sounding places.

Not my father, though. With his eyes and ears always open, he discovered that there was a Jewish rescue committee headed by Rezső

Kasztner, who had brought 380 Jews to Budapest from Kolozsvár for some sort of exchange. I do not know if he actually met Kasztner, but he certainly made some useful contacts and as a result we took refuge in the Aréna Street synagogue with hundreds of others who had put their hope in Kasztner. But even this did not satisfy my father's instinct for survival. Just as he had left me on my own in the Kolozsvár ghetto when he slipped out to get the fake disability certificate, he now left me on my own in the synagogue while he went once more in search of rescue, although this time I did not have to hide from any gendarmes.

He returned with a small slip of paper granting us permission to move into the camp in Kolumbusz Street, where the contingent from Kolozsvár was being held. I know that no money changed hands because my father had none. It is possible that he had cajoled or pestered one of the leaders of the Kolozsvár group, another distant cousin, called Jenő László, to allow us to join. In any case, trying to look as if we were not Jews without their yellow star, but expecting to be arrested at any moment, we hurried through the hostile city until we reached the Kolumbusz camp in one of the southern suburbs. The SS guard, after a brief glance at my father's slip of paper, opened the gate and waved us in. For the sake of a faint hope of rescue, we had voluntarily exchanged our uncertain freedom for certain captivity in the hands of our worst enemies. It was a desperate gamble which some, including my father, were prepared to take, and others not. Those who took it survived, while many of those who did not died. But at the time nobody could anticipate the outcome.

I remember a big gymnasium, a smaller villa and a number of wooden huts in a shady garden, which would have been quite idyllic, had they not been crammed full of tense and anxious people. I now know that we were in the Wechselmann Institute for the Deaf-Mute that had been converted into a temporary camp for 'privileged' Jewish captives. The huts had been built within days by the architect László Devecseri, who joined the inmates together with his family. The people milling around me had arrived from Kolozsvár a few days before my father and I were admitted. Despite their relief at having escaped from the ghetto, they were reeling under their recent ordeal and deeply apprehensive of what the future might bring. They did not know where they were going next, but they were impatient to be on their way and at the same time afraid to leave an unkind but familiar world behind. Of course I was not conscious of all this, but I shared the general restlessness.

As it happened, Kolumbusz Street was where I experienced my worst air raid. The Allied planes came in the night and we had to stay in our makeshift huts as there were no shelters to go to. It began with the wails of nearby sirens, soon followed by the hum of heavy bombers. We sat in complete darkness, while the bombs rained down, inexorably repeating a tune that started with a long whistle, continued with a moment of deep silence and ended with a deafening explosion. As the planes came closer, the whistles became louder, the pauses more ominous and the explosions more powerful, making the ground shake like an earthquake. The tune is now familiar to all the audiences of war films, but this was not a film and I certainly was not used to it. I trembled and whimpered, and there was nothing my father could do to help me. Eventually it did end and we were unscathed, but to this day my stomach contracts for a moment when I hear a factory siren announcing a change of shift.

On 30 June 1944 the group held in Kolumbusz Street, including my father and me, left for Bergen-Belsen, although of course none of us had heard of it or knew that this was our destination.

CHAPTER 4

The First Steps

Relief for refugees

The name of Rezső Kasztner is synonymous with one of the most astonishing episodes of the Holocaust in Hungary. Although he did not act alone, Kasztner was the outstanding figure in a small group of Zionists who embarked on an unlikely attempt to halt the extermination of the Jews by bribing and hoodwinking the SS. In fact, each side tried to trick and bluff the other – the Jews seeking to save lives, the Germans engaged in daylight robbery and mass murder. The SS played a ruthless cat-and-mouse game, collecting payments and promising concessions, as the death trains were continually leaving for Auschwitz. Nevertheless, the Zionists, considering the formidable obstacles facing them, scored some remarkable successes.[1]

The beginnings were relatively modest. From the spring of 1942 more and more Jews from German-occupied Poland, Slovakia and Yugoslavia were fleeing to Hungary. They came with nothing but the clothes they stood in, having lost their jobs, their homes and their families, running for their lives, in constant fear of being stopped by the police or reported by passers-by and sent back to their own countries, where the Germans or local collaborators were waiting to throw them into concentration camps or summarily execute them. By

November 1943 they numbered between 12,000 and 16,000. On arrival the refugees needed to be fed, clothed, housed, hidden from the authorities and supplied with false identity papers, before they either managed to build a new – albeit temporary – existence in Hungary or continue their flight to Palestine via Romania and Turkey.

When the law-abiding official leaders of Hungarian Jewry found themselves unable to meet the needs of this influx of desperate refugees an informal group of Zionist mavericks took matters into their own hands. In January 1943 they constituted themselves formally as a 'Relief and Rescue Committee', in Hebrew 'Vaadat Ezra ve' Hazalah' or just 'Vaada'. The chairman of the organisation was Dr Otto Komoly, a highly respected civil engineer, veteran officer of World War I and president of the Hungarian Zionist Association. Dr Rezső (also known as Rudolf or Israel) Kasztner was the executive vice-chairman. Other members included Joel and Hansi Brand, Moshe Schweiger, Samu Springmann, Shulem Offenbach, Tzvi Szilágyi, Endre Biss and representatives of the Polish and Slovakian refugees and of the different branches of the *chalutz* (young pioneer) movement.

The Vaada had built up clandestine contacts with numerous underground organisations abroad. Two members – Samu Springmann and Joel Brand – had particularly useful foreign connections. Springmann was a well-known Budapest jeweller who employed a network of messengers – diplomatic couriers of the Hungarian foreign ministry and the neutral states, members of the Hungarian and German intelligence services, double agents and smugglers, who were usually rewarded with substantial bribes – to carry information and money between Hungary and various other countries. In particular, he kept in touch with the representatives of the Jewish Agency in neutral Istanbul and through them with the Jewish Agency in Palestine.

The Jewish Agency, which had been founded in 1929 to assist immigration to Palestine under the British mandate, would eventually become the first government of the state of Israel, dominated by the Mapai (Labour) party. Its leaders included David Ben Gurion and Moshe Shertok, who were to take office as the first prime minister and the first foreign minister of Israel (by which time Shertok had changed his name to Sharett). In Istanbul its chief representative was Chaim Barlas, charged with assisting the relief and rescue of Jews in German-occupied countries. Setting up the link to Istanbul was Springmann's greatest contribution to the cause of Hungarian Jewry. He escaped to Palestine shortly before the German occupation.

Brand was a drifter and playboy who at various points in his life had flirted with communism and dabbled in the black market. While his wife Hansi (née Hartmann) ran a small knitwear business, he spent much of his time drinking and gambling in the cafés and night clubs of Budapest. Educated in Germany, he spoke the language like a native and since the beginning of the war had often been seen in the company of German officers. He was particularly close to Josef Winninger, an agent of the Abwehr, the Wehrmacht's counter-intelligence unit. He also hobnobbed with a shady multiple agent called Bandi (András) Grosz, who worked for the Poles, the Japanese and the Americans as well as for the Abwehr, the Gestapo and the SS, and who ran errands for Springmann; and his further contacts in the murky world of espionage included a number of Hungarian officers. It was a louche way of life and an asset in saving Jews.

In the summer of 1941 one of Hansi's sisters and her husband were expelled from Budapest, among thousands of other Jews deemed to be aliens, and transported to Hungarian-occupied Ukraine. Before they could fall victim to the notorious Kamenetz-Podolsk murders, Brand met a Hungarian counter-intelligence agent called József Krem who, for a substantial bribe, smuggled them back into Hungary in the boot of his car. Similar rescues followed and the Vaada, in addition to looking after illegal refugees in Hungarian territory, found itself actively engaged in smuggling people across the borders. The code word for such enterprises was *tiyul*, meaning 'excursion' in Hebrew.

In addition to the Jewish Agency in Istanbul, the Vaada had two important contacts in neutral Switzerland: Nathan Schwalb, the representative of Hechalutz, the organisation of young Zionist pioneers, and Saly Mayer, a wealthy retired businessman, former president of the Swiss Federation of Jewish Communities and representative of the American Jewish Joint Distribution Company (Joint for short), a charity set up to provide financial assistance for Jews facing hardship or danger abroad. Mayer in particular was to play a key role in Kasztner's work.

It was through Istanbul and Switzerland that the Vaada received most of the funds needed for its work with the refugees. It was also through Istanbul and Switzerland that it tried to alert the world to reports that were reaching Hungary about the unfolding Holocaust, although the responses were to prove slow and inadequate. In November 1943 Kasztner and Springmann, over a glass of schnapps in one of Budapest's luxury hotels, met a German businessman who had been introduced to them by a certain Rudi Sedlaczek, a Viennese dentist working as an Abwehr agent. The visitor was running factories in Poland and Czechoslovakia which produced goods for the Nazi war effort, but which were primarily intended as safe havens for their apparent Jewish slave labourers. He had come to set up escape routes and financial cooperation with the Vaada, but what made the meeting particularly important was that Hungarian Jewish leaders heard for the first time what was happening in the extermination camps in concrete detail. 'Smashing the skulls of children with one's boots is not the military way,' the visitor told his appalled listeners, before he explained that in Auschwitz Jews were being 'gassed and burnt' according to a 'scientific system'.[2] This account confirmed Kasztner's and Springmann's worst suspicions, but also offered some slight grounds for hope. Apart from the horrors, it contained a reference to Himmler's new policy of sparing those fit for slave labour, which they promptly recognised as a respite that might be used for rescue operations. Contacts between the Vaada and the visitor continued for a while, but no significant joint action followed. The visitor's name was Oskar Schindler.

From time to time the Vaada worked together with other organisations, but no permanent cooperation developed. Fülöp Freudiger was the president of the Orthodox community. As head of a large and influential group of Jews, he initially provided assistance of various kinds to the Vaada. This lasted until August 1944, when he made a special deal with the SS and escaped to Romania with some fifty friends and relations. Occasionally the Vaada also combined forces with Moshe Krausz, a member of the powerful religious Mizrahi party and head of the Palestine Office in Budapest. However, rivalry and personal hatred between Krausz and Kasztner damaged their common cause during the war and contributed significantly to Kasztner's troubles after it. Mainstream Hungarian Jewry, represented by the Jewish Council, disapproved of the Zionists on social and political grounds. Thus the Vaada faced the German onslaught more or less alone. But within the Vaada itself – not surprisingly, given its mix of strong characters with very disparate mentalities and backgrounds – there were also acute tensions, both psychological and ideological. The deep discords throughout the Jewish community made dealing with the common enemy even harder.

By early 1944 a fairly clear division of labour had developed in the Vaada. Brand was mainly responsible for helping refugees. Springmann looked after the courier network and finance. Kasztner was in charge of foreign relations. Large sums of money were contributed by a wealthy baroness, Edit Weiss, not herself a member of the Vaada.

Since Schindler's visit in November 1943, if not before, the Vaada had suspected that it might be possible to ransom Jewish lives from the Nazis, and this became very likely soon after the German occupation. The Vaada decided to bribe the Germans. Upright, honest citizens in normal peaceful times do not engage in bribery and corruption, but these times were far from normal and peaceful.

Faced with the Holocaust, the Vaada could not afford the luxury of contemplating the morality of dealing with the Nazis. Prompt action had to be taken. Lives had to be saved, and one of the options, however repugnant, was negotiating with murderers. In fact, once Komoly's calls for help had been turned down by indifferent, hostile or impotent Hungarian dignitaries, it was the sole option. Ironically, the Germans had become the Jews' last and only hope.

Opening gambit

The Nazis did not let the grass grow under their feet. As soon as the German troops had occupied Hungary, Eichmann and his crew began to organise the destruction of the last surviving Jewish community within their reach. In response to this immediate threat, the members of the Vaada were now faced with the near impossible task of trying to save the Hungarian Jews.

Their own attempt was preceded by a similar attempt in Bratislava, the capital of Slovakia, where the rabbi Michael Dov Weissmandel and the Zionist activist Gizi Fleischmann had tried to come to an arrangement with Eichmann's deputy, Dieter Wisliceny. In the summer of 1942 the Nazis suspended the deportation of 25,000 Jews still alive in Slovakia. They did so at the urgent request of the Slovak government who needed the surviving Jews to keep their economy afloat, but Weissmandel and Fleischmann believed that the respite was due to a bribe of 20,000 US dollars (today worth about 230,000 dollars or £115,000) they had paid to Wisliceny. A larger rescue operation now seemed possible. An ambitious 'Europa-Plan' was formulated, and the Vaada in Budapest informed through secret channels of communication.

On 19 March, as the German troops were approaching Budapest, the Abwehr agent Josef Winninger took Joel Brand into protective custody, together with the Vaada's cash, its correspondence with Istanbul, Switzerland and Bratislava, and the reports it had received

on German atrocities from refugees, all of which had been hidden
in Kasztner's apartment. He may have intended to protect Brand
from arrest by other German units or to secure all the valuable material for himself. On the same day Komoly and Kasztner fled with
their families from the waves of arrests to an apartment at 15 Semsey
Andor Street, which belonged to Endre Biss and where they were
joined a few days later by Joel and Hansi Brand. The Jewish-born
Biss had been brought up as a Catholic and had registered the apartment – which he had been using as a shelter for Polish fugitives –
as the office of a Lutheran organisation.

In Bratislava Wisliceny approached Weissmandel and Fleischmann
about the possibility of finding likely partners to deal with in Hungary.
He was directed to Freudiger, the head of the Orthodox community, and Nissan Kahan, the representative of the Zionists, in Budapest.
Nothing came of these meetings. More fruitfully, Weissmandel also
drew Kasztner's attention to the possibility of a deal with Wisliceny.
Kasztner and Brand therefore asked Abwehr representatives
Winninger and Johann Schmidt to sound out Wisliceny whether the
Judenkommando was 'prepared to negotiate with the illegal Jewish
rescue committee on an economic basis about the moderation of the
anti-Jewish measures,' as recorded in Kasztner's own *Bericht*.[3] The
would-be rescuers were reduced to bargaining with mass murderers
for the lives of their victims as if buying or selling merchandise. Of
course, to the SS, we were precisely that – not human beings but at
best a potentially valuable commodity.

On 5 April (or possibly a little earlier) Kasztner and Brand were
received by Wisliceny in Winniger's private apartment. They bluntly
asked Wisliceny on what conditions, if any, the Judenkommando would
be prepared to 'a) spare the lives of the Hungarian Jews; b) refrain
from concentrating the Hungarian Jews in ghettos; c) refrain from
deporting the Jews from Hungary; d) allow Hungarian Jews with
foreign visas and entry permits to emigrate'.[4] Lying through his teeth,
Wisliceny replied that while the Germans insisted on radically

removing the influence of Jews in all areas, they would not enforce ghettoisation and deportation. It would be 'possible to negotiate about the preservation of the Jewish substance'. In fact he knew that the Hungarian authorities, in collusion with the Judenkommando, had already instructed the Hungarian police and gendarmerie to register the Jews for ghettoisation and deportation. Wisliceny explained that the German 'highest authorities' were not interested in 'small-scale emigration', but if Kasztner and Brand were to prepare a plan involving the departure of 'at least 100,000 Jews', he would try to make it 'digestible' in Berlin.[5] Kasztner and Brand, for their part, were aware that the Jewish Agency had 30,000 immigration permits to Palestine at its disposal and hoped to persuade the Germans that these meant whole families, some 150,000 individuals.

In return for allowing 100,000 Jews to emigrate, Wisliceny, on behalf of the Judenkommando, demanded 2 million US dollars (today worth nearly twelve times that amount), of which ten per cent would have to be paid in Hungarian pengős within a week to demonstrate the Jewish side's 'good will' and ability to deliver. Schmidt and Winninger, who were also present, demanded a ten per cent commission for the Wehrmacht and one per cent each for their own services. The exchange rate was to be that of the black market, which amounted to 6.5 million pengős for 200,000 dollars at the time. Wisliceny also indicated that the 2 million dollars were only an advance on further payments.

To enable the Vaada leaders to carry on the negotiations unhampered by the anti-Jewish laws, the SS supplied them with 'immunity passes'. They were exempt from the obligation to wear the yellow star. They were allowed to use cars and phones, and to ignore the curfew imposed on Jews. They could travel freely wherever they liked. These privileges were not always respected by German or Hungarian gangs, but on the whole they enabled Kasztner and his associates to do their undercover work without the constant threat of arrest and deportation.

In response to Wisliceny's demands, Samu Stern, the president of the liberal Jewish community of Budapest and de facto secular leader of Hungarian Jewry, summoned a procession of rich Jews to his office and managed to raise some 5 million pengős, which was supplemented by 1.5 million from the Vaada's own rescue fund. But he was unable to meet Wisliceny's deadline, which enraged the Germans.

On 9 April Kasztner and Brand called at Winninger's apartment to deliver the first 3 million pengős, somewhat less than 100,000 dollars. Wisliceny had been replaced by the more senior Hermann Krumey and Otto Hunsche. Kasztner began to suspect that the SS were treating the proposed deal as important official business rather than just a bit of private extortion. It is difficult to tell how far, if at all, the SS intended to keep their part of the bargain, but it was obvious that they were playing a double game. Even as Krumey and Hunsche were receiving the Jewish money in Budapest, Wisliceny was in the northern town of Munkács, overseeing the Hungarian authorities' preparations for the round-up of the Jews of Carpatho-Ruthenia. The ghettoisation, which Wisliceny had emphatically ruled out, in fact began in that part of the country on 16 April.

On 21 April Kasztner and Brand delivered another 2.5 million pengős, leaving 1 million still outstanding. Krumey threatened to break off negotiations, and Hunsche in particular was full of righteous anger. Eventually they granted a deferment with Krumey promising that a number of Jews would be allowed to emigrate provided there was proof that either a neutral state or the USA was prepared to accept them. Kasztner and Brand produced a telegram from Chaim Barlas in Istanbul to the effect that a ship was ready in the Romanian port of Constanţa on the Black Sea to take 600 holders of British entry 'certificates' to Palestine. The Germans stressed that any group departure would have to be disguised as deportation for the benefit of the Hungarian authorities and that the whole enterprise, on pain of death, had to be kept a 'Reich secret'.[6]

Normally, immigration certificates were sent for distribution to

Moshe Krausz at the Palestine Office, but Kasztner was not prepared to leave a matter of such crucial importance in the hands of his rival. He therefore assigned the task of listing appropriate recipients to Otto Komoly and Ernő Szilágyi. In the event the list grew to almost three times its original size and underwent numerous amendments. Kasztner himself kept the option of making the final decision in many cases.

Half of the 600 permit holders were to be brought from the provinces to a 'privileged camp' in Budapest by SS men. On 2 May Krumey demanded a list of 300 and at the same time undertook to allow 100 more to emigrate on payment of a further 10 million pengős, or 3.5 million dollars, which it would be 'child's play' for the Jews to raise.[7] On 3 May Kasztner travelled to Kolozsvár to select 300 men, women and children with the help of local Jewish leaders. In response to fierce protests, a provisional list was prepared which included small contingents from other provincial towns.

On the same day the ghettoisation of Jews began in Kolozsvár. So it was that this first stage of Kasztner's negotiations coincided more or less with my confinement in the ghetto of Kolozsvár, my escape to Budapest, and my admission to the Kolumbusz group.

As it happened, Kasztner was driven to Kolozsvár by the same Abwehr agent, Rudi Sedlaczek, who had earlier brought Schindler to several meetings in Budapest. Kasztner was deeply distressed by what he saw on the way:

> Everywhere on the roads we met small groups of Jews. They travelled on ox-drawn and horse-drawn carts crammed full of the wretched possessions of their poverty. Most of them were walking. Young and old men and women dragged themselves along tired and exhausted. Their faces were pale as on Yom Kippur, their eyes sad and miserable. Behind them gendarmes with fixed bayonets. They were being led to the ghettos in the cities: the collection point and last stop before deportation.[8]

During his stay in Kolozsvár, Kasztner discussed the prospects ahead with the leaders of the local Jewish community. Looking back on the events up to that point, he claims to have told them that the next steps after ghettoisation would be deportation and extermination. The details of the discussion are not known, but it is clear that the leaders did not pass on the message to the rest of the community. Ten years later this omission was to play a decisive part in Kasztner's tragedy.

It was also during this stay in Kolozsvár that Kasztner met Wisliceny who, with characteristic mendacity, complained that Eichmann had removed him from the negotiations and put him in charge of ghettoisation because the Jews 'thought too well' of him.[9] When Kasztner asked point blank whether the wholesale deportation of the Hungarian Jews was imminent, Wisliceny prevaricated. Once they had returned to Budapest, he told Kasztner that we would all be deported. That was on 8 May – my eleventh birthday. The deportations started in earnest one week later.

Meanwhile Joel Brand had received an amazing offer from Eichmann.

CHAPTER 5

Trucks for Lives

The Brand mission

Early on the morning of 25 April Joel Brand was summoned by Adolf Eichmann. At 9 o'clock an SS sergeant in a black Mercedes picked him up at the Opera Café and drove him to Eichmann's headquarters at the Majestic Hotel. The account that follows is based on Brand's own recollections as retold by Alex Weissberg. Although not always accurate, Weissberg's story is broadly confirmed by Kasztner's own report and other documents.[1]

Today Obersturmbannführer Adolf Eichmann is remembered from a number of portraits either as a ruthless young officer in SS uniform or as a bald, aging prisoner being tried in Jerusalem. Brand described him as being about forty, of medium height and slim build, with fair hair, thin lips and a thin nose. But for his 'steel blue, hard and sharp' eyes, which 'seemed to drill through you,' he could have been 'a clerk in an office'. His speech was like a 'machine gun; he would rap out a few words and then pause'.[2] At this meeting, after a few brief introductory remarks, Eichmann put forward his infamous 'goods for blood' proposal.

I suppose you know who I am. I was in charge of the 'actions' in Germany and Poland and Czechoslovakia. Now it's Hungary's turn ... I have investigated you and your people in the Joint and the Sochnut, and ... I am prepared to sell you one million Jews ... Goods for blood – blood for goods. You can take them from any country where there are Jews left ... What do you want to save? Men who can beget children? Women who can bear them? Old people? Children? Sit down and talk.[3]

His head reeling, Brand replied that he was unable to provide any goods as all Jewish factories and businesses had been closed down. He asked if Eichmann would accept money instead, and how much. But Eichmann insisted:

I'm going to Berlin the day after tomorrow, and I'll discuss the matter again with our leaders. In the meantime you must decide what kind of goods you can offer us ... Go abroad and get in direct touch with your people and with representatives of the Allied Powers. Then come back to me with a concrete proposal.[4]

Brand suggested that he might go to Istanbul, where the emissaries of the Palestine-based Jewish Agency were best placed to act as a link between the Jews under German rule and the Allies. Eichmann agreed, with a sinister reminder that Brand's mother, wife and children would remain behind as hostages to ensure his return.

On 8 May Eichmann summoned Brand again. He now had 'assent from the highest levels' for the negotiations to proceed.

What I would like to get are army trucks. You want to have one million Jews? ... I'll make you a fair offer. You deliver me one army truck for a hundred Jews ... That makes a total of ten thousand trucks ... They must be brand new and equipped for winter conditions.[5]

Amidst declarations that the trucks were needed for the 'Eastern Front exclusively' and would 'never be used in the West', Eichmann assured Brand:

> If you return from Istanbul and tell me that the offer has been accepted, I'll dismantle Auschwitz and bring ten per cent of the million I've promised you to the frontier. You can take them away and bring me the thousand trucks afterwards. And we'll go on like that, delivery followed by payment. A thousand trucks for every hundred thousand Jews.[6]

As the discussions continued, Eichmann and Brand agreed on a ransom of 10,000 trucks, 200 tonnes of tea, 800 tonnes of coffee, 2 million cases of soap, an unspecified amount of tungsten and some other goods needed for the German war effort.[7]

Eichmann summoned Brand again on 14 May. This time Otto Klages was also present and, to Brand's surprise, handed over 50,000 US dollars and 270,000 Swiss francs together with a number of letters intercepted by the Germans in transit from Switzerland to the Vaada. This gesture was intended to demonstrate the reliability of the German 'business partners'.

Brand's last meeting with Eichmann took place on 15 May, when Eichmann told him that the deportations from Hungary had just commenced: 12,000 Jews would be taken away every day. He announced that the transports would be sent to Austria or Slovakia, rather than Auschwitz, to await Brand's return. 'If you come back in a week's time, or shall we say two weeks at the latest, and bring me a positive decision, then I'll blow up Auschwitz, and the people I am deporting now will be sent to the Spanish frontier. If you don't come back or aren't here in good time, they'll all go to Auschwitz.'[8]

When Brand reported back to his Vaada colleagues, they were dazed by the sudden prospect of rescuing a million Jews. But soon they regained their scepticism. It was impossible to believe that the

Nazis could offer such a deal in earnest or that the Allies would consent to it. However, there was still a chance to benefit. On the one hand, Brand in Istanbul might alert the world to the Holocaust and persuade the Allies to take action to save the Jews still surviving in German hands. On the other hand, by dragging out the negotiations – through bluff, prevarication and deception, their only weapons against the overwhelming power of state-sanctioned robbers and murderers – they might keep large numbers of Jews alive until the approaching collapse of the Third Reich.

As for Eichmann, he too could hardly have believed that the deal would come off, and it is likely that he did not even want it to. He might not have objected to grabbing a substantial ransom, preferably without honouring his side of the bargain, but for the real reasons behind his offer, or at least for some plausible hypotheses, we must look further afield.

It is certain that Eichmann acted with the knowledge, and to some extent on the orders, of his superior, Heinrich Himmler. But what did Himmler himself really expect from the deal? It is possible that at this eleventh hour, realising that the war was all but lost, he decided to play the part of the surviving Jews' saviour in order to secure better treatment for himself: his subsequent suspension of the deportations and exterminations may also point in this direction. It is equally possible that he wanted, and actually managed, to trick his victims into cooperating in their own destruction: by raising false expectations of rescue, he made any resistance to the deportations appear unnecessary. Two further hypotheses take into account the possible effect of the offer on the course of the war itself. One of these involves propaganda: Himmler sought to engineer a refusal in order to score a resounding psychological victory by shifting the blame for the obliteration of Europe's Jews to the Allies and the Jewish organisations of the free world. The other has even wider implications: there seems to be a strong case for believing that Himmler was trying to drive a wedge between the Western Allies and the Soviet

Union, with the aim of concluding a separate peace with Britain and
the USA and concentrating on defeating the Red Army. In this last
context it has been argued that Brand's mission was only a cover for
the far more important mission of Bandi Grosz, who was to travel
to Istanbul and establish contacts between senior German intelligence officers and their British and American counterparts. Whatever
motivated Himmler in letting Eichmann make this staggering offer,
it is certain that the Germans were grossly mistaken in attributing
any influence in international affairs to the Vaada. But the Vaada, of
course, did nothing to undeceive them.

On 17 May Obersturmbannführer Hermann Krumey drove Brand
and Grosz to Vienna. Two days later they were flown by German
courier plane to Istanbul. Before their departure Hansi Brand had
been summoned by Eichmann for the first time. He ordered her to
treat the deal strictly as a secret of the Reich and to inform him
immediately if she received any news from Istanbul. She was to stay
in Budapest with her family, reporting to his office daily. In short,
she was Eichmann's hostage. On the same day Hansi 'decided that
it was not for a woman to bear such responsibility'[9] and Rezső
Kasztner obtained an audience with Eichmann to introduce himself
and to continue the negotiations together with her.

The fiasco in Istanbul

When the Vaada informed the Jewish representatives in Istanbul
about Brand's impending journey, a coded telegram came back in
reply explaining that 'Chaim' was ready to meet him. The Vaada
understood this to refer to Chaim Weizmann, the distinguished
President of the World Zionist Organisation. Hopes were riding
high. But when Brand landed in Istanbul he was shocked to find
that the man awaiting him was Chaim Barlas, the head of the Jewish
Agency's local rescue committee, or the Istanbul Vaada. On their
arrival Grosz had immediately been spirited away from the airport
by some of his own contacts, while Brand, who had no Turkish

visa, was denied admission to the country until Jewish Agency officials managed to obtain a temporary permit for him.

At an emotional meeting in the Pera Palace Hotel, Brand told the horrified local representatives of the various Zionist groups all that was by then known in Hungary about the Holocaust, mainly from the accounts of the *Auschwitz Protocols* of Rudolf Vrba and Alfred Wetzler. He urged his listeners to obtain the Allies' immediate agreement in principle to hold discussions with the Germans about their offer. While Brand had no illusions about the chances of the deal itself, he believed that a simple oral promise could hold up the deportations for a while, and the pretence of continuing negotiations would buy enough time for the remaining Jews to survive until the end of the war. Describing how each day 12,000 Hungarian Jews were being carried in the most inhuman conditions to their deaths, Brand called for a man of the stature of Weizmann or Shertok to come to Istanbul forthwith in order to give the Germans the impression that significant progress was being made. He demanded that the Allies bomb the gas chambers and crematoria of Auschwitz and the railway lines leading to them.

Over the next few weeks a number of urgent appeals were made to the British and US governments by leading members of the Jewish Agency, but produced no results. Supplying strategically important goods to the enemy was out of the question. The request that the British and US governments string the Germans along by declaring, at least in appearance, their willingness to engage in negotiations was also turned down. Proposals and counter-proposals flew to and fro between the representatives of Jewish organisations and more or less important diplomats and politicians in Istanbul, London and Washington, but to no avail. In late June Moshe Shertok travelled to London to ask for a 'carrot to be dangled before the Germans.'[10] What he experienced was typical of the whole process. The foreign minister, Anthony Eden, assured him that Britain would do all it could to save the Jews, but in fact the British government had already decided early in June to have nothing to do with the offer. On 11 July Prime Minister Churchill reiterated that there should be 'no negotiations of any kind on this subject' and instructed Eden that with regard to the Holocaust – 'probably the greatest and most horrible crime ever committed' – 'declarations should be made in public, so that everyone connected with it will be hunted down and put to death'.[11] The American authorities, acting partly on the advice of the British, were no more helpful. They informed the Soviets of Eichmann's undertaking to use the trucks on the Eastern front only, and the Soviets flatly refused to allow any negotiations to proceed. The US Ambassador to Moscow, in formal diplomatic language, reported to Washington on 19 June that the Soviet government did 'not consider it expedient or permissible to carry on any conversation whatsoever with the German government on the question touched upon'.[12]

Shertok's and Weizmann's joint appeals in late June and early July for bombing raids on Auschwitz were rejected by Eden and the Foreign Office. A similar request put forward on their behalf in late June by Henry Morgenthau, US President Roosevelt's Secretary of the Treasury, was refused by the War Department.

The main reason for the Allies' refusal to negotiate, or even to appear to negotiate, was their insistence on an unconditional German surrender. Any negotiation would have breached this principle, and a deal, if one had materialised, might well have had an adverse effect on the Allies' conduct of the war. The reasons for refusing to bomb Auschwitz were complex. The success of such an operation was uncertain and the Allies were reluctant to divert resources from existing strategic plans. There were misgivings about the influx of vast numbers of refugees in the event of an agreement and perhaps not a little indifference to the fate of the Jews. Immigration by large numbers to either the USA or to Britain and the Empire was restricted by the enforcement of a rigorous quota system, which neither the Americans nor the British were prepared to relax. The British were particularly worried about the possible effects of masses of Jews arriving in Palestine, which was under their control at the time. In London, on 31 May, the Cabinet Committee for Refugees informed its US counterparts that any negotiation might 'lead to an offer to unload an even greater number of Jews on our hands'.[13] In Cairo, in late June, a British politician, hearing about Eichmann's offer, asked Brand in amazement: 'What should I do with a million Jews? Where should I put them?'[14] According to Brand, the politician was Lord Moyne, Minister of State for the Middle East. In any event, the reaction was typical of the views held in most influential circles.

The Western Allies decided that the most likely motive behind Eichmann's offer was to cause a split between them and the Soviet Union. After many secret discussions, the deal was finally rejected. The *New York Herald Tribune* of 19 June lambasted the idea as a devious German scheme to subvert the unity of the Allies. The next day the London *Times*, among others, delivered the following rebuttal under the heading 'A Monstrous "Offer"':

> It has long been clear that, faced with the certainty of defeat, the German authorities would intensify all their efforts to blackmail, deceive, and split the allies. In their latest effort . . . they have reached a new level of fantasy and self-deception. They have put forward, or sponsored, an offer to exchange the remaining Hungarian Jews for munitions of war . . . The whole story is one of the most loathsome of the war. It begins with a process of deliberate extirpation and ends, to date, with attempted blackmail . . . The British Government know what value to set on any German or German-sponsored offer . . . the German 'offer' seems to be simply a fantastic attempt to sow suspicion among the allies.[15]

The very public rejection of the top-secret offer put a sad end to Brand's mission.

★

Brand himself had been harassed by the Turkish authorities from the moment he arrived in Istanbul. His hopes of meeting an important member of the Jewish Agency were dashed when Moshe Shertok in Palestine was unable to obtain a Turkish visa. It was finally decided that he should meet Shertok in Aleppo, Syria, half-way between Turkey and Palestine, and he left Istanbul by train on 5 June. Before he reached the Syrian border two members of the Jewish underground organisation Irgun joined the train at Ankara and warned him that he was about to fall into a British trap. Brand saw no alternative but to continue his journey. On 7 June, immediately after crossing into Syria, he was detained by British forces, who suspected him of being a Nazi spy. He was finally allowed to meet Shertok in Aleppo in the presence of British intelligence officers. Brand told Shertok in great detail about the progress of the Holocaust and the efforts of the Vaada. Shertok was profoundly moved, but had little comfort to offer. When he explained that the British intended to take Brand to Egypt as their captive, Brand called out in despair: 'Don't you realise what you're doing? This is plain murder! Mass murder! If I don't go back, our best people will be slaughtered . . . I am here as the delegate of a million people condemned to death. Their lives depend on my return.' Deeply distressed at the thought of what was happening to the Jewish masses, he was equally disturbed by the prospect of Eichmann's reprisals against his own family: 'My wife! My mother! My children! They will be the first to go.'[16] It was no good. Shertok promised to have the matter taken up at the highest level in London, but although he kept his word and did all he could to secure Eden's support, he was unsuccessful.

Brand, guarded by a British officer, was taken by rail through Palestine to Cairo, where he was interrogated day after day, week after week, by the British about his relations with the Germans and about the Jewish Agency. The ordeal lasted more than three months. It ended on 5 October, when Brand was given the choice between going to Palestine and returning to Hungary. With the Jewish Agency's cooperation he took the first option. Had he taken the second, he would in all likelihood have been immediately put to death by Eichmann.

However, shortly before leaving Istanbul for Aleppo, Brand had scored a small success. He had managed to persuade the Istanbul Vaada to draw up an 'interim agreement', dated 29 May, which stated that negotiations to resolve the legal and political difficulties were making progress. The document urged the Germans to cease deportations and to allow Jews to emigrate. Probably because of courier problems, it did not reach Budapest until 5 July, three days before the deportations from the whole of provincial Hungary were completed.

While Brand was detained in the Middle East, his associates back in Hungary suspected him of desertion. They could not begin to imagine the military, diplomatic and political reasoning behind the Allies' refusal to come to their aid, even by merely pretending an interest in the German offer. Brand never fully succeeded in clearing his name. With less than full justification, he accused both the Allies and the Jewish leadership in Palestine of deliberately betraying him. Bitter and disillusioned by his failure to gain the recognition he thought he deserved, upset by quarrels with his wife Hansi, envious of Kasztner's achievement, he died in Israel in 1964.

After the fiasco of Brand's mission Kasztner, supported by Hansi, became the undisputed leader of the Vaada's rescue operations.

CHAPTER 6

The Merciless Task

The two sides of Rezső Kasztner

Although technically vice-chairman of the Vaada, Kasztner was in effect its prime driving force. In order to understand his extraordinary relationship with the Germans it is necessary to appreciate his own contradictory personality.

Rezső Kasztner was born on 14 April 1906 in Kolozsvár, as I was a quarter of a century later, and he attended the Jewish *gymnasium* there, as I did for a year before Jewish education and so many other things came to an abrupt end in Transylvania. After obtaining a law degree in his early twenties he worked as a journalist and Zionist activist. He was a regular contributor to the *Új kelet* (New East) newspaper and a member of Ihud, a conglomerate of centre-left parties, which had close links to the Mapai (Labour) party in Palestine. Kasztner had joined the Barisia Zionist youth movement at the age of sixteen and by the time he was twenty-six he had become one of its leaders. In 1937 he married Erzsébet (nicknamed Bogyó, Hungarian for 'berry'), the daughter of Dr József Fischer, the wealthy president of the Jewish Religious Community in Kolozsvár and a member of the Romanian parliament while Jews were still allowed to participate. On joining the family, Kasztner was given the assignment of breaking

up a relationship between Bogyó's younger sister Vica and Joel
Nussbecher – or Joel Palgi, as he called himself after his emigration
to Palestine – who was later to play an unfortunate part in Kasztner's
destiny. Vica also emigrated to Palestine, where she married Pesach
Rudik.

In 1940, soon after the annexation of Transylvania by Hungary,
Kasztner moved to Budapest where he continued his Zionist activities. In 1942 he was conscripted and served for six months in a
slave-labour unit of the Hungarian army, building fortifications in
Transylvania. After his release he resumed his work as a Zionist and
leading member of the evolving Vaada.

I never knew Kasztner personally, and he would hardly have taken
much notice of an eleven-year-old if we had actually met. As I listened
to the adults talking about him later in Bergen-Belsen, I had visions
of a superman who would one day tear the barbed wire apart with
his bare hands and lead us out of the camp past our astonished
guards, much as Moses had led the Israelites out of Egypt. The real
Kasztner was a rather different person.

Those who knew him remember Kasztner as a complex individual, whose remarkable strengths were accompanied by equally
remarkable weaknesses. Rivka Bar-Yosef, a member of the young
Zionist group led by Kasztner before the war, describes him as
unquestionably 'sharp-witted and shrewd', but claims that 'he often
made promises he couldn't keep'. Rafi Ben-Shalom, a member of
the Zionist youth resistance in Hungary, who frequently encountered Kasztner in rescue operations, recalls that he was 'exceedingly
courageous', noting that the other side of his courage could be
described as 'megalomania'.[1]

Joel Brand, one of his closest associates, had at least two good
reasons to criticise him: Kasztner was not only Brand's rival within
the Vaada, but he also had an affair with Brand's wife Hansi while
Brand was pursuing his hopeless mission abroad. Nevertheless, in
his memoir, *Advocate for the Dead*, he paints a picture of Kasztner

that is even-handed enough to be believed. To Brand, Kasztner seemed the 'prototype of the snobbish intellectual who lacks the common touch'. Quick rather than reliable, he was sometimes slapdash in manner and 'not always an easy man to work with'. However, 'when he really put his mind to something', Brand wrote, 'he was able to achieve things that at first seemed almost impossible . . . he showed marvellous courage at critical moments'.[2]

Fülöp Freudiger, in a report he wrote soon after his own escape to Romania, described Kasztner as 'dictatorial in nature, jealous of the successes of others and terribly lax vis-à-vis deadlines and compliance with agreements.' In the same piece, Freudiger acknowledges that Kasztner was also idealistic and competent, 'a man of vision . . . selfless and always willing to take personal risks'.[3]

Understandably, the most sympathetic character witness is Kasztner's daughter Zsuzsi. In my conversations with her it was clear that she idolised both her parents. She readily accepted the charge of arrogance that is often levelled against her father, but she repeated what she had earlier said in an interview about him: 'On one hand he was a very, very good person. He liked to help people. On the other hand he was arrogant, very arrogant, and rightly so because he was extremely smart and intelligent and handsome and charismatic.'[4] She was less willing to accept the charge of untruthfulness, preferring to see her father as a dashing gambler who relied on clever stratagems and good luck rather than crude dishonesty. Interviewed by the academic Ann Pasternak Slater, she said much the same thing: 'He was not a liar. But he played poker!'[5]

After Joel Brand's departure for Istanbul, Kasztner's negotiations with the SS became increasingly intensive. He was frequently summoned to Eichmann's headquarters or himself requested permission to attend. It is not surprising that he found these occasions extremely stressful, but he forced himself to appear undaunted. A characteristic anecdote illustrates his ability to put on a brave face and treat the all-powerful murderers as his equals, even though he was quaking in his boots. When he complained to Hansi Brand about Eichmann's intimidating habit of smoking during their encounters, she advised him to do likewise. He did, and this display of self-assurance, however fake, achieved its aim. After the war Eichmann himself, for what it was worth, praised the cold-bloodedness and panache with which Kasztner had 'smoked cigarettes as though he were in a coffee house'.[6]

There is general agreement that Kasztner was ambitious, overbearing and devious, but also that he had a sharp mind, remarkable diplomatic skills, enormous courage, the ability to make difficult decisions and the determination to perform his task without regard to his own comfort and safety. Many of his traits may seem less than admirable in our relatively normal circumstances, but in those chaotic times they were precisely what was needed to carry on a relationship with the Germans which one member of our Bergen-Belsen group, Shoshana Barzel, has called a 'story of mutual fraud'.[7] Another member of the group, Eva Speter, describes him as a 'man without scruples', a womaniser and a liar, a 'man with an ego like a balloon'. But, in the perverse situation prevailing, she believes that Kasztner's more objectionable qualities made him 'the best contact man with the Germans – the man who could bribe them and go with the Germans to have girls and drink and play cards and take care to lose on the card games'.[8]

Eva Speter may be overstating the alleged levels of dishonesty and debauchery, but it is certain that Kasztner would not have achieved much if he had used only polite, honest approaches. The same point is made by Alex Barzel, who later became one of Kasztner's greatest champions in his misfortune. He too sees Kasztner as 'arrogant, patronising and aggressive', but stresses that 'it was actually because of his character that he was capable of doing great things during the Nazi occupation'. Outside the boundaries of conventional behaviour, Kasztner proved a remarkable individual, very different from the supine Jewish masses: 'To take any action under the conditions of the German inferno, you needed to have a very special personality, leadership and decision-making ability and especially, no small measure of *chutzpah*.'[9]

Historians who have written about Kasztner emphasise more or less the same ambivalence. The most thorough study, particularly of Kasztner's experiences in Israel after the war, is Yechiam Weitz's *The Man who was Murdered Twice*, published in Hebrew in 1995 and yet to appear in English. Weitz's detailed account is both objective and sympathetic. He does not deny that Kasztner 'obsessively tried to take centre stage', but he points out that Kasztner's behaviour in the storms of the Holocaust cannot be judged by the standards of more ordinary times. He attributes Kasztner's astonishing ability to stand his ground against the Nazi criminals to both the positive and negative sides of his character:

> A man must possess some extraordinary traits to dare to enter the lion's den and to maintain contact with S.S. officers, in particular when his hands are empty and he has nothing to offer in return for the Jews he wants to save. To do this, he had to have courage and nerves of steel. But he needed other, more problematic, traits – cunning and the ability to lie without blinking an eyelash – traits which are usually considered negative and harmful, but were absolutely vital in the hell that was Budapest.

Finally Weitz pays homage to the extraordinary strengths and inner resources Kasztner revealed by rejecting several opportunities to stay securely in Switzerland, when the Germans allowed him to cross the border to raise money from Swiss sources, and by returning 'to the Nazi hell, daring again and again to enter the office of the master murderer' in order to continue his rescue work.[10]

The Ark
While Brand desperately sought some sign of real or pretended Allied willingness to negotiate with the Germans, the Vaada in Budapest

tried equally desperately to convince Eichmann that the hold-ups were only temporary. Kasztner, often accompanied by Hansi Brand, called on Eichmann at frequent intervals, and a bizarre relationship developed between the tiny group of Jews and the exterminator of millions.

Kasztner and Hansi made a tremendous effort to stand up to Eichmann as his equals, although it was clear that he could have put them to death with one pen stroke. They gambled with thousands of lives, including their own, concealing their fear behind a show of boldness, their hatred and disgust behind diplomacy and cunning. While Eichmann deceived, blackmailed and bullied them, they tried to bluff, hoodwink and trick him. They met his lies, broken promises and open threats with subterfuges of their own. He treated them with contempt because they were Jews, but he also had a sneaking respect for them because he believed that they had a secret power. The mighty SS grossly overrated the importance of Kasztner and his small band of frightened Jews. They pretended to represent the American Jewish Joint Distribution Committee, and the SS fell for it. As Kasztner wrote, 'the Joint was the embodiment of their ideas of "Jewish World Power", the "Jewish World Conspiracy" and "Jewish Wealth"'.[11] Having been brainwashed by their own propaganda, the Nazis believed in the omnipotence of 'World Jewry', whose secret agents they took the Vaada to be.

Soon after Brand's departure Kasztner and Hansi plucked up enough courage to warn Eichmann that any delay in the arrival of the Kolozsvár contingent in Budapest would harm the approaches to the Jewish Agency and the Allies in Istanbul. When they complained about the inhumane treatment of the deportees from Carpatho-Ruthenia Eichmann replied that if up to a hundred people had been squeezed into the cattle trucks it was because the Jews in that region had many small children, who did not need much space. Asked to halt the deportations, he declared that he was 'not that stupid'; if he did, the 'people abroad' would stop negotiating.[12] On 22 May

Eichmann specified his plans for the 600 holders of Palestine entry certificates. As the German leadership had promised Amin al-Husseini, the Grand Mufti of Jerusalem, that no Jew would be allowed to emigrate to Palestine, the group would travel through Germany and occupied France to Spain, and from there to Africa. What happened afterwards was not his concern.

On 27 May three agents of the Hungarian secret police again raided Endre Biss's apartment, which served as a hiding place for the Vaada. They found a large sum of US dollars, Swiss francs and Hungarian pengős, supplied from Istanbul and Switzerland to finance escape operations. Fortunately, they missed a suitcase full of forged identity papers, also kept there by young *chalutzim* (Zionist pioneers) engaged in rescuing refugees. Kasztner and his wife Bogyó, Hansi Brand and her sister, and several others were arrested and taken to police headquarters on Svábhegy Hill in Buda. It transpired that a group of Polish and Slovakian Jews had been caught by Hungarian gendarmes trying to cross into Romania with false documents. They had been brutally questioned and one of them had given away the name of the printer. On his arrest, the Vaada was identified among his contacts.

Kasztner and his companions were held for five days before the first of them, Hansi Brand, was questioned. The interrogator was the head of the secret police, Péter Hain. He confronted Hansi with the printer who admitted that she had paid him for printing false documents. Hain then concentrated on Hansi's connections with the rescue work of the *chalutzim* and the Germans' reasons for sending her husband to Istanbul. Hansi later recalled in her testimony at Eichmann's trial that 'this kind of half questions, half beatings, continued for about seven hours', but she 'did not tell them anything', because she 'did not want to be the only person who would jeopardise' the Vaada's only chance to save people. She refused to answer, even when she was beaten so badly that she was unable to walk for weeks after.

Next morning it was Kasztner's turn to be questioned. After the first five minutes the secret policeman in charge hit him in the face and began to kick him. At that point the phone rang and soon an SS Scharführer (staff sergeant) appeared at the door. He took all the Vaada captives to the nearby SS headquarters, and two hours later they were free. As Kasztner was to discover, the SS, afraid that the captives might betray to the Hungarians the 'Reich secret' of their intended sale of Jews, had gone as high as Prime Minister Sztójay to secure their prompt release.

While Kasztner was under arrest, a telegram arrived from Brand announcing that the 'interim agreement' was on its way. Kasztner again asked Eichmann to suspend the deportations, which had by then removed all the Jews from Carpatho-Ruthenia and northern Hungary. Eichmann replied: 'That's out of the question. On the contrary, I'll continue the deportations at full steam.'[13] Kasztner then demanded that the selected Jews from the provinces be brought to the capital without delay. Eichmann promised again, but on 3 June he summoned Kasztner and claimed that because of difficulties with the Hungarian government he could not bring any provincial Jews to Budapest. When Kasztner reminded him that he had already given orders for the departure of the Kolozsvár group Eichmann replied: 'Yes, but I rescinded the order yesterday. Is that clear? Now I have no more time for you!'

At this point a deeply frustrated Kasztner took stock of the situation. He began with a list of Eichmann's breaches of promise:

First we tried to prevent or at least delay the deportations. The Germans promised, and we paid, paid a great deal. But they did not keep their word.

Then we asked them at least to allow six hundred people to emigrate. Again they agreed and promised to bring three hundred prominent people to Budapest from the provinces. They did not keep their word again. And by now more than 300,000 Jews have been sent to Auschwitz, without one of the three hundred being saved.

Kasztner continued with a somewhat cryptic reflection that goes a long way to explain his actions:

> It is not only the rescue of a few hundred Jews from the provinces that is at stake. If Eichmann cannot be forced to give in here and now, then, by putting our money on the German number in this game of roulette with human lives, we were naïve losers, just as so many others before us in occupied Europe. Then paying so many millions was a foolish delusion. But the loser in this game is also called traitor.[14]

After the war Kasztner was accused of betraying the bulk of Hungarian Jewry to save his own family and friends. In fact he was trying to prevent the deportation of the masses who had not yet been deported to Auschwitz. Our relatively small group from Kolozsvár and elsewhere was meant to act as a test case. If the Germans were to release us, their apparent willingness to deliver might encourage the Allies to show an interest in Eichmann's far-reaching offer; which might in turn persuade the Germans to delay the deportations. Thus Kasztner intended to use the rescue of a few hundred to save many thousands more. If he was clutching at straws, it was better than doing nothing. He was driven to distraction by Eichmann's cruel tricks, but he pulled himself up time and again because he felt that by abandoning his efforts he would betray not only the small contingent from Kolozsvár but all the surviving Jews who might still be saved.

Eichmann's cat-and-mouse games are graphically described in Hansi Brand's testimony.[15] Between May and September, either with Kasztner or on her own, she met him more than fifteen times and, like Kasztner, was infuriated by his lies. She recalled how Eichmann 'kept stressing that what a German officer promises, he will always honour. But he did not honour anything'. The Vaada felt helpless in the face of his deceitfulness: 'Everything we did, all our work, was like a daily, laborious tilting at windmills. What we had established on one day . . . the next day was found to be nothing at all.' His perfidy had been apparent right from the start of Brand's mission. Having promised that in the case of the first transports from Hungary 'Auschwitz would not operate, in order to provide a basis for nego-tiating', he had 'started immediately with the gassings'. In response to complaints about his persistent failure to honour his undertakings he threatened to continue the gassings – which were happening anyway – and for good measure told Hansi: 'You are perfectly free to telegraph your husband that I am letting the mill run – no one should think that I am afraid.'[16] Once Hansi begged him to spare children being sent to Auschwitz and, having received a blunt refusal, burst out: 'You probably do not have any children, and that is why you have no pity on them.' He replied: 'You are taking a great liberty, Mrs Brand; if you speak to me like that, I advise you to stop coming to see me.'[17]

In fact Eichmann never had any intention of sparing Jews. He may have been prepared to let a few escape in order to facilitate the destruction of the many, but he objected to any rescue on a larger scale. Hansi remembered that he was 'very angry and upset' about Brand's failure to return from Istanbul, but 'very pleased that this transaction had not come off', because that gave him 'a free hand' to 'quite happily dispatch' the Jews.[18] Later, when Himmler called a halt to the deportations, Eichmann tried to sabotage the order. It is not clear whether he was taking an independent initiative against Himmler's wishes or obeying orders from Kaltenbrunner and Müller, following Hitler's own determination not to leave a single Jew alive.

When Kasztner heard Eichmann's bad-tempered retraction of his agreement to bring the 300 Jews from Kolozsvár to Budapest, he decided to bluff. He asked Krumey and Klages to intervene and threatened to inform Istanbul that there was no point in continuing the negotiations. Later that morning he was summoned by Eichmann. With Hunsche, Krumey, Wisliceny and Novak in attendance, Eichmann threw a 'fit of rage', which Kasztner let pass without any response. When he had calmed down, the following exchange took place:

'What do you really want?' Eichmann begins the conversation at last.
'I must insist on our agreements being kept. Will you bring the people suggested by us from the provinces to Budapest?'
'Once I have said *no* it's no!'
'Then there's no point in continuing to negotiate.'
I pretend to be getting up.
'You're a bundle of nerves, Kasztner. I'll send you to Theresienstadt to recover. Or do you prefer Auschwitz?'
'It would be pointless. Nobody else would take my place.'
'You must understand me, I've got to clear this Jewish filth out of the provinces! It's no use arguing or crying.'
'Then our arguments in Istanbul won't be any use either.'
'What good are these few Jews to you?'
'It's not only these few. Things in Istanbul aren't going well because you're pressing ahead with the deportations. You must provide proof that your offer is serious. What do these few Jews matter to you?'[19]

For an hour Eichmann alternated between appearing to give in and banging the table in new fits of rage. Then he suddenly offered to send 100–200 Jews from Kolozsvár to Theresienstadt. They were to leave with a train of deportees heading for Auschwitz in order to deceive the Hungarian authorities. Putting the blame on the Hungarian secretary of state, he explained: 'I can't act the Jew-saver here. I promised László Endre that no Jew will return to this country alive.'[20]

When Kasztner refused, Eichmann's deputy Dieter Wisliceny intervened. The SS, he said, had told the Hungarian authorities that a dangerous Zionist conspiracy had been discovered, whose members had to be kept apart from Jews being sent to work in the Reich. Smiling with 'satisfaction about the diplomatic genius of the master race', Eichmann finally conceded: 'All right. The Kolozsvár people are coming to Budapest.'[21]

This concession was followed by two hours of haggling. Eichmann agreed that 'about two hundred' could be brought to the capital. They were to travel with their luggage in unsealed cattle trucks and stay in a camp guarded by SS. On his way out Kasztner bumped into the SS Scharführer who was to escort the group to Budapest and promised him a generous reward if 'about two hundred' turned out to be considerably more.[22]

The negotiations had been conducted on the understanding that the transport would consist entirely of people holding entry certificates to Palestine or other documents permitting travel abroad. Eichmann demanded a list of all the individuals to be brought to Budapest from Kolozsvár, rejecting the suggestion that it should be compiled by the Kolozsvár Jewish Council. Thus Komoly and Szilágyi had the impossible task of selecting 388 people out of 18,000 who were by then in the ghetto. They were assisted by Zsigmond Léb, the former president of the Kolozsvár Orthodox Community, who happened to be in Budapest. With studied understatement Kasztner wrote about a 'painful and complicated operation that did not take place without inner struggles'.[23]

The selectors would have preferred to save only children, but were obliged to include mostly adults in order to maintain Eichmann's fiction of a 'conspiracy'; at the same time they could not bring themselves to break up families. After long, heated debates they agreed to choose from the following categories: 'a) deserving figures in Jewish public life; b) people who had served the Jewish community in general or made sacrifices for Jewish social causes; c) widows and orphans of slave labourers.'[24] Eventually they produced a list of about 250 families. This was subsequently modified in the Kolozsvár ghetto: some people were added by the local Jewish leaders or by bribed German and Hungarian officials, while others already on the list had meanwhile been deported to Auschwitz. Understandably there were angry charges of nepotism which were to continue long after the war.

It was to house the group from Kolozsvár that the Vaada had acquired and enlarged the premises of the Wechselmann Institute for the Deaf-Mute in Kolumbusz Street in southern Budapest. Kasztner described the arrival of the group as a momentous event in the history of the Holocaust. Instead of being deported to their deaths in Auschwitz, these Jews had been brought to a safe haven to await the outcome of a mad gamble with their lives:

On 10 June a special train with 388 Jews, dirty, ragged, some half beaten to death, arrived in Budapest from the Kolozsvár ghetto. We met them with trucks. In the camp, which was scarcely finished, they found hot food, a place to sleep and – peace. Within a few days they began to look human again. Subsequently the camp in Kolumbusz Street became a unique phenomenon. The five SS guards had been ordered to treat the inmates humanely. They carried out this order as faithfully as they would have done the opposite.[25]

As the deportations continued in the provinces, Budapest was teeming with frightened Jews, some numbly awaiting their fate, others frantically trying to hide or to find ways to escape. But while chaos ruled outside, within the camp there was an unreal sense of calm:

In the midst of this madness, in Kolumbusz Street there was a mysterious, fantastic island of peace and security: the 'privileged camp', a world secluded by bars. At the gate an SS man stood guard. Behind him, in the shaded garden, quite undisturbed, were the 388 Jews from Kolozsvár, later joined by the prominent Jews from other provincial ghettos.[26]

The task of the guard was not to prevent Jews leaving but to stop anybody else entering. Originally, permission to join was granted by the Judenkommando on the advice of the Vaada. Gradually the Vaada smuggled in more and more fugitives without asking for permission. More huts were erected in Kolumbusz Street and two new camps set up in the Aréna Street and Bocskay Street synagogues. About 2,000 Jews were thus able to live in relative security, at least for a few months.

Meanwhile Eichmann continued to press Kasztner for a clear statement about Brand's progress in Istanbul. Although Kasztner believed less and less in a positive outcome, he was determined to 'continue to tell Eichmann that the negotiations abroad would eventually succeed'. In order to 'gain time – and perhaps human lives' he intended to raise more money, gold and foreign currency from Hungarian Jews.[27] He called on Eichmann to protest against the relentless exterminations in Auschwitz. Nobody abroad believed any longer that the Germans had ever been serious about the rescue plan, he protested.

'What has got into you?' Eichmann roared. 'Perhaps you think the Reich has enough food to feed hundreds of thousands of Hungarian Jews for months, or staff and doctors to look after the sick? For such a thing the Americans should look for a less smart partner than me.'

'It's my duty to ask you', I continued, 'what will happen if an agreement comes into being in Istanbul from one day to the next. If you have the Hungarian Jews gassed, where will you get the "merchandise" to supply in exchange for the trucks?'

'Don't worry. There are the children between twelve and

fourteen. We're letting those live. You know, in a year or two they'll also be big enough to work. But I can also supply Polish Jews or Jews from Theresienstadt. You can leave this to me.'

With astonishing nerve Kasztner retorted:

'I'm convinced that this way you won't get other countries to make any concessions. Quite on the contrary. If you have any interest at all in this transaction you must supply proof of your good will . . . We demand that you guarantee the lives of 100,000 Hungarian Jews, including small children, old people and sick people. As a proof of our willingness to make a sacrifice, we offer you about five million Swiss francs in jewellery, foreign currencies and pengős. We'll deliver these successively in proportion to your services in return. Guaranteeing the lives of these 100,000 will have a favourable effect on the negotiations. But above all else, the transport to Palestine must be got under way.'[28]

When Eichmann inquired where the money would come from, Kasztner lied that it would be raised abroad. He asked for the group to be taken via Romania to Palestine. Eichmann reiterated that the emigration would have to look like deportation to satisfy the Hungarians and that he would not allow any Jews to emigrate directly to Palestine because of the German government's promise to the Grand Mufti. He proposed instead that the group should spend a few weeks in the detention camp of Strasshof near Vienna and then travel, through France and Spain, to Lisbon and western Africa. He also agreed to allow surviving Jews from provincial centres other than Kolozsvár to be brought to Budapest according to lists provided by the Vaada.

To raise the 5 million Swiss francs, the Vaada sold 150 places to rich Jews who, at the risk of arrest and torture, had defied orders to deliver all their assets to the Hungarian authorities. Thus the rich contributed most of the ransom for the rest. The assets were collected at the Síp Street offices of the Jewish Community by a special committee that included Otto Komoly, Hansi Brand, Shulem Offenbach and others. Regular raids by Hungarian secret agents pretending to be Jews made these meetings extremely hazardous.

On 20 June three suitcases containing 200,000 US dollars, 100,000 Swiss francs, various other foreign currencies, gold, diamonds, share certificates and 13.5 million Hungarian pengős were delivered by Kasztner, Offenbach and Hansi Brand to Klages at the Gestapo headquarters on Svábhegy Hill. It was on that occasion that they first met SS Obersturmbannführer Kurt Becher, who was to become Kasztner's chief partner in the continuing negotiations and a significant actor in his subsequent tragedy. Hansi later recalled that she had asked Klages, who seemed 'decent' to her, for advice on a secure place for the suitcases. Klages volunteered to take them into safe keeping, and in due course they found their way to Becher. Soon after the war most of the money and valuables disappeared and were never traced.

Kasztner and Becher met again between 25 and 27 June. Becher was so impressed by Kasztner's extravagant promises that he decided to muscle in on the deal, although for some time Eichmann remained Kasztner's closest contact. While Eichmann kept asking for news from Istanbul, Kasztner kept repeating that the Allies and the neutral states were keeping a keen eye on the 'Palestine transport', on whose fate their own response to the wider German demands depended. In a slow and laborious process of bluffing and haggling, Kasztner persuaded Eichmann to approve the departure of 1,300 Jews. With a hard-won air of confidence hiding his dread of Eichmann's u-turns, he offered a ransom of 100 dollars per head. Eichmann demanded 200 dollars and raised this to 500 dollars, while Becher, who was also present, demanded 2,000 dollars. Eichmann and Becher were constantly in touch with Himmler, each jockeying for a better position. Finally Himmler fixed the price at 1,000 dollars per Jew.

It was agreed that the group should be a mixture of people from the provinces and the capital, and the Germans again insisted that the departure should be made to appear like a deportation to the Hungarians, who would regard any rescue deal struck by the Germans as betrayal.

Kasztner promptly handed Eichmann a memorandum which listed the following stipulations. The group would travel via Germany and France to a neutral country, after spending a few weeks in the 'privileged camp' of Strasshof. Thirty-five cattle trucks would be provided for the 1,300 passengers, who would be allowed to take 50–80 kilograms of luggage each. While they were in Germany they would receive the same food rations as German civilians. They would not be obliged to wear the yellow star or to work. They would elect their own leaders and handle their affairs with autonomy. Physical abuse would not be permitted. To supplement their diet, they would carry one and a half truck loads of tinned food with them. After more nerve-racking bargaining Eichmann agreed to let the group leave Budapest at 6 pm on 30 June.

Once again the Vaada was obliged to compile a 'final' list. The community was rife with whispers, rumours and fantasies. Word had got round that Vaada members could grant access to Kolumbusz Street by merely signing a slip of paper. This surprisingly casual procedure may suggest either indifference or lack of rational organisation on the part of the Nazis, who did not always live up to the conventional image of German efficiency. Day and night Kasztner and his associates were beleaguered by masses of frantic people, begging, cajoling or badgering them and fighting each other for a place. Those who managed to get one may well have felt like László Devecseri, who knew that by delivering himself and his family into German hands he was 'taking a gamble' that could easily end in death, but who decided to do it because 'staying in Hungary was much more dangerous'.[29] Others refused an invitation to join because, as Hansi Brand explained, they 'did not seriously believe that the transport would really reach a neutral foreign country' and 'they were simply afraid'.[30]

A U S W E I S   No. 4/9/.B

für . . . *Ellenbogen Judit*

Teilnehmer des I. Transportes besonderer Aussenarbeiter.

Den . . . . 1944.

Meinberg

Identity document issued by Vaada

In due course two other categories were added to those established by the Vaada. One consisted of some fifty individuals to whom Becher had issued protective passes against large payments and who had to be included in the transport on Becher's orders. The other included a considerable number of people who – like my father and I – had not been invited but had found a way into Kolumbusz Street through personal contacts or sheer persistence, or who managed to join the departing group at the marshalling yard or on the way to the Austrian border.

The train left Budapest late on 30 June 1944. By then we were nearly 1,700. As Kasztner put it, we 'represented a miniature cross-section of Jewry living in Hungary at the time', enhanced by 'those who had rendered outstanding services to Jewry' and therefore 'were to be honoured by special consideration'. That was how the group became 'so heterogeneous and yet so comprehensive' that Kasztner called it a 'Noah's ark' long before the phrase 'Schindler's ark' became famous.[31]

Kasztner described the selection process as a 'merciless task' and there is no reason to doubt his sincerity in claiming that he and his associates 'tried to carry it out according to the best of our conscience in full awareness of our tremendous responsibility.'[32] Unfortunately, there was no way of saving some without leaving others in the line of fire. This applied equally to the anonymous masses of deportees and to the three young people who became famous through the disastrous 'parachutist affair'.

The parachutists

In January 1944 the Vaada had been informed of an agreement between the Jewish Agency and the British mandatory power in Palestine to send a small mission to Hungary to help local Jews prepare for self-defence and resistance. In March three Jewish volunteers were parachuted into Yugoslavia. They were Joel Nussbecher (later known as Joel Palgi) and Peretz Goldstein, both of whom had emigrated to Palestine from Kolozsvár, and Hanna Szenes, originally from Budapest. Nussbecher was twenty-six, Szenes twenty-three and Goldstein nineteen. They had worked in a kibbutz, but also held ranks as British officers. Szenes was a highly gifted poet.

After their arrival in Yugoslavia they spent three months with the anti-German partisans led by Tito, before continuing their journey to Hungary. In response to a coded telegram from Istanbul, Moshe Schweiger, the head of the Hungarian branch of the illegal Jewish army, the Hagana, had instructed them to report to a Zionist contact in Újvidék (Novi Sad) as soon as they had crossed the border. In addition to the mission tasks set them by the Jewish Agency, they were to radio military information to the British forces.

The first of the three to reach Hungary, on 9 June, was Hanna Szenes. In the meantime all the Jews of Újvidék, including the appointed contact person, had been deported and Schweiger arrested. As soon as Szenes had crossed the border, an official, whom the Vaada had mistakenly regarded as a friend, handed her over to counter-intelligence and she was taken to prison in Budapest. A few days later Nussbecher and Goldstein entered Hungary and approached the same official. They gave him their radio equipment before they set out for Budapest, unaware that they were being watched at every step. They arrived on or about 20 June and took a room in a small hotel. Their first visit was to Kasztner, who had been one of their leaders in the youth movement in Transylvania.

Kasztner immediately recognised the threat that the arrival of Nussbecher and Goldstein represented to his delicate negotiations with the SS. In the weeks since his brief detention the Vaada's responsibility for the rescue work had grown substantially and if he were found to be 'implicated with the whole Rescue Committee in military espionage'[33] he would be laying the project – and possibly his own life – on the line. He persuaded Nussbecher and Goldstein to leave and arranged to meet them again the next day. Two hours later three Hungarian secret policemen called on his landlady and ordered her to keep a discreet eye on the two visitors if they were to return.

When Nussbecher and Goldstein came to the Jewish Community building the next day, as agreed, they spotted agents of the Hungarian secret police among the crowd in the corridors and fled. Nussbecher later called on Kasztner and was hidden in a private apartment. Goldstein also managed to find a hiding place. Then Kasztner took a bold gamble. To allay any German suspicions, he told Otto Klages, head of the SS intelligence in Budapest, that the two young men were working with the Vaada,[34] and he sent Nussbecher to the Gestapo pretending to be a representative of the Jewish Agency from Istanbul. The trick seemed to work, but after the first meeting Nussbecher was arrested by Hungarian agents. Meanwhile Goldstein had come out of hiding, and on 28 June Kasztner and Hansi Brand smuggled him into the Kolumbusz Street camp to see his parents. The Hungarians, having found Nussbecher, rightly believed that Kasztner and his friends had also hidden Goldstein. On the morning of 30 June Kasztner, Hansi Brand, Offenbach, Biss and Biss's wife were arrested and taken to Hadik Barracks, the notorious interrogation and torture centre of the Hungarian counter-intelligence.

Kasztner was repeatedly asked where Goldstein was. When he refused to answer, the interrogator threatened: 'If you don't answer, the other one, this Nussbecher or whatever his name is, will be shot in ten minutes.' Kasztner replied: 'Give me and Mrs Brand some time for reflection. Release us for a few hours. Meanwhile my friends will stay here with you as hostages. We'll both be back in a few hours.'[35]

Kasztner and Hansi went to Kolumbusz Street and explained the situation to Goldstein. He had no hope of hiding indefinitely; the Germans knew where he was and had threatened to send everybody in the camp – including his parents – to Auschwitz, unless he came forward; if the Vaada was discovered to be involved with British officers on an espionage mission it would be the end of any hope of continuing negotiations with the SS. It is not known how much pressure Kasztner and Hansi put on Goldstein. In the end he decided to surrender.

At the same time Kató Szenes, Hanna's mother, was desperately trying to free her daughter. She herself had been arrested by a Hungarian detective in June and unexpectedly confronted in prison with Hanna. It was an attempt to blackmail Hanna into giving details of her mission. But even when her captors threatened to kill her, Hanna persisted in her refusal to answer any questions. When Kató was released she repeatedly called at Kasztner's office, but was told each time by his secretary, Lili Ungár, that he was not available.

Nevertheless, the Vaada did try to pull strings behind the scenes as far as was possible without harming the main cause. For example, Hansi Brand later recalled that she and Kasztner had interceded with Eichmann on behalf of the three captives, but he had replied that 'the matter was not within his competence'.[36] Eventually, just as it was beginning to look as if they were getting somewhere, a dramatic change in the political situation crushed their hopes for good.

On 14 October, István Oláh, the personal secretary of the Hungarian minister for war, gave his staff orders to prepare the release of the paratroopers and promised Kasztner that they would be free in a few days. One day later the ultra-fascist leader Ferenc Szálasi overthrew the Hungarian head of state, Horthy, and the Arrow Cross party's reign of terror began. As a result of the coup, the preparations to release Hanna were halted, and she was executed by firing squad on 7 November. Just as she had refused to confess, she also refused to beg for clemency. About two weeks after her execution Goldstein and Nussbecher were deported. Nussbecher managed to jump out of the train and escape. He went into hiding and survived the war. Goldstein disappeared without a trace. For Kasztner, the affair resurfaced disastrously ten years later, when he was accused of deliberately betraying the paratroopers. In fact he had done as much as he could to save them without jeopardising his main objective. Given the choice between making a possibly futile grand gesture on behalf of three individuals and quietly pursuing the faint hope of saving thousands, he opted for the latter.

The Strasshof group

While Kasztner was haggling with Eichmann about the fate of his 'ark', another opportunity came along. This operation turned out to be less spectacular than our eventual release, although the numbers involved were much larger and there has been a fair amount of controversy whether Kasztner actually saved them or was taken for a ride by Eichmann.

On 14 June Eichmann told Kasztner that he was prepared to put 30,000 Hungarian Jews 'on ice' in Austria as a sign of good will. In fact he had just been ordered by his superior, Kaltenbrunner, to send 30,000 slave labourers to the neighbourhood of Vienna to build fortifications against the approaching Red Army. The labourers had been requested by the mayor of Vienna, Karl Blaschke, and Eichmann had to obey. Nevertheless, he demanded 200 US dollars per person from Kasztner for not sending them to Auschwitz. Kasztner, unaware of Kaltenbrunner's order, offered 100 dollars for each Jew who remained alive. It was agreed that two contingents, 15,000 from Budapest and 15,000 from the provinces, would go to the detention camp of Strasshof. Able-bodied men and women would have to work, but those incapable of work would also be kept alive and families allowed to stay together. Their living expenses were to be defrayed by the Vaada.

Six trains carrying a total of 18,000 Jews, who had somehow avoided deportation from the ghettos of southern and eastern Hungary, were taken to Strasshof between 25 and 28 June, and those who were strong enough set to work in various industrial plants nearby. Kaltenbrunner had written to Blaschke that the arrangement was subject to the possibility of a 'Sonderaktion' or 'special operation', the grim SS euphemism for extermination. No doubt Eichmann would have been happy to oblige, but this never happened, even though the group contained a striking number of elderly or sick people and children, who would normally have ended up in Auschwitz. During the last months of the war Strasshof was supervised by Krumey from an office in Vienna. When Kasztner saw him in January 1945, he reported that some 15,000 inmates were still alive and conditions in the camp relatively bearable. Ultimately some 12,000 were liberated by the Soviets. Shortly before the arrival of the Red Army in Vienna all the documents in Krumey's office were destroyed.

There has been a great deal of debate about Kasztner's role in this matter. According to Biss, Kasztner was 'hypnotised' by Eichmann's power and therefore failed to realise that he was paying for what Eichmann had to do in any case.[37] Similarly, the judges in Eichmann's trial suggested in their verdict that Kasztner had fallen for a 'simulated concession'.[38] Hungarian historians disagree most sharply: István Fischer claims that Kasztner was 'simply shafted', while László Karsai and Judit Molnár maintain that thanks to him 'several thousand people, including many incapable of work, were directed towards Vienna'.[39] Among western experts, Raul Hilberg talks of a qualified 'success' on Kasztner's part, and Yehuda Bauer conjectures that it was 'perhaps because of the Kasztner negotiations' that the Jews in question were sent to Austria rather than Auschwitz.[40] In my view Eichmann was indeed obliged to send labourers to Austria, but Kasztner managed to save the lives of many potential victims of Auschwitz by including them in the transports. Shlomo Aronson's judgement seems to get the balance right, with regard to both this case and some others: 'Kasztner's strategy did yield results when combined with German needs for working hands, war material, and foreign currency.'[41]

Choosing who should be saved again posed a huge moral problem. Kasztner was acutely aware of this: 'Once again we were facing the hardest dilemma that ran through our entire work like a red thread: should we leave the selection to blind chance or try to influence it?' Kasztner's answer to this agonising question – which he calls 'the most terrible ever to confront our consciences' – was to entrust the task to a committee of the Vaada and to follow agreed guidelines. As he puts it, 'the weak human hand writing the name of an unknown person on paper, thereby deciding over life and death, needed truly holy principles to support and guide it'. Whether holy or not, the principle agreed by the Vaada was to save men 'who had worked all their lives for the *Tzibur*' (the Jewish community), women 'whose husbands were in "work camps"', and 'children, especially orphans.'[42]

However, the lists prepared by the committee were not final. Some of the people who had been selected withdrew, preferring to stay in their hiding places, while others begged, cajoled and harassed the selectors until they were included. Names were further added or removed by ghetto leaders, corrupt German officers or, on a whim, by Eichmann himself. Blind chance also played its part. On one occasion a train due to take 3,000 Jews from the ghettos of Győr and Komárom to Strasshof went to Auschwitz, and another train, scheduled to deliver a similar transport from Debrecen to Auschwitz, went to Strasshof instead. By force of habit, the SS Scharführer escorting the first train had directed it towards Poland and when the mistake was discovered at the Slovak border Eichmann decided that it might as well continue its journey. To make up the shortfall, the second train was sent to Austria. Kasztner saw these changes to the original lists as a 'mercy of fate'[43] which relieved the human selectors of some of the guilt.

Two days after the last train to Strasshof had left Budapest we started our own journey to an unknown destination.

CHAPTER 7

From Budapest to Bergen-Belsen

The cattle trucks

On the afternoon of Friday, 30 June 1944, in a heat wave unrelieved by the occasional cloudburst, we were taken from Kolumbusz Street to the Rákosrendező marshalling yard in eastern Budapest. Most of our luggage and some old, ill or crafty people travelled on open lorries. The rest of us walked, escorted by SS soldiers. My father with his stiff knee and I with my short eleven-year-old legs did what we could to keep up, because the alternative was unimaginable. Local residents watched us from the pavements or from behind pots of geraniums on their balconies. Their expressions ranged from indifference through curiosity to undisguised hatred and malicious glee. Although we had been allowed to take off our yellow stars, there could be little doubt that we were a bunch of stinking Jewish parasites who were at last being excised from the healthy body of the Hungarian nation. When we arrived at the marshalling yard we were shocked to find that the train that awaited us was made up of cattle trucks.

Our group from Kolumbusz Street was followed by contingents from the Aréna Street and Bocskay Street synagogues; from Bocskay Street, instead of 150 permit holders, all 450 inmates turned up.

Others arrived piecemeal from all over the city while we were waiting to leave. Two young *chalutzim* bound for a slave-labour camp deserted from the train on the next track and joined ours. As we were pulling away, two Polish orphans, Yitzhak and Abner Weinberg, aged five and three, were pushed through the door by their aunt in the desperate hope that a stranger would take care of them.

Boarding the cattle trucks was a chaotic affair. People pushed and shoved to secure positions near the door and the few air vents. Later arrivals forced their way in, while those already established refused to give way. Families were separated and luggage lost. There were arguments, insults and swearing. While some tried to make the best of a bad job by helping their fellow-sufferers, the majority demonstrated that shared misfortune does not necessarily produce compassion or consideration for others.

The train consisted of thirty-five cattle trucks. One was reserved for our leaders and their families, another for patients, the third for the SS guards, and the fourth for supplies. This left thirty-one trucks to transport almost 1,700 people. The trucks, intended for military use, carried a notice '36 men or 8 horses'. In each, between fifty and sixty of us, with up to 50 kilograms of luggage, were crammed into 20 square metres of floor space. A few makeshift benches had been hastily knocked together before our departure, but for most of us there was only the bare floor. We took turns standing, sitting and lying down, because there was not enough room for everybody to stretch out. My father managed to shield me on one side, but I was constantly being kicked from the other by a man who, in his turn, was trying to protect a little girl. Every kind word or gesture was eclipsed by a tussle or a row. The darkness added to the confusion and discomfort. There was one bucket holding 15–20 litres of water and another serving as a lavatory. Both were too small.

At that stage we were not yet hungry. Our leaders had stored 500 kilograms of cured meat, 1,000 kilograms of tinned meat, and similar amounts of cheese, jam and bread in the supply truck. For the journey they had distributed 2 kilograms of bread, 500 grams of cheese and several tins of liver pâté per person, and many of us had further provisions of our own. Unlike the trains to Auschwitz, ours was not sealed from the outside and the doors were often left open during the journey. This made us a little more comfortable both physically and emotionally. Our greatest comfort, of course, was the hope of soon being in Spain or Portugal and then on our way to Palestine. But that hope was too faint to overcome our fear of the Nazis and our sense of having lost everything that had made us feel at home in the world.

Judy Jacobs, who was seven at the time, paints a powerful picture of the nauseating conditions: 'The stench in the cattle car became worse. Nobody died in transit, but people fainted and people felt sick and people vomited . . . and this just went on and on.'[1] Vera John-Steiner, who was fourteen, remembers above all else the effects of overcrowding on formerly 'lofty human beings': 'There were people crying and asking for a little more space. And everything was about not suffocating. People really didn't talk, they were just saying, "I can't breathe. I am hurt. I am old. Give me more space."'[2] The indignity of our conditions is graphically evoked by Naomi Herskovitz, who was fifteen:

> We were awaited by cattle trucks, cattle trucks, and we were told: 'Get in.' We said: 'What's this? Are we cattle?' . . . Then we got into this train, about eighty people, it was summer, very hot, terribly crowded. Somebody put a bucket into the middle of the truck and said: 'This is the toilet.' I had a high fever, I had diarrhoea and didn't know what to do. As I said at the beginning, we were brought up to be very modest . . . and suddenly I should sit on this bucket in the middle of eighty people and relieve myself in front of them? . . . I realised that I was only a number and no longer a human being.[3]

For George Brief, who was six, 'the single most horrible symbol of anything and everything remained those trains'.[4] But it was also possible to resist the 'feeling that all the things one was used to suddenly no longer existed' by calling on inner resources. Shoshana Hasson, another seven-year-old, adds a heartening note to the misery: 'One had to try somehow not to cry and not to disturb and not to panic and not to be terrified and to keep going in this train that runs and runs and with this noise of the wheels and it isn't clear where we are going and nobody knows where we are going.'[5]

We finally left towards 11 pm, having been delayed by a four-hour air raid. We travelled all night, but in the morning we were amazed to find ourselves still in Budapest – to be exact, at Ferencváros station, normally a few minutes' journey from Rákosrendező. To dodge the continuous air raids, we had been shunted to and fro between junctions while we thought that we were on our way to liberty. In the early afternoon the train made a proper start and at sunset we arrived in Mosonmagyaróvár near the Austrian border. Here we were to experience one of the worst frights of the journey.

Auspitz or Auschwitz?

In Mosonmagyaróvár the train stopped in a siding and did not move for three days. In the summer heat most of us decided to camp in the open. We were guarded by Hungarian policemen and gendarmes, more to protect us from attacks by anti-Semitic local people than to prevent escapes. We bought food from the local peasants, in addition to the rations distributed by our leaders. Compared with the cattle trucks, sleeping under the stars was almost idyllic, although sanitary conditions were bad: it was not until the last day that latrines were dug and we no longer had to use the wheat fields. A baby girl was born by candlelight in one of the cattle trucks. The Orthodox men shaved, because their beards often provoked harassment by malicious Hungarians and Germans. There were constant rumours about what was going to happen to us, but in fact nobody knew anything.

During this halt a formal administration was set up. Since the start of Kasztner's negotiations, the Jews from Kolozsvár had occupied a privileged position, and were much resented for it. More or less automatically József Fischer, the head of the Kolozsvár contingent and Kasztner's father-in-law, became the leader of our entire group. Fischer in his turn appointed a team of aides, from his 'closest circle', as the anonymous author of a highly critical memoir, entitled 'Deportation to Bergen-Belsen' puts it.[6] A set of 'Camp Rules' ('Seder Hamachaneh'), drafted by some of the many lawyers and politicians among us, was issued on 3 July. The frequent use of Hebrew terms reflected the ideology and practices of the Zionist organisations which dominated our entire group.

First in command was the 'camp leader', Fischer himself, assisted by a number of deputies and secretaries. One level down came the heads of various sub-units and their deputies. Below these, each cluster of six cattle trucks had its own head and deputy head, as did, yet another level lower, each individual cattle truck. Any requests or complaints had to be made through official channels. We were forbidden to leave our temporary camp without a permit from the camp leader. We had to get up promptly at 6 am, tidy ourselves and our surroundings as far as possible, and all eat our breakfast at the same time. From 8 am to noon and from 3 to 6 pm the adults – with some carefully defined exceptions such as old people or pregnant women – had to be available for any chores the leaders might require them to do. The hours betweeen noon and 3 pm were allocated for lunch and rest, and those between 6 and 9 pm for dinner and preparations for bedtime. By 9.30 pm there had to be complete silence. Order and discipline had to be strictly observed under supervision by the heads of the various units. Women were forbidden to wear trousers, shorts, swimsuits or lipstick. Only the dedicated latrines and cooking places could be used. Any illnesses had to be reported to selected doctors or officials. Nobody except the appointed leaders was allowed to disseminate any news or issue any directives.

Compliance with the rules was assured by an internal police force of young men wearing armbands, whose orders had strictly to be followed. Disobedience carried severe penalties.

The purpose of such elaborate rules and regulations was, no doubt, to preserve a semblance of control, order and security in the middle of chaos, but what strikes me most today is the deep gulf between the delusion of power fuelling these bureaucratic games and the real plight of 1,700 people who had been robbed of their accustomed way of life, their possessions and their rights, and were sleeping rough in a field around a train of cattle trucks that might at any moment take them to the gas chambers.

On the fourth day we were ordered to get ready to leave. That was when the first great panic erupted. In fact this panic is one of my own clearest memories of the journey. As we were collecting our possessions from the fields a fierce debate started about our next destination. Somehow a rumour had arisen that we were going to Auschwitz and the pessimists among us were petrified. The optimists argued that we were going to a place called Auspitz and there was nothing to worry about, although to me they seemed as frightened as the pessimists. Each party claimed that it had heard its own version from the train driver or one of the guards. At the same time a grim Hungarian pun was making the rounds: 'Auspitz – Auschwitz, Cion – cián' (Zion – cyanide). To anticipate what later became one of the most contentious issues in the history of the Holocaust, this black joke puts paid to the claim that the Hungarian Jews did not realise what awaited them in Auschwitz until they were actually there.

As the panic grew, Fischer obtained the guards' agreement for László Devecseri, who had false Aryan identity papers, to return to Budapest to alert Kasztner. The rest of us boarded the train, which left in the evening for a still unknown destination. Miriam Buck, a language teacher in her thirties, recalls the atmosphere in the cattle truck that night:

Auspitz and Auschwitz, a difference of a few letters, could mean life and death . . . Had we been cheated? . . . The train clattered along in the dark night, with its human cargo writhing in despair. Hysterical women cried fitfully. Men stared impassively into space. Miraculously, nobody jumped out of the train.[7]

One day later Devecseri caught up with us near the Slovak border and delivered the reassuring message that we were not going to Auschwitz. To our huge relief, those who knew their geography confirmed that we were heading west towards Austria, rather than north towards Poland. The next evening we arrived in Vienna, where we were given a hot meal. Meanwhile some passengers had lost their nerve and used the occasional stops to get off, and others, who had heard rumours about the transport being a 'privileged' one, had taken their places.

Gradually, the shock of Mosonmagyaróvár wore off. Another followed in Linz.

Linz

On the seventh morning after our departure from Budapest the train stopped in Linz, the home of Mozart's 36th symphony, although music was not on our minds. We were ordered to get out as we were going to have a bath. We were marched to a military delousing and disinfecting station on the outskirts of the city. Our luggage followed on lorries. When we reached our destination men and women were separated. The women had to go into the building first and were not seen again until early afternoon. The men waited in the courtyard. I remember the heat, the crush, the pain in my knee, which I had cut on the metal step as I was climbing out of the cattle truck, and a general sense of confusion about what was happening around me. At one point we heard women screaming inside and an SS guard explained with a grin that they were being gassed. As in Mosonmagyaróvár, there was panic, because many of the adults had already heard of apparent shower rooms proving to be gas chambers.

Eventually we were ordered to walk indoors in groups of 250–300, undress, hand over our clothes to be disinfected, and wait again. I remember feeling vulnerable and embarrassed as I was standing naked next to my naked father, hemmed in by a crowd of naked men of all ages, shapes and sizes. We were then ushered into the next room, where we were cursorily examined by a doctor and sprayed with Lysol that made our eyes water and our skin burn. Finally, we were sent in groups of forty or fifty into the last room, where we were given a hot shower. I cannot say that I was particularly relieved when the holes in the ceiling produced water, because I knew nothing about the possible alternative, but many of the adults felt as if they had been given a new lease of life.

It was bad enough for the men. William Stern, who was two years younger than I, recalls that 'those spraying us were both male and female German soldiers, something which brought a great deal of embarrassment to the hundreds of men who were undergoing that process'.[8] A vivid passage in a letter from one member of the group, who is known only as Willy, brings back all the physical discomforts: 'Imagine: Hundreds of people completely undressed, body crammed against body in a low, stuffy, overheated hut, waiting for hours and hours for our turn to be shorn, bathed and disinfected in a barbarous manner.' The writer also recalls the fear we all shared: 'You can't imagine how many evil premonitions, how many whispered horror stories circulated among us shocked people in those endless hours.'[9]

But for the women it was even worse. Brought up in a more modest age than today, they were profoundly embarrassed by their enforced nudity. Ester Jungreis describes how she felt as a girl of eight in this situation: 'It was such a terrible thing to see your mother stripped . . . I just kept on looking down, as I was so afraid to look up. I just couldn't bear to see her nude and stripped and so were all the other

people.'[10] But that was not all. Many boys of up to twelve or thirteen who had no male relatives were sent in with the women, while
male guards and prisoners carrying luggage to be disinfected walked
freely up and down among them. As George Revesz reports, for his
mother the 'first step of degradation' came with the lewd remarks of
the soldiers: 'you are naked and a bunch of loud-mouthed SS making
comments which girl looks okay and which girl doesn't look okay.'[11]
Vera John-Steiner was particularly shocked by the viciousness of the
Ukrainian female attendants who dragged the women in front of a
male SS doctor before pushing them into the showers: 'To have
women be so brutal and scream and hit and to tear the clothes off
us if we weren't quick enough, was quite scary.' She was also deeply
worried about the possibility of sexual abuse: 'I, personally, was so
afraid of being violated in my body that I wasn't thinking that much
about the gas.' She concedes that nobody was actually raped, but she
regards the examination by male SS doctors as something pretty
close to it: 'We were violated, because supposedly they were looking
for lice in our vaginas.'[12] In contrast, Herskovitz was greatly relieved
when she saw German soldiers in the shower room as a sign that
nobody would be gassed. But her elation gave way to distress when
she realised that the Germans despised Jews to such an extent that
they were left completely cold by hundreds of naked Jewish women:
'We're naked, we're ashamed, we have no name, only a number . . .
Holding us, standing us under the water, touching us everywhere so
that we get clean everywhere is another humiliation. "They aren't
human beings . . . we don't perceive you as women. They are cattle,
a number."'[13]

   The worst psychological damage was done to the fifty or so women
who were first to be examined. Their heads were viciously shorn bald
by the attendants, and some of them also had their pubic hair removed
under the pretext of delousing. Apparently the attendants believed
that we were on our way to Auschwitz and they wanted to prepare
us suitably for that destination, until they were informed about our

'privileged' status. According to Szidonia Devecseri's reminiscences, it was during this process that a guard remarked: 'Now you're going into the gas chamber.'[14] The uproar the men had heard while waiting outside was the panic that followed the cruel joke.

Initially this treatment seemed to confirm the women's fear that they were about to be killed. But when that fear proved to be unfounded the loss of their hair was felt by many as the most profound disgrace: 'Money, work, home – it was easier to part with all this than with one's hair. It was the only ornament left, beauty, woman-hood itself',[15] writes Miriam Buck. The shock is even said to have cost one young woman's life. Eva Breslauer, seventeen years old, contracted pneumonia and, having lost her will to live, died four weeks after our arrival in Bergen-Belsen.

No member of our group was deliberately killed by the Germans, either in Linz or elsewhere, but what Linz meant, in particular to the women, is again summed up most accurately in a few words by Miriam Buck: 'After about six hours we returned to our men, exhausted, hungry, but alive . . . Only one thing had been killed in us: our human dignity.'[16]

It was about 9 o'clock when, shaken and worn out, we all got back to the cattle trucks and were given some food. We had eaten nothing all day. Our disinfected luggage came back in disarray. Many of us were to recover our belongings only after our arrival in Bergen-Belsen, or not at all. It has been claimed that some of our leaders had stayed on the train while we went to the showers, because they knew what might happen there and were not having any of it. Be that as it may, by the time the train resumed its journey in the dark towards an unknown destination, the euphoria of being clean and ungassed had given way to a general mood of dejection.

The train rattled on for two more days, often held up by Allied bombing or giving way to troop carriers. Finally, on the afternoon of Sunday, 9 July 1944, it stopped next to a long, bare concrete struc-ture surrounded by trees but with no buildings in sight. We did not know that at the time, but we were looking at the platform of the German army training ground of Bergen-Hohne, which doubled as the station for the concentration camp of Bergen-Belsen. Nor did we know that we were about to enter the place that was to become the epitome of the Holocaust, second only to Auschwitz.

Belsen

Unlike Auschwitz, Bergen-Belsen was not an extermination camp. While the Jews deported to Auschwitz were either gassed on arrival or killed more slowly by slave labour in atrocious conditions, Bergen-Belsen was originally intended to keep Jews alive for exchange – or blackmail – purposes. The horrors that were to make 'Belsen' a byword for the concentration camp system as a whole came late and were caused by wilful neglect and criminal indifference, rather than by an active policy of mass murder. The Bergen-Belsen I knew during the second half of 1944 was relatively bearable in comparison with the hell that opened in front of the advancing British troops in April 1945.[17]

Early in 1943 the German Foreign Ministry had floated the idea of exchanging some 30,000 Jews with contacts abroad for German nationals in Allied hands. In April Himmler gave orders for 10,000 'exchange Jews' – more accurately, hostages – to be confined in a special camp. On Lüneburg Heath near the small towns of Bergen and Belsen, 30 kilometres north of Celle in the Hannover District of Lower Saxony, the SS converted part of an existing prisoner of war camp into a camp for 'privileged' Jews. The correct designation for such an institution would have been *Zivilinternierungslager* (civilian internment camp), but the SS called it an *Aufenthaltslager* (detention camp) in order to circumvent the Geneva Convention, which guaranteed the Red Cross and other international commissions right of access to the first type but not to the second.

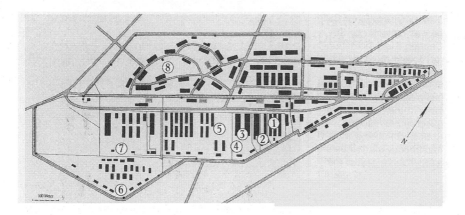

Ground plan of Bergen-Belsen camp (in September 1944)

1. Männerlager (Men's Camp)
2. Neutralenlager (Neutrals' Camp)
3. Sonderlager (Special Camp)
4. Ungarnlager (Hungarian Camp)
5. Sternlager (Star Camp)
6. Frauenlager (Women's Camp)
7. SS-Kleidermagazin und Werkstätten (SS Clothing Store and Workshops)
8. Kriegsgefangenenlager (POW Camp)

The camp covered a roughly triangular area of about 1,800 metres in length and up to 800 metres in width. It was surrounded by two parallel barbed-wire fences set about 5 metres apart, with a clearing between them, which was probably mined, and a watch tower every hundred metres. Beyond the perimeter a dense forest stretched into the distance. The main gate was near the eastern corner, and a central roadway ran south-west from it, with buildings on both sides. The first cluster of buildings, on the right, contained the baths and the disinfection station, the living quarters of the SS, the staff canteen, offices, stores, tool sheds and a prison. At varying intervals there were kitchens. About 80 long, low-slung wooden huts left of the central roadway housed the inmates.

At the time of our arrival the camp was divided into five compounds, separated by barbed wire fences. Counting from the main gate, the first compound was the 'Männerlager' (Men's Camp), which held some 500 prisoners, predominantly Russian and Polish, who had been brought in from other camps in various stages of illness and exhaustion. Next came the 'Neutralenlager' (Neutrals' Camp), with some 250 Jewish men, women and children from non-combatant countries such as Spain, Portugal, Turkey and Argentina. This was followed by our own 'Ungarnlager' (Hungarian Camp), which consisted of hut number 11 and half of number 10. The other half of number 10 was the 'Sonderlager' (Special Camp), occupied by some 350 Polish Jews who had been left behind when a larger contingent was moved to Auschwitz. A concrete wall inside the hut made communication between us and the Poles even more difficult than the barbed wire outside. The fifth, and largest, compound was the 'Sternlager' (Star Camp), with some 4,100 'exchange Jews', of both sexes and all ages, from Greece, Yugoslavia, Albania, France, North Africa and, above all, Holland: not surprisingly, it was called 'star camp' because the people in this group had to wear the yellow star on their civilian clothes.

From early August contingents of women evacuated from Auschwitz were put up in the 'Frauenlager' (Women's Camp), consisting of hastily erected tents to serve as temporary accommodation, before they were redirected to various labour camps in the neighbourhood. On the night of 7 November the tents were destroyed by a violent storm and the women – 8,000 by then – were moved partly into the Star Camp and partly into the 'SS-Kleidermagazin' (SS Clothing Store). To accommodate more, the 'Kriegsgefangenenlager' (POW Camp) became part of the Women's Camp in January 1945. Three months earlier, in October, a number of new huts, surrounded by fresh barbed wire, had been erected between the Star Camp and our own compound. When a new contingent of exhausted women arrived to occupy them, we heard on the grapevine that they were Dutch and had also come from Auschwitz. I now know that one of them was called Anne Frank.

As the Allies closed in on Germany from all sides, the Nazis continued to waste precious material and human resources on moving the inmates of outlying concentration camps to camps within the Reich. The conditions in which these human beings were transported hundreds of miles – squeezed into sealed cattle trucks, piled onto open goods wagons, or stumbling on foot with SS thugs abusing them verbally and physically – are now too well known to be described yet again in detail. Bergen-Belsen was one of the most common destinations for such transports, and the number of inmates soared. When we arrived on 9 July 1944 there were some 5,200 in the various compounds. By the time we left on 4 December the total was about 15,250. By 1 January 1945 it had risen to 18,500, by 15 January to 22,300, and by 1 March to 41,500. When the British took charge on 15 April they found 40,000 inmates in the main camp and 15,000 in the military barracks nearby.

In line with these growing numbers, conditions deteriorated rapidly. From May 1943 to December 1944 there were some 2,000 deaths, in January and February 1945 about 8,000, in March 18,000, in the first two weeks of April 10,200, and from liberation on 15 April to mid-June 13,000. This makes about 51,000 dead out of a total of between 110,000 and 120,000 who spent time in Bergen-Belsen. The records are incomplete, mainly because the SS destroyed all the files before liberation, but they are reliable enough for historians to agree roughly on these figures.[18]

The first commander, from April 1943, was Hauptsturmführer Adolf Haas. He seems to have been as decent a human being as a high SS officer in charge of a concentration camp could be, but on 2 December 1944 he was replaced by Hauptsturmführer Josef Kramer, who is generally described as the most brutal type of Nazi. After a lengthy career in other concentration camps Kramer had become the commander of Auschwitz-Birkenau in May 1944, and the gassing of most Hungarian Jews took place there under his supervision. When he came to Bergen-Belsen he was accompanied by several of his subordinates from Auschwitz, including the notorious female SS supervisor Irma Grese. He immediately turned Bergen-Belsen into a 'regular' concentration camp with all the characteristics – slave labour, sadistic punishments and lethal living conditions. I had the good fortune of leaving the place two days after Kramer's arrival. Tens of thousands were less lucky.

It is true that there were no gas chambers and no deliberate mass murders in Bergen-Belsen. The 51,000 who died there were killed by overcrowding, starvation and disease. But they would not have died if the SS had not allowed – or indeed caused – these things to happen. As the numbers grew, nothing was done to make the camp habitable. Up to five inmates had to sleep in a bunk or on top of each other on the concrete floor in the ramshackle huts, with rain dripping through the roof and refuse piling up inside and out. Food rations dwindled, water for drinking and washing became more and more scarce, medical supplies ran out, latrines overflowed, heating was non-existent, clothes turned into rags infested with lice. Roll calls of up to five hours in the open in all weathers added to the misery. As the SS looked on indifferently, thousands and thousands died of typhus, dysentery, tuberculosis, starvation or exhaustion. Initially the bodies were burnt in the crematorium, but as their numbers grew larger they were either buried in mass graves or stacked with layers of wood between them and set on fire with diesel oil. Finally they were either thrown on heaps of other decomposing bodies or left to rot where they had dropped. For four days before liberation 2,000 inmates who could still walk worked in teams of four, dragging bodies to mass graves, directed by SS officers, beaten by Kapos and cheered on by two bands of captive musicians forced to play dance music.

When it became clear that the Germans had lost the war Hitler gave orders for the concentration camps to be defended or blown up together with all their inmates. In March 1945 Himmler, in a belated attempt to save himself from punishment, issued directives for the camps to be handed over to the Allies without a struggle and with the inmates unscathed. In Bergen-Belsen a truce was agreed between the British forces and the garrison, and on 15 April 1945 British soldiers took possession of the camp. The majority of the SS had left beforehand, but 50 soldiers and officers and 30 female supervisors remained behind. They included Kramer and Grese, who were soon put on trial and hanged.

The sight that awaited the British troops was horrifying. At the trial of the culprits, Medical Officer Brigadier H. L. Glyn-Hughes testified as follows:

> There were various sizes of piles of corpses lying all over the camp . . . The gutters were full and within the huts there were uncountable numbers of bodies, some even in the same bunks as the living . . . Some of the huts had bunks but not many, and they were filled absolutely to overflowing with prisoners in every state of emaciation and disease. There was no room for them to lie down at full length in each hut. In the most crowded there were anything from 600 to 1000 people in accommodation which should only have taken 100.[19]

And an extract from Lieutenant-Colonel M. W. Gonin's diary reads:

> Corpses lay everywhere, some in huge piles where they had been dumped by the other inmates, sometimes singly or in pairs where they had fallen as they shuffled along the dirt tracks . . . One saw women drowning in their own vomit because they were too weak to roll over and men eating worms as they clutched half a loaf of bread purely because they had to eat and could scarcely tell the difference between worms and bread . . . Men and women crouching down just anywhere in the open relieving

themselves of the dysentery which was scouring their bodies, a woman standing stark naked washing herself with issue soap in water from a tank in which the remains of a child floated.[20]

This was what made Belsen synonymous with the Holocaust, and this was the fate I was spared, with many others, thanks to Rezső Kasztner.

Arrival

On the morning of Sunday 9 July 1944 our train stopped at its final destination. An SS Oberscharführer (staff sergeant) with an Alsatian on a lead ordered us to get out of the cattle trucks, adding for emphasis: 'Hurry up, it isn't Sabbath today!'[21] The platform of Bergen-Hohne stood in open countryside and bore no name. Today it looks much the same as it did then and is regularly used by German and NATO military. The last station sign we had seen before reaching it was that of Celle, which is why many people in the group were to claim in retrospect that we had to walk about 30 kilometres to the camp. In fact the distance was about seven kilometres and the march took less than two hours, but given our condition, this was hard enough. Judy Jacobs remembers it vividly:

After a while, the train stops and the doors open, and again, there is a lot of this obscene nasty yelling and intimidation and we are in a heavily forested area ... We are told to walk in perfect formation, maybe four or five abreast, in straight lines, with whips in the hands of the guards ... Every 30 seconds, somebody would yell another insult at you ... I cannot tell you how long we walked, but it seemed like a tremendously long walk ... because by this time we were dehydrated and underfed and we had been sitting up in these cattle cars so our bones and joints were creaky and everything else – and we were not really in the best of shape anyway.[22]

Some of our heavy luggage and provisions were transported to the camp by lorry. The old, the sick and the very young were supposed to go the same way, but there were not enough lorries for all, and in addition much of the space available was taken up by our able-bodied leaders. I remember, once again, my father hobbling along with his stiff leg and me trying to keep up, terrified of the SS guards and the dogs straining at their leads. The road ran straight through an endless forest. From somewhere behind the trees we heard men shouting and rifles firing. I now know that it was only a German army exercise, but at the time the sounds seemed to suggest something much more ominous.

I have only a vague memory of how I felt on arrival in the camp, but the accounts of various other members of the group ring many bells. Judy Jacobs recalls the characteristic features of the camp, permeated by her sense of being trapped beyond redemption: 'It was your stereotypical camp – the long narrow barracks, the barbed wire, the separation between camps, the mines between the barbed wire fences so that if anybody would escape, there would be no hope or prayer that they would go anywhere.'[23] The sarcastic remarks of the semi-anonymous Willy recall the sense of isolation and claustrophobia that I shared, within the limits set by my ignorance, with the adults: 'Here they were, in Bergen-Belsen, those smart Jewish VIPs, in a compound surrounded by guards, electric wire fences, watch towers with searchlights and revolving machine guns, and not a sound, not a breath of theirs could reach the world outside.'[24] For all our fears, we had left Hungary in the belief that we were on our way to Palestine, and some of us were still so confident that they threw loaves of bread across the barbed wire to the other inmates watching our arrival. But to the majority Bergen-Belsen looked very different from the Promised Land and even I, for all the haziness of my ideas of Palestine, was deeply disappointed. Edith Goldstein expresses the shock eloquently:

When we reached Bergen-Belsen after a march, a gate rose, we walked through and it was closed behind us. Then another, and another. And we realised that there was no way out of here, that we would never again get out of here. The end, this was the end, they had deceived us and we understood that it was the end.[25]

Nor did we feel any better when we heard that other groups, too, had been assured of leaving within a fortnight and were still here eleven months later.

Our compound was about 500 metres from the main entrance, between the Men's Camp and the Special Camp on one side and the Star Camp on the other. The inmates of the Men's Camp were the worst sight. Edith Goldstein conveys the feelings of many of us as we marched past these people on the verge of death by starvation and exhaustion, who were called 'Muselmänner' in concentration-camp slang, possibly based on the prostrate position by which Muslims at prayer are supposed to express their submission to their fate: 'We met "Muselmänner", who were only skin and bones . . . And we realised that quite soon we would be like them, that this was the future awaiting us.'[26] Miriam Buck also mentions the pitiable condition of these particular prisoners: 'They were hollow-eyed, grey-cheeked living corpses, with death written on their faces.'[27]

Once we had reached our own compound we were ordered to line up between our two huts. A desk with a typewriter had been set up in the open and some members of our group prepared a register. There remains some uncertainty about the size of the group. Kasztner writes that 1,684 passengers left Budapest, and it is usually assumed that 1,684 were rescued from Bergen-Belsen. In fact we do not know exactly how many were on the train when it started its journey, while the number of those who finally made it to Switzerland was about 1,670. However, it is almost certain that on our arrival in the camp we numbered 1,684.[28] As for the register, no proof of identity was required and the only details we had to supply were our names, dates of birth, nationalities and occupations.

As we were to discover in due course, nationality was the most important issue. In the negotiations with the SS the Vaada had described all of us as Hungarians, which was essential in view of the absurdly legalistic procedures of the Germans in the midst of the most arbitrary terror. In reality more than one-third of us were not strictly Hungarian nationals. Some had had several nationalities due to the shifting borders since the First World War, while others were fugitives from neighbouring countries and were using false identities. Ann Pasternak Slater, in her meticulous article, counts 5 Austrians, 23 Italians, 33 Poles, 48 Yugoslavs, 115 Czechs, and 173 Romanians in a list of 1,350,[29] and the full 1,684 included further non-Hungarians.

Word had come down from our leaders that we should all describe ourselves as Hungarians, but there were some who hesitated. In the large contingent of Transylvanians in particular many regarded themselves as Romanians, and there was a lot of speculation and agonising. Shaul Ladany recalls: 'Never will I forget the frantic debates and deliberations as everyone tried to decide what nationality to declare.'[30] I also remember my father dithering. Finally, either by another lucky gamble or because there seemed to be a deceptive safety in numbers, he opted for Hungarian. This was probably one of the factors that eventually saved our lives.

On the day after our arrival Jenő Kolb, in his diary, referred to 972 women or girls and 712 men or boys; this included about 320 children of all ages from newborn to fourteen.[31] According to Thomas Rahe, 16 per cent (about 285) were children under fourteen, 43 per cent (about 600) were men and 57 per cent (about 800) were women.[32] Many of the children were orphans, looked after by relatives or friends of their dead parents, representatives of religious or political organisations, or strangers who took pity on them as they were deposited on the train and left to fend for themselves. The age range, in Pasternak Slater's view, was 'scrupulously balanced', with

lfd. Nr.	Name	Vorname	Geburts- datum	Geburts- Ort	Natio- nalität	Beruf	Kz
961	Lefkovits	Zoltán	12.2.22.	Nyiregyháza	ung.	Arbeiter	56
962	Legmann-Stern	Lea	9.3.07	Mármarossziget	ung.	Haushalt	56
963	Legmann	Ladislaus	2.1.01	Kisbács	ung.	Landwirt	56
964	Lewy	Gabriel	12.6.42.	Kolozsvár	ung.		56
965	Leiner	Judit	2.3.31.	Kassa	ung.		56
966	Leitner	Felix	8.10.21	Nagyvárad	ung.	Student	56
967	Leitner	Marianne	31.1.24.	Nagyvárad	ung.	Studentin	56
968	Leitner-Blau	Rosa	3.6.95.	Nagyvárad	ung.	Haushalt	56
969	Leitner	Alexander	5.11.89.	Nagyvárad	ung.	Kaufmann	5
970	Lew	Peter	29.7.30.	Técső	ung.		56
971	Levy	Georg	4.12.12.	Nagyvárad	ung.	Mach,Ing.	56
972	Lewy-Moskovits	Irene	21.9.13.	Kolozsvár	ung.	Haushalt	56
973	Lewy	Judit	11.4.44.	Kolozsvár	ung.		56
974	Lichtig	Mor	5.20.90.	Csarne	ung.	Kaufmann	56
975	Lichtig-Langer	Sara	5.5.92.	Salgow	ung.	Haushalt	56
976	Lichtig	Felice	19.1.21.	Lipiany	ung.	Schneiderin	56
977	Lichtig	Elsa	26.12.21.	Kassa	ung.	Photograph	56
978	Lichtmann	Emerich	10.2.40	Szabadka	ung.		56
979	Lichtmann	Hedda	26.12.37.	Szabadka	ung.		56
980	Lichtmann	Mira	31.8.43.	Szabadka	ung.		56
981	Lichtmann-Klein	Roza	29.4.04.	Hajdunánás	ung.		56
982	Lichtmann	Tibor	19.11.36.	Szabadka	ung.		56
983	Liebermann	Zoltán	12.5.95.	Kassa	ung.	Kaufmann	56
984	Liebermann-Pickel	Dora	20.	Huszt	ung.	Kindergärtnerin	56
985	Link	Arnold	26.1.04.	Nagytapolcsány	ung.	Beamter	5
986	Láthaue-Gereben	Edith	07.	Budapest	ung.	Haushalt	5
987	Lock	Alfred	7.11.22.	Wien	ung.	Elektrotechn.	5
988	Loker-Berger	Margarethe	15.12.89.	Budapest	ung.		5
989	Löb	Ernest	28.2.206	Zilah	ung.	Ing.	5
990	Löbl	Georg	31.7.31.	Szabadka	ung.	Schüler	56
991	Löb	Isak	29.7.96.	Kendermező	ung.	Agronom	56
992	Lühl-Fränkl	Klara	9.12.11.	Obecse	ung.		5
993	Löb	Ladislaus	8.5.33.	Kolozsvár	ung.		5
994	Löwenstein	Zoltán	25.6.36.	Galánta	ung.		5
995	Löwenstein-Pollák	Edith	4.10.11.	Kemence	ung.	Haushalt	5
996	Löwenstein	Emma	24.3.42.	Budapest	ung.		5
997	Lewy	Agnes	1.9.29.	Budapest	ung.		5
998	Löwinger-Löwinger	Hedy	31.7.10.	Verbove	ung.		5
999	Löwinger	Samu	17.8.07.	Vác	ung.	Kaufmann	5
1000	Lustig-Rosenberger	Julie	12.8.08.	Kolozsvár	ung.		

One page from the list prepared on our arrival in Bergen-Belsen the emphasis on saving children and young adults. Arranging the ages by decades, and not quite reaching 1,684, she counts 60 under three, 213 between four and fourteen, 362 between fifteen and twenty-four, 310 between twenty-five and thirty-four, 270 between thirty-five and forty-four, 221 between forty-five and fifty-four, 130 between fifty-five and sixty-four; 50 between sixty-five and seventy-four, and 11 between seventy-five and eighty-two.[33]

The range of occupations was equally wide, although the list is as unreliable as that of the names, for similar reasons. To give just one example, Egon Mayer's website lists my father as a 'farmer',[34] which he never was: I suspect that he described himself as such because he assumed that, in a group of would-be pioneers planning to carve the new state of Israel out of the desert, a farmer would look more valuable than a small business man. A selection from Pasternak Slater's compilation may adequately reflect the diversity as a whole: 187 housewives, 139 students, 113 employees, 84 merchants, 77 dress-makers or seamstresses, 40 workmen or labourers, 36 lawyers, 35 doctors, 32 schoolchildren, 27 teachers, 25 tailors, 18 nurses, 17 rabbis, 16 engineers, 12 gardeners, 12 chemists, 10 secretaries, 9 professors, 7 locksmiths, 7 milliners, 7 mechanics, 7 hairdressers, 5 manufacturers, 5 florists, 5 electricians, 4 printers, 4 economists, 4 dentists, 4 watch-makers, 3 furriers, 3 architects, 3 shoe-makers, 3 painters, 3 carpenters, 2 accountants, 2 bakers, 2 cooks, 2 actors, 2 photographers, a weaver, a glazier, a singer, a cabinet-maker, a butcher, a contractor, an agronomist, a musician, an exporter, a candy-maker, a glove-maker, a journalist, a blacksmith, an occupational therapist, an artist, a translator, a librarian, and many more.[35]

True to the Vaada's selection criteria, the group included many religious or political leaders of the defunct Jewish communities and their families. Although the Neologues were in the majority, there was also a strong Orthodox – or even ultra-Orthodox – element, 126 individuals according to Jenő Kolb. The most active political sector was that of the Zionist parties, of all shades from far right to far left:

Kolb counts 199 Zionists from Transylvania and 230 from Budapest.[36] As already indicated, the internal affairs of our group were managed by Zionists in accordance with their political beliefs – not always with the approval of non-Zionists.

It was this chequered group, then, that queued up in Bergen-Belsen on 9 July 1944 to be registered. It was not fun, but we were spared a much worse queue that hundreds of thousands had to join elsewhere in order to have numbers tattooed on their forearm.

When we had all been duly registered, our leaders directed us to our quarters. These consisted of two long wooden huts, divided into a number of large rooms with concrete floors, tiny windows, and three-storey bunks arranged in tightly packed squares. In spite of hastily issued guidelines, securing a place to sleep was a free-for-all. People were pushing and shoving to capture whichever of the three bunks – bottom, middle, top – they thought most desirable. Some families or cliques who got there first spread themselves so widely that others were obliged to obtain their fair share by force. The anonymous memoir 'Deportation to Bergen-Belsen' accuses the dominant set of Zionists from Kolozsvár in particular of grabbing more space for themselves and their fellow-Transylvanians than they were entitled to.[37] The huts were dark, cold and smelly. As we soon found out, they were also infested with bedbugs, fleas and lice. Willy's comment may seem entertaining in retrospect, but the experience was far from funny: 'In the huts hundreds of thousands of starving lice were waiting for us. They sucked themselves into our as yet well-padded bodies and crawled into everything. The struggle against the lice was quite fruitless. They always remained in the majority and so came out on top.'[38] Miriam Buck sums up our impressions on arrival, which did not improve with the passing of time: 'No colour, no beauty, no comfort, not the smallest place where one felt at home . . . Being confined in this bare, cold place was almost as bad as the lack of food. One gnawed our bodies, the other our souls.'[39]

At about 8 o'clock in the evening we were told to assemble in the open space between the two huts. What followed was the *Zählappell*, the first of about 150 roll calls we were to endure. With the exception of the gravely ill, we all – men, women, children, old people, babies – had to line up, five deep, and wait to be counted. We had been given some bread and coffee substitute, but we were still hungry. We were exhausted from the long journey in the cattle trucks. We were confused and afraid. As we stood waiting, there was a thunderstorm that left us drenched. SS officers, who either wanted to harass us or were genuinely innumerate, counted us again and again. The ordeal lasted until 10 o'clock, when we were finally allowed to go to our bunks.

The roll calls are remembered by every member of our group as one of our most traumatic experiences. Ervin Heilper's recollection is very close to my own: 'The Zählappell lasted for hours. They counted us and didn't let us go until we could stand on our legs no more. And so long as the number wasn't right or something, we stood there. Then it started raining. It was pretty tough, but not too bad . . . in proportion to what could have happened in another camp.'[40] Indeed, compared with the ordeals of people in other camps, our sufferings were relatively light. Nevertheless, this initial roll call – and the others following it day by day – had a profoundly demoralising effect on us. Mrs Tibor Adler remembers: 'They counted us like animals. It was humiliating for people to be treated like numbers, which of course we were for them.'[41]

As a valuable commodity, our own group was relatively well off, as were the inmates of the 'Neutrals' Camp' and the 'Special Camp'. Those of the 'Star Camp', whom the Germans regarded as being less likely to produce a lavish ransom or rewarding exchange, were having a much harder time. They were allowed to wear civilian clothes but were stigmatised by the yellow star, given worse food, forced to do slave labour – such as unearthing tree roots, digging drains, performing kitchen duties and, above all, dismantling millions of shoes to recycle the leather – and all this while they were shouted at and beaten by SS soldiers and Jewish Kapos. Worst off were the inmates of the 'Prison Camp', who wore convicts' uniforms and who were systematically starved and worked to death.

Our group was lucky enough to suffer less than most others during the five months of our stay, and when we left for Switzerland early in December, the most deadly ordeals were yet to come for the many thousands left behind. Nevertheless, finding ourselves behind barbed wire in Bergen-Belsen rather than on our way to freedom in Palestine left us in deep shock and bewilderment.

CHAPTER 8

Life in the Privileged Camp

Creature comforts

Because the Germans regarded us as a valuable commodity, we were treated better than most other inmates of Bergen-Belsen. We were allowed to keep our own clothes and were not obliged to wear prison issue or the yellow star. Apart from keeping our compound in order, we did not have to work. We regularly marched to the showers, which we gradually learnt to trust, even though the women never got over the embarrassment of being supervised by male German soldiers. We were relatively well fed and permitted to engage in some cultural or religious activities. We ran our own internal administration and were not constantly being bullied by SS guards or Jewish Kapos. Men and women slept in separate huts, but families could spend the days together. For all that, five months in Bergen-Belsen was not a holiday in the country.

Our days were carefully mapped out. We were woken at 6 am and the food bearers delivered breakfast at about 7. After tidying the huts and the courtyard we had to be ready for the *Zählappell,* the roll call, which could take place at any time between 9.30 and 11.30 or later. After lunch, which came between 11.30 and 12.30, we were free for a variety of activities until supper arrived between 5 and 6 pm.

Bedtime was at 9 pm, followed by lights out at 10.[1] This pattern was sometimes disrupted when the roll call overran or when Allied planes flew over the camp to bomb German cities and we were ordered into the huts, probably to spoil our pleasure at seeing our friends in the sky. But basically it was repeated day after day with soul-destroying monotony.

As to the dreaded *Zählappell*, every morning we had to turn out of the huts and, in ranks five deep, stand in the open until the SS guards had counted us and were satisfied with the number. This could take up to two or three hours and if they miscounted, which often happened, they started again. Depending on their mood or character, they did so either in a quiet businesslike manner or with insults and curses. It was bad right from the beginning and it got worse as both the weather and our own condition deteriorated. It is remembered with revulsion by every member of the group, perhaps most eloquently by George Brief, for whom it comes 'next in line to the cattle cars' in the 'list of horrible memories':

> They would line us up in the courtyard surrounded with these towers and the SS and the guards, and you had to stand and stand and it would rain and even snow and you had to stand and stand there until the SS officers will go by and they will count the prisoners as if there was a way to disappear from there. And at least in my memory these things were incredibly long, incredibly trying and cold and threatening.[2]

To me the word *Zählappell* means aching legs, a merciless north wind cutting through soaked garments, a little fear and endless boredom. Nor did I find much comfort when we were finally allowed to return to our quarters.

The 1,684 of us were crammed into huts 10 and 11. Each hut was divided into eight large rooms, but three rooms in number 10 belonged to the Polish Special Camp. This left us a total of thirteen rooms of about 180 square metres each, which should have meant 130 people to a room, with 1.4 square metres of living space per head. In reality we were more tightly packed because some rooms were set aside for other functions. One served as the office of our internal leaders as well as a store for clothes, food and medical supplies, and a sick bay. Another contained a number of perforated lead pipes, where we could wash ourselves and our clothes with trickles of cold water. A third, the residence of our leaders with their families and friends, held only 70 people. As a result of all this, each of the remaining ten rooms had to absorb up to 160 people.

As far as possible, people from the same geographical areas or with similar religious or political affiliations were allocated to the same rooms. Men and women were segregated, although the young pioneers often disregarded this rule. I have a vague memory of being in room 10B, which seems to tally with the fact that A and B held men and boys from Kolozsvár.

The largest area in each room was taken up by three-storey bunks arranged in blocks of four, with narrow passages between them. Near the entrance was a table with a few chairs, and at the back a single toilet, which we all had to use after nightfall, when we were forbidden on pain of death to leave the huts in order to walk to the latrines 60 metres away. From the nearest watch tower, which happened to be just outside the perimeter wall close to the latrines, a soldier with binoculars and machine gun kept us under constant surveillance. The searchlight sweeping the huts from dusk to dawn was a particularly sinister feature. Edit Goldstein's recollection of what it was like to live in such conditions is very close to my own:

I got a top bunk under a slanting roof. It was impossible to sit up . . . There was no light and no air. When it started raining, the rain came in, straight onto my bunk. I put my food bowl where the rain came in, but then it came from somewhere else . . . Eventually our things went mouldy. There was no chance of airing them because if I hung something up outside it would have immediately been stolen ... In front of the toilet there were long queues. People were freezing and if it wasn't one's turn in good time, there were great problems.[3]

Jenő Kolb's diary captures the ambience in the huts at night perfectly in two thumbnail sketches. The first describes the different sounds produced by sleepers: 'They cry, wail, talk, grind their teeth, laugh, issue commands ... moan, puff, snore.' The second suggests our increasingly miserable state of health: 'Each of them breathes differently and they can all be recognised by their different liquid WC sound. Their shuffle as they go to the toilet after the soup. Nothing but skeletons with guts distended by gas and inflamed bladders.'[4]

Szidonia Devecseri's description of a typical night in her hut would be hilarious if the circumstances were not so distressing. The rabbi's wife tries in vain to stop her children, aged four and eight, fighting in her bunk. Her neighbours, kept awake by the din, swear at them. A woman screams because a mouse has run over her face. Bedbugs drop from the higher bunks onto the lower. Another woman screams because the little boy in the bunk above her has spilled the jam jar he uses as a chamber pot all over her. Somebody has whooping cough. Another little boy begs his mother not to beat him because in his sleep he wet the bunk he shares with her. She does and he squeals. A former night-club dancer tells dirty stories about her ex-colleagues to the refined Orthodox language teacher, who does not know whether to block her ears or to laugh. A spoilt rich wife has hung her clothes on all available nails, leaving no room for anybody else. The passage ends with: 'In 24 out of 24 hours there is never a minute's silence. By daybreak the noise has somewhat abated, and I ache as I imagine the much greater torments of the people who have been deported elsewhere, including our own loved ones.'[5]

I too have memories of such nights, including the fury of the man in the bunk below me when I drenched him with the contents of my own jam jar. I also remember the narrow bunks reaching up to the ceiling, the bare bulbs that gave hardly any light, the bumpy palliasses, the rough blankets that were rumoured to have been made out of human hair, the bedbugs and the lice, the sniffs, coughs, burps, farts, sighs, groans and screams, the whispered arguments and the sudden roars of abuse, the constant flushing of the toilet, the tinkle of jam jars being filled, the dripping of water through the leaky roof, the howling of the wind through every crack in the walls, the beam of the searchlight flashing through the small window at regular intervals, men shouting and dogs barking in the distance, and myself lying in the cold, damp, smelly darkness. But unlike the adults I do not remember thinking that this was no way for human beings to live.

There were two latrines, one for men and one for women, near the perimeter fence, overlooked by a watch tower. Toilet paper was in short supply and we had to make do with pages torn out of books and bits of wrapping. I had already got over the shock of using a latrine together with dozens of other people in the Kolozsvár ghetto, but to many the experience remained traumatic. Somehow a tomato plant managed to grow near the latrine outside the perimeter fence. Although it died long before we left the camp, it was taken to be one of the few encouraging signs in the general bleakness. Shaul Ladány is one of those who were struck by the incongruity: 'I will never forget the latrine and the stench that rose from it, or the tomato plant that grew outside the high voltage fence.'[6]

The misery of living in those huts was compounded by the misery of starvation. The daily ration we were given by the Germans consisted of about 330 grammes of bread, 15 grammes of margarine, 25 grammes of jam, 1 litre of soup, 1.5 litres of coffee substitute and occasionally a small piece of cheese or sausage. Children under fourteen received additional rations and some milk.[7] The provisions we had brought with us supplemented these rations, but still fell far short of what we needed. To make matters worse, as time passed, both the rations and our own reserves became smaller.

The bread came in grey loaves reminiscent of bricks, both in shape and weight. A ration of 330 grammes a day may seem generous, but the loaves were extremely heavy and their nutritional value minimal. Some of us divided them into equal parts for the whole week, while others did not have the strength of mind to wait and finished them in two or three days. There were scientific debates about whether two thick slices or three thin ones were more nourishing. Rulers were used to ensure accuracy. As we became more and more hungry, the bread, such as it was, seemed more and more desirable. Ági Hendell describes it as being 'made of mud and sawdust' but 'the best thing that you ever tasted in your life.'[8] Our leaders built up reserves against possible emergencies by retaining part of our bread allowance and keeping it fresh by regularly replacing the old loaves with new ones.

The coffee, which was distributed for breakfast in the early morning and for supper in the late afternoon, was made of some unknown substitute. I can still hear one of the officious officials in our hut, Jenő Tyroler, barking twice a day: 'Coffee! Fall in, everybody!' We fell in, but what we were given had little in common with coffee, except the colour. Ben Hersch speaks for all of us by calling it 'black water that was sometimes warm and sometimes not – not bad tasting, just tasteless.'[9]

The daily soup was brought from the camp kitchen in containers holding 25 or 50 litres. It was made of unpeeled turnip, mangold and various other root vegetables that we had never seen before, except perhaps in the form of cattle feed. Olga Munk recalls: 'We got the stuff that they feed to the animals – I don't even know how you say it in English. It was cut in small pieces and there was dirt in it – it wasn't even washed – and that is what we had to eat. But we had to eat something.'[10] On our lucky days we found some potato peels and even potatoes in the general mess. On still luckier days there were some scraps of meat among the vegetables.

Initially, we were unable to eat this soup. We left it in the containers, threw it away, or tried to hand it to our less well-off neighbours on the other side of the barbed wire. But as we got hungrier we were only too glad to have it. Edit Goldstein remarks drily: 'At first nobody wanted to eat this stuff. It was for pigs, not human beings. A day or two later we were queuing up for it.'[11] Like everybody else, I too was starving, but there were some vegetables – a kind of turnip and a variety of beetroot in particular – that I simply could not eat. My father gave me a large part of his other rations instead.

The distribution of food was extremely contentious. 'Malnutrition and constant hunger made everybody irritable, and an innocent word was enough to set off a quarrel even between friends' is how the anonymous author of 'Deportation to Bergen-Belsen' sums up the situation.[12] Kolb's diary reports daily scenes of 'tumult, confusion, shouting and unprecedented scuffles – for a plateful of vegetables with a few scraps of meat.'[13] Jack Gross's recollection is as graphic as it is accurate:

> There were fights, for instance, when you stood in line to get your bowl filled with that slop from noontime, and people were so hungry that they were fighting, 'You gave him more! You gave me less! Why did you give him more? Why did you favour him?' And they were grabbing things from each other's hands and they were also stealing.[14]

Obeying the law of gravity, the solid substances in the soup remained near the bottom of the containers. As a result, everybody wanted to be served as late as possible, and the pushing and shoving at times developed into full-scale brawls. But such momentary outbreaks were less serious than the resentments caused by corruption on a larger scale. The angry author of 'Deportation to Bergen-Belsen' in partic-ular claims that the food bearers, in addition to their extra rations, were stealing 30 or 40 litres of soup a day, with the connivance of our leaders, who were themselves misappropriating deliveries and allowing tailors and shoemakers to demand extortionate payments in kind for their essential services.[15] I was not aware of the finer points, but I watched people coming to blows more than once over food and still remember the mixture of fascination and shock I felt when I first saw blood on the face of a distinguished lawyer after such an encounter.

The humiliation and shame that could result from hunger is illustrated in two poignant memories of William Stern, who was a child at the time. At one point he recalls his astonishment at watching 'a previously very well-to-do and honourable gentleman . . . licking out with his finger the bottom of the food containers because the amount that was rationed to each one was obviously not enough for him'. At another point he describes his own 'deep feeling of guilt' when, running between the huts to deliver jam sandwiches made by his mother to his father, he 'would secretly lick off part of the jam, trying to spread the balance on the sandwich, so as to satisfy my craving for something sweet'.[16]

One day fifteen barrels of stale mussels were dumped in front of the huts. People went wild, grabbing the slippery molluscs by the handful, stuffing them into their pockets and withdrawing from the fray briefly to suck them out of their shells before returning for more. Although, in Kolb's words, this exotic feast was 'foul-smelling, like the sea shore at low tide',[17] I longed to take part in it, but my father would not let me for fear of food poisoning.

Constant hunger led to an unabating preoccupation with food. In our waking hours we never stopped talking about great meals we had had or were going to have once we were back in civilisation, and by night we dreamt about them. Recipes for the most sumptuous dishes were exchanged and some of our rations recycled with great ingenuity. Delicious 'cakes' were created out of bread, margarine and jam for birthdays and the high Jewish festivals. It is less certain that 'fishing the potatoes out of this soup thing and making some kind of a potato salad type concoction which would go on the top of the bread' actually produced 'sandwiches which were more nutritious than it would have been just drinking the soup', as Emanuel Mandel recalls.[18]

One group of people who suffered even more deprivation than the rest were the smokers. From time to time our rations included cigarettes, but never enough. There were endless debates about whether non-smokers should have the same allowance as smokers, or women as men. On one occasion the allocation proposed by our leaders almost provoked a revolution. Some people smoked cigarettes recycled from discarded butts, while others tried to use tea leaves. Those most addicted sold essential food and possessions for cigarettes.

Things started with simple barter and soon developed into a complex economy that closely mirrored the economy of the world outside. Goods and services were exchanged for other goods and services, or for IOUs in American dollars and Swiss francs, to be redeemed after our hypothetical liberation. There were booms and slumps, inflation and deflation, and there were middlemen, agents and brokers, who made handsome profits. And for a common currency there were cigarettes.

Although prices varied, this extract from Miriam Buck's table[19] gives a good idea of the market value of cigarettes and what they could buy:

4 pieces of toilet paper	1	cigarette
1 supper	1–2	cigarettes
1 lunch	3–4	"
1 onion	3	"
1 tin of tomatoes	5	"
1 portion of butter (30 gr)	8	"
1 pair of woollen socks	25	"
1 loaf of bread (2 kg)	50	"
1 pair of womens' shoes	150	"
1 pair of men's shoes	200	"
1 men's suit	270	"

In the service sector of this economy tailors and shoemakers played an important part. As our captivity continued, our clothes and shoes began to wear out. Many of us had only brought summer things, believing that we would be taken from Budapest straight to Spain and Palestine, and as the weather got wetter and colder, the tailors and shoemakers found themselves increasingly in demand. Winter clothes were made out of blankets. Planks, either supplied by the Germans or taken from the bunks, were shaped into wooden soles and attached with leather straps or strips cut from tin cans to ragged shoes: I had a pair of these myself and remember how stiff they were and how tall they made me feel as I tried to walk on them. The craftsmen were paid in cigarettes, food or other commodities, either by the customers in the way of private enterprise, or by the leadership, who allocated special rations to them, turning their work into something like a nationalised industry. There were also amateurs, including women who developed unexpected skill in creating new clothes by sewing together patches taken from old ones, or unravelling knitware that had become unusable and knitting new items out of the wool.

Just as we were better fed than most inmates but still suffered from starvation, we were also healthier than most others, but many of us suffered from various illnesses, which got worse as time passed. Kolb's diary reports colds and infections of the intestines on the day after our arrival in Bergen-Belsen, and fainting fits, scarlet fever, a gastric haemorrhage, a stomach ulcer, encephalitis and a gynaecological operation in August and September.[20] Szidonia Devecseri lists more and more cases of measles, whooping cough, stomach problems.[21] In addition, there were a number of mental patients, the most conspicuous being a young man called Gyuri Mező, who knew the whole Hungarian railway timetable by heart and recited it on the slightest provocation. People with deformities included two hunchbacks, both of whom happened to be cantors. Naturally, physical disorders also affected our emotions and the relations between different individuals. Kolb again provides some telling illustrations:

The majority are ill, thin, hungry and nervous. I think Dávid
has developed thyroid problems as a result of starvation. His
eyes bulge, he is quick-tempered and in his agitated state even
violent. This is also how Rosenberg behaved when he had fallen
out with Federit and later with Neumann, but his case was made
worse by a stomach ulcer.[22]

The lack of proper hygiene resulted in skin ailments. My father
and I were among the many who contracted scabies. The relentless
itching kept me awake at night and drove me to distraction by day,
until Dr Valerie Stark gave us some ointment and cured us. Having
examined both of us from top to toe, to my great embarrassment,
she also ordered us to get rid of any hair on our bodies, and I
remember my father struggling with a blunt safety razor, latherless
soap and cold water to obey her command.

Although epidemics were to become rampant after our departure, we did not suffer any major outbreak. Once measles started
to make the rounds among the children and threatened to spread
to the adults, but the doctors suceeded in checking it before it
had claimed too many victims. We were all vaccinated against
cholera with serum we had brought with us. But mass vaccina-
tion against typhus could not go ahead, because although we had
the serum, the surgical spirit was not available. By sheer luck, we
were spared the typhus that killed thousands in the last months
of the camp.

Medical services were overseen by an SS doctor holding the rank
of captain. Apart from occasional disagreements, he got on well with
our own doctors. In the Star Camp next to us, which was occupied
by Dutch Jews, there was a primitive clinic. Despite the strict ban
on communications between the different compounds, we were
allowed to attend this clinic for dental treatment, and in some cases
children were taken across for surgery by our own doctors. Three
middle-ear operations and one intestinal operation are reported to

have been carried out by doctors Kalocsay, Hermann and Schwartz 'with the support of the SS doctor'.[23]

As the Vaada's selection was meant to represent Hungarian Jewry as a whole, it comes as no surprise that there were about thirty-five doctors – including such renowned specialists as the radiologist Ferenc Polgár, the physician Sándor Braun and the ophthalmologist József Hamburg – and several pharmacists among us. We also had fairly large stocks of medical supplies, although we lacked equipment and many essential drugs. If I remember the group as a relatively healthy one, this may be in part due to the ignorance of a relatively healthy boy of eleven. It must have felt very differently to the adults, who knew, and the sick, who suffered.

'Overcrowding, shortages. Many doctors, no organisation . . . Difficulties obtaining medicines'[24] is how Kolb's diary describes the conditions in which the doctors had to do their work. Nevertheless, their commitment is praised by many, including Judy Jacobs: 'The doctors tried to do as much for healthcare as was possible, remembering that – for the most part – there were no supplies, no medication, no instruments.'[25] Jacobs's father, Dr Adalbert Gondos, provided a striking example of the ingenuity needed to cope with such a situation: 'I had an infection on my leg and there were no antibiotics, and my father concocted a sulfur ointment from Vaseline and smashed sulfur pills and it worked.'[26] Olga Munk, whose son had dysentery, pays tribute to the dedication of a 'wonderful doctor' who, against the strictest German orders, ventured out of his hut to help her: 'He came at night and he risked his head to see my child and he had medication with him and gave it to him, so he survived.'[27]

Doctors had the enviable power to requisition food. If they felt that a patient needed more nourishment they could prescribe extra rations. This may have improved the health of some, although it could be abused, as it was by a smart twelve-year-old. David Kohn had been bedridden with a fever for three weeks. A doctor diagnosed general debility and prescribed an extra ration of semolina. David later confessed that he had promptly 'recovered, but stayed in bed all the same'.[28] Some years later David became my stepbrother, when a marriage was arranged by relatives between his widowed mother and my widowed father.

I too had a slightly high temperature for a while, and my father worried that it could be a sign of the TB that had killed my mother. He took my temperature twice a day, and more than once the borrowed thermometer broke in the process. Being an honourable man and a non-smoker, my father reimbursed the owners in cigarettes, while I thought sadly of the extra food we could have bought if he had not bothered with thermometers in the first place.

In a group of that size, over five months, there were bound to be births and deaths. At least three people died in our compound, and one abortion was carried out by a female doctor without instruments. About eight children were born – several by candlelight in the huts during air raids – in addition to the one delivered in the cattle truck on our way to the camp.[29] Egon Mayer lived through our captivity in his mother's womb and was born in Switzerland in January 1945. He later became a distinguished professor of sociology in New York City University, the creator of the Kasztner Memorial website and the author of several chapters in draft for a book on Kasztner, which sadly remained unfinished when he died of cancer in 2004.

It appears that many women in our group stopped menstruating, as women did in other concentration camps, either for psychological reasons or owing to malnutrition. At the time I was not aware of this, either because I was too young to be interested or because the topic would not have been discussed openly. In the men's quarters, where I was living with my father, there would not have been much talk about such matters in any case.

Segregation in the huts naturally had an effect on our sex lives. At eleven I knew nothing about this subject either, and the recollections of others largely ignore it. Some of the young male and female pioneers shared their accommodation and a few memoirs briefly

allude to their uninhibited lifestyle. I remember hearing of a female
SS supervisor making an angry scene, with verbal abuse, blows and
objects sent flying, when she found a man in the women's hut one
afternoon: I now guess, although I had no idea at the time, that she
had probably found them together in a bunk. At a relatively early
stage of our stay Kolb notes in his diary: 'Young men and women
lie down together at night. There will be many pregnancies, we have
no contraceptives. Sexual needs announce themselves. We seriously
consider introducing an institutional sex day.'[30] Later he hints at what
happened when the lights had to be turned off in case of air raids:
'Generally we spend the last two hours in total darkness – lectures
etc. are cut short, we undress in pitch darkness. From an erotic point
of view this has many advantages, which are in fact made use of.'[31]
But on the whole there does not seem to have been a great deal of
sexual activity. An obvious reason must be the lack of privacy, although
stress, depression or malnutrition would have played their part. There
were rumours that we were being fed bromide in our rations to calm
us, but this seems unlikely.

Self-rule

As a privileged group we enjoyed a degree of autonomy within the
camp. Generally the SS guards entered our compound only for
the daily *Zählappell*. I can visualise two of them, in particular, who
also appear in many memoirs. One was tall and bad-tempered. He
took every opportunity to abuse and intimidate us, and we hated
him. As he had either a hare lip or a scar caused by some accident,
we called him 'Cut Mouth'. His second nickname was 'Betar' after
one of the most aggressive right-wing Zionist organisations. The
other was small, cross-eyed and as kind as a German concentration-
camp guard could be. He always had a pipe in his mouth and was
often laughed at by the rest of the Germans. We called him 'Popeye'.
He too had a second nickname, 'Mizrahi', the designation of a
religious Zionist party.

Many of us remember Popeye with affection. One day he discovered that a young girl was missing from the roll call because she could no longer bear to stand in the puddles in her worn-out shoes. The next day he handed her a paper bag which turned out to contain another pair, old but serviceable and more or less the right size. Sometimes he also brought food for the children and old newspapers for the adults. Once, when I was lying in my bunk with a temperature and he came to count the absentees from the roll call, he gave me an encouraging pat that I remember to this day. None of us knew his real name and I have never been able to find out what happened to him after the war. Some memoirs, including Alex Barzel's, claim that he was a British spy who was sending intelligence to Britain about the German war effort.[32] But Popeye was exceptional. More typical is an incident reported by Joseph Berger. When Berger, who was seven at the time, kicked a ball over the fence, the guard returned it to him, but only after sticking his bayonet through it.[33]

There were female SS supervisors, who were supposed to check the cleanliness and tidiness of the huts. We hated one of them even more than Cut Mouth. Miriam Buck describes her as a pretty blonde in her early twenties, but 'her eyes were as hard as steel and her mouth had an evil laugh, full of contempt and hatred'. She called us nothing but 'dirty Jews'. She hit a child of three in the face because he did not stand up straight when she entered the hut, and she tore up an old woman's prayer book with a cruel laugh. If the blankets did not lie impeccably flat on our bunks 'a hail of punishment (withdrawal of bread rations) came full of lust out of her hard mouth'. Buck was 'horrified to see university professors, world-famous physicians, venerable rabbis with long beards, standing to attention, caps in hand, while this young girl stared at them arrogantly and abused them in the most obscene terms'.[34] Lili Szondi-Radványi remembers how, finding an unwashed cup, she yelled: 'I'm going to break you. If you don't get your act together in eight days you'll be wearing yellow stars and working.'[35] The description in Kolb's diary probably refers to the same person: 'White fur gloves, high boots, uniform, culottes, cap pulled down over half her face, swaying walk, flirtatiousness, in between she whistles, shouts, is in high spirits, throws dishes, threatens withdrawal of butter, messes up the bunks, tells how she hit two people in the face in the other compound.'[36] None of the reminiscences mention an SS woman by name, but this particular specimen is likely to have been the notorious Irma Grese, who had come to Bergen-Belsen from Auschwitz with camp commander Kramer and was hanged with him by the British soon after the war.

Under the terms of the autonomy negotiated for us by Kasztner, the commander's orders were delivered to our internal leaders, who transmitted them to us and determined the practical details of our everyday lives. In fact, our group was organised like a miniature state, with political parties, a government, a hierarchy of officials, a judiciary, a police force, a written constitution, elections, intrigues, string-pulling, log-rolling, in short everything that it takes to run a democracy. The only snag was that we were all prisoners of the undemocratic Nazis, who could withdraw our privileges, and indeed send us to Auschwitz, at the drop of a hat. The earnestness with which this collection of helpless people on the brink of extermination played at politics, with agendas and minutes, motions and amendments, points of order, chairman's actions and votes, was as absurd as it was necessary for maintaining self-respect. It was a farce, but it kept us going, as long as we managed to forget that the bubble might burst at any moment.

In Bergen-Belsen the men appointed as our leaders in Mosonmagyaróvár continued to run our affairs according to the rules introduced at that time. It was not a smooth operation. There were constant clashes, both personal and political. The worst distrust existed between the contingent from Kolozsvár, which contained most of the leading Zionists, and that from Budapest, which formed the majority of the people. Quarrels between the youth groups, mainly on the left, and the established figures, more to the right, were also frequent, as were the squabbles between the more religious and the less religious factions. On 22–23 July an 'action committee' of twenty-six members and an 'executive' of six were elected. The executive consisted of Moshe Rosenberg, Ferenc Kauders, Hillel Danzig, Jenő László, Éli Kohn and, as its head, József Fischer. Contentious issues were decided by autocratic decree from Fischer.

After long debates an impressive set of new rules[37] was agreed in October. It consisted of twenty-five clauses spread over six closely typed pages, referred to as our 'constitution'. The complex bureaucracy, described in pedantic officialese, seemed more appropriate to a small state than to a group of less than 1,700 Jews behind barbed wire and at the mercy of the SS. But it gave us – at least the adults – something to do and to argue about. It also gave us a deceptive sense of control over our own destiny and helped to prevent anarchy.

The 'constitution' was based on the understanding that our group would be led in the 'Jewish national spirit' – i.e. along Zionist lines – and that our governing body had absolute discretion over our 'skills, expertise and assets within the camp'. The governing body was to be elected by secret ballot. It was to consist of the camp leader, two deputy leaders and fifteen other members. Ten sub-committees, each with its own area of responsibility, were to cover all aspects of our lives: central and local administration, law and order, the economy, food supplies, health, education, religion and welfare. Their heads were chosen by the governing body from its own members. There was also to be a supervisory board of three members, who were not part of the governing body. As camp leader, in German *Lagerältester* or *Judenältester*, József Fischer was to have particularly far-reaching powers. Law and order were to be kept by an internal police force and any breaches punished, for instance, by withdrawal of rations or having to sleep on the bare boards of a bunk. Applications (e.g. for medicines), complaints (e.g. about the police) and appeals (e.g. against punishments) had to follow precise procedures.

By mid-November the draft had been accepted and it was time

for elections. After a heated campaign with long speeches, manifestos and arguments, 52 electors, themselves elected by the numerous political parties represented among us, voted for the new governing body. If we accept Kolb's somewhat inaccurate list, this consisted of the following 21 individuals, including some ex-officio members: József Fischer, Dov Braun, Jenő László, Ferenc Kauders, József Gottlieb, Dezső Hermann, Ferenc Pártos, József Weinberger, Adolf Schlesinger, Béla Zsolt, Jenő Kolb, László Somogyi, Lajos Gottesmann, Alex Vas, Mose Rosenberg, Ede Márton, György Polgár, Sándor Leitner, Leo Stein, Eduard Izsák and Lipót Blau.[38] Soon after, the sub-committees were formed, with Kolb himself responsible for education and culture. On the whole, the newly elected officials were identical to those in charge before, and things continued in much the same way.

As might be expected, there were many complaints about unfairness, bullying, nepotism or downright corruption levelled against the leaders. I suspect that to some extent they served as scapegoats for the hardships of the camp, but given the situation in which we found ourselves it would be surprising if they had been completely innocent of any abuses. The most extreme charges are those in 'Deportation to Bergen-Belsen'. I believe that they are exaggerated, but may contain some grains of truth, even though their relentlessly bitter tone suggests a deep personal grudge on the part of the anonymous memoirist.

According to this jaundiced catalogue, Fischer filled all the key positions in the administration with his own followers, who in turn considered themselves absolute rulers; the clique at the top enjoyed lavish meals, while the majority was starving; individuals responsible for everybody's welfare diverted basic necessities to their own cronies, and food supplied for all was sold to some who could pay in hard currencies and valuables; members of the governing body placed their names first on the lists for anticipated departures; the internal police intimidated the community by impromptu raids and harsh penalties. The anonymous critic sums up his allegations as follows:

The leadership saw to it that there was constant terror in the camp. Any freedom of speech was stopped and any criticism punished. All the time the 'powers that be' preached the necessity of solidarity, while they themselves were only after their own personal advantage.[39]

Although I think this writer, pursuing his private vendetta, overstates his case, there are more moderately phrased but no less critical remarks by others which also indicate a strong discontent smouldering beneath the surface. Kolb suspects some members of the governing body of selling communal food reserves on the black market and trying to hide their shady deals by either supporting other culprits or attacking innocent individuals.[40] He further notes that many of the medicines we received from the Red Cross shortly before our release were withheld from the community but were suddenly available to solvent buyers.[41] Hermann Adler adds that three-quarters of the nutrient Starkosan, which was a gift from the Red Cross for all of us, found its way into the private stores of some of the leaders, who also profiteered by selling a proportion of the communal bread they claimed to have kept in reserve for everybody.[42]

It is impossible to prove the truth of such accusations. Kolb is probably right in finding grave faults all round, rather than picking on the leaders alone: 'Not much honesty, lack of order, lack of a system, a phlegmatic flouting of rules.'[43] But if this was the general mood, our elders and betters did nothing to create a better one. Edit Goldstein condemns their attitude in a brief understatement: 'The leaders of the camp didn't mingle with the people.'[44] They were indeed resented by many for the relative physical comforts they had secured for themselves and for their supercilious and authoritarian treatment of the rest of us. The smell of real coffee being brewed behind closed doors in their quarters is remembered by several witnesses as a symbol of the eternal gulf between rulers and subjects that existed even in our miserable situation.

Culture

Many members of our group had belonged to the intellectual and artistic elite of Hungarian Jewry, and the comparatively large amount of luggage we had brought with us included books, stationery and devotional objects. As we were not obliged to work, a makeshift but active cultural life developed in our compound right from the start.

Books of all kinds – philosophical and historical studies, religious writings, Hungarian and foreign literary classics – were read aloud in communal sessions or lent to individuals by their owners either as a friendly gesture or in exchange for cigarettes or food. A large proportion of the limited amount of paper available was used to produce bureaucratic documents – regulations, agendas, minutes, records of court proceedings – but some was left for more creative artistic purposes. The constant flow of cultural events ranged from light entertainment to high-minded educational projects. A number of key personalities stand out in my own memory, corroborated by the recollections of others.

The most eminent of several psychologists in the group was Leopold Szondi, the founder of the school of 'fate analysis'. He spent much of his time developing his theories, conducting courses, counselling patients and fine-tuning his famous Szondi test. I was one of many who had to select the most appealing and the least appealing pictures of assorted mentally ill patients, while he produced a graph that assessed my own personality based on my choices. I quite enjoyed doing this, although I found all the faces equally repulsive.

István Irsai, a well-known graphic artist, occupied himself by decorating the huts for the Jewish festivals, preparing posters for our elections and drawing ironic postcards showing typical aspects of the camp – the watch towers, the huts, the three-storey bunks, the iron food containers, the inedible wild carrots, the diminishing loaves, the patchwork garments, the dream of Palestine – always seen through a grid of barbed wire.

The renowned writer and journalist Béla Zsolt delivered lectures about literature, history and politics and analysed the progress of the war with the help of bits of newspaper or oral reports supplied by the guards in exchange for cigarettes, which he hated to part with as he was the heaviest smoker in the group. Gathering his admirers about him, Zsolt promised them posts in a government he would head as prime minister when we returned to Hungary. My father was to be minister of finance. Zsolt never became prime minister, but he at least was elected to the Hungarian parliament. He died soon after, having written *Nine Suitcases*, his great Holocaust memoir, which I had the privilege of translating into English many decades later.

Two professional singers, Dezső Ernster (later of the Metropolitan Opera, New York) and Hanna Brand (Joel's sister), gave recitals in the huts, often in the dark after lights out. George Bishop pays a particularly warm tribute to Ernster: 'In the middle of the night to all the desperate people and all the hungry people and so forth, all of a sudden came this heavenly voice singing Verdi and Wagner . . . From his bunk he sang for ten minutes, fifteen minutes to us and that was beautiful.'[45] Kolb recalls a third singer and her uplifting defiance: 'Fridays are terrible, there is no electric light and by 4 o'clock it is dark . . . But in our hut Margit Salgó sings jazz songs.'[46] Choral singing was one of the most common cultural activities. Members of the Zionist youth movements performed the Hebrew songs of their various political associations. Others sang Yiddish or Hungarian folk songs or popular hits. For obvious reasons instrumental music was extremely rare, although Kolb reports playing the violin once or twice. The pianist Tamás Blum made up for not being able to play by giving talks on musical history.

Two members of the group recited poems from memory while we lay in our bunks in the dark: Erzsi Palotai, who was a novelist, but whose greatest successes had been her readings of modern Hungarian poetry, and Hermann Adler, himself a poet, who remarks that he was paid for his appearances in 'breadcrumbs'.[47] Another poet, Ferenc Ábrahám, published his own poems, including some written in Bergen-Belsen, under the title *Rabságban* (In Captivity). The edition is unique in that there was only one copy, made out of margarine boxes, tin cans and scrap wire. It is now in the Bergen-Belsen memorial museum. At the time it could be borrowed for a few cigarettes or a lunch.

Some events evolved spontaneously, while others were carefully planned and orchestrated by the leadership. For example, in mid-October representatives from each room in the two huts met to discuss structured ways of spending the evenings on cultural activities. They noted that in 10b, 10c, 11b and 11c there were already discussions and talks, while in 10a singing lessons could be had and in 10c religious study was taking place all day. The outcome of the meeting is not known.[48]

With so many Jewish intellectuals crammed into a few hundred square metres, there was bound to be an abundance of lectures and debates. I was not interested in adults holding forth, but wherever I went there were groups of people listening to a speaker or arguing, in the open while the weather was fine and in the tight communal areas of the huts when it became cold and wet outside. The lectures are mentioned in most memoirs. Edit Goldstein recalls 'young, old, religious, secular, artists, singers, journalists, psychologists, doctors, all kinds of interesting people who gave talks'.[49] Kolb's diary bristles with detailed lists and critical comments. A terse example is: 'Dov Braun gives a talk on biology, Buk on sociology, Hermann on the structure of society', followed two days later by 'Szabó's bad lecture about sabre-rattling.'[50]

The lectures and debates often had a political motivation. Kolb himself was active in 'Gordonia', a non-Marxist Zionist labour movement. He mentions, among others, a series he and his fellow-Gordonians mounted with the intention of creating an intellectual climate favourable to Zionism: 'Anti-Zionism is on the rise. Against this we are organising cultural lectures: The Development of the

Zionist Idea (Jenő Kolb, Dezső Weiss, Ede Márton, József Hamburg).' He then lists the following speakers and topics: 'Farkas Engel: The intellectual movements of the 19th century; Komlós: The tragic fate of Hungarian Jewry; Buk: The road of two thousand years; Dov Braun: Buber; Mandel: Hebrew literature, etc. Lajos Márton´s seminar: The history of Palestine in the age of the Bible; a Chernishevski evening; a Yiddish evening in the women's huts, etc'.[51]

On 2 November we celebrated the 27th anniversary of the Balfour Declaration, which had promised the Jews a homeland in Palestine. In the course of the day József Fischer commemorated that historic event in Hungarian and in Hebrew in an address to our governing body, and in the evening speeches and discussions took place in every room of the two huts.

Not all these events were political. At Szondi's initiative, a 'Study Group' including intellecuals of all persuasions was set up with the aim of 'humanising the individual and attempting to humanise the masses'.[52] Each member was to investigate the meaning of humanism in a given area (religion, philosophy, law, literature, art, sociology) and a debate followed. Szondi himself spoke at length about the concept of humanism in the light of depth psychology. But soon the original topic was forgotten. Kolb complains about the loss of common purpose: 'For three days of discussions in rain and frost . . . not a word about humanism – they all talk about their own interests and hobby horses . . . Fischer defends Zionism, Polgár the common human values, Zsolt calls nationalism syphilis and leprosy.'[53]

We also had some lighter entertainments. To quote Szidonia Devecseri, 'in spite of all . . . miseries, vacillations and despair, we sometimes tried to conjure a little bit of merriment into our huts'.[54] As the outstanding example of such diversions I remember a series of productions that I did not entirely understand but thoroughly enjoyed as I was lying in my bunk in the dark. This was 'Rádió Ajvé'

(Radio OyVay), a spoof review based on the sophisticated political and literary cabarets of Central Europe. Featuring mock news, satirical sketches and humorous songs, it poked fun at the more conspicuous members of our group, the German guards, the food, the latrines, the weather, the quarrels of the political parties and many other topical issues, including at least one item by Ferenc Ábrahám, which Kolb thought 'witty, but rather too spicy'.[55] The jokes about some characters called 'SSK' baffled me. I knew that they were scurrilous and had something to do with the German female supervisors, but that was all. I have discovered since that 'SSK' was the Hungarian abbreviation of 'SS whore', but I still don't know exactly what the jokes said about them.

The group included about 300 children and 30 teachers, and it was decided soon after our arrival to organise lessons. On 21 August the school for the Neologue majority was formally opened, immediately followed by a *cheder* and a *yeshiva* for the Orthodox minority. In theory, one or two hours of lessons a day were compulsory, but uneven attendance and shortage of teaching materials made them less effective than the organisers had hoped. In good weather classes took place in the open and the lack of paper was somewhat alleviated by the possibility of writing in the sand with our fingers or small sticks. When autumn came we were transferred into the overcrowded huts and the lessons gradually ran out of steam. I must admit that I do not remember going to school in Bergen-Belsen. One of the teachers, Lili Szondi-Radványi, gives a vivid sense of the difficulties of teaching in such conditions:

I pull out my newspaper – the only text book I have – from beside my paillasse and walk to a table in the other corner of the hut, which is the school. Unfortunately not every pupil has a pencil, and paper is at a premium. Some children do not come to school because their feet are frozen, some have no shoes. Only six or eight of fifteen are present . . . We start doing sums, which requires neither paper nor pencil. A modern teacher always invents tasks related to the prevailing situation. I ask how many food bearers there are if each of five rooms in the men's hut provides six bearers, or how many decilitres of soup one person gets if there are 50 litres to share and a hundred people in the room.[56]

Kolb supplies a sobering account of the limited success even of an uncommonly committed and energetic teacher:

Mrs Kudelka makes plans, issues directives, organises; she can't live without being active . . . Yesterday she held exams: the first five children got commendations. They have forgotten an enormous amount and can hardly read or do sums any more. Their memory is blurred, like that of the adults. Their imagination revolves round mundane things and they can hardly imagine the future, that is, a normal life.[57]

An important part of the education was devoted to Zionism. For the younger children the method was fun and games. This is how it seemed to Ági Hendell, who was ten at the time: 'Every afternoon somebody of the Zionist people got all the kids together and they taught us Hebrew and we sang songs and they occupied us.'[58] But there was more to it than that. The Zionist movements – the left-wing Hashomer Hatzair, the religious Mizrahi, the right-wing revisionist Betar and various others – were intent on educating, or indoctrinating, the children for a life as pioneers in Palestine, each according to its own exclusive ideology.

This was not to everybody's taste. Many resented the relentless Zionist propaganda and, if they were Orthodox, its disregard for religious values. Jack Gross, who was fourteen, remembers: 'Because it was a Zionist organized group – it was forced on us to take Hebrew lessons, to get to know about Palestine, about the geography, not learning Torah, but just about what concerns the Zionists' objectives.'[59] As for young people who were neither Zionist nor Orthodox, Kolb remarks that 'the non-Zionist bourgeois youth also wants to be occupied: art, music, literature, etc.' The programme of a 'youth seminar' that he quotes included 'the physiology of the human body', 'introduction to Hebrew literature', 'literature between the two world wars', 'history of music' and 'Jewish history'.[60]

Among the most frequent activities were language courses, for adults as well as children. Given the dominant role of Zionists in a group apparently bound for Palestine, Hebrew lessons were the most popular, but English, French and even German lessons were also well attended. Edit Goldstein, a particularly versatile teacher who taught all four languages, had brought English, Hungarian, German, French and Latin dictionaries in her luggage.

One form of education that was largely lacking was physical. In our condition – not to mention the lack of facilities – we had neither the desire nor the energy to take much exercise. Nor were Jewish intellectuals, of whom there were so many among us, particularly keen on sports. Nevertheless, mainly in the early months of our captivity, the youth groups engaged in volleyball, gymnastics and folk dancing, sometimes interrupted by bad-tempered guards. Some pioneers made primitive weapons out of boards from the bunks and stolen bits of barbed wire and exercised with them in the wash room. This was not meant to be a game, but rather preparation for self-defence if the SS tried to murder us before the Allies arrived. It helped to keep up the young men's morale but amounted to little more than shadow-boxing.

Naturally all this could give us only momentary respite from the miseries of the camp. As our physical and emotional condition worsened, our cultural activities also declined. Nevertheless, while they lasted, they did a lot to keep up our morale. Hermann Adler writes tersely: 'We felt that we were human beings.'[61] Vera John-Steiner uses the same image: 'I felt like I belonged to a people, rather than what they were trying to make us into, which was animals.'[62] These activities indeed helped us preserve our self-respect and sanity in the middle of all the squalor and deprivation. But had we not been rescued when we were, no amount of culture could have kept us human.

Religion

Although the majority of the group was not religious, many among us clung to the Jewish rituals, whether from belief, a sense of tradition, or sheer despair. We celebrated the great festivals, prayed, and studied religious texts. The devotional objects we had been able to bring with us – Torah scrolls, Bibles, copies of the Talmud, *tallitot* (prayer shawls) and *tefillim* (phylacteries) – were in frequent use.

For the great Jewish festivals the huts were transformed into temporary synagogues. The main synagogue was the sick bay, from which the patients were evacuated for the duration. The naked light bulbs were festooned with Stars of David cut out of cardboard. An eternal light was made of a tin can and the burner of a tea warmer. The walls were hung with home-made posters bearing religious inscriptions. A women's section was curtained off and the concrete floor covered by blankets masquerading as oriental rugs. Other rooms were adapted in a less flamboyant but similar way.

The most important festivals in the Jewish calendar are Rosh Hashana (New Year) and Yom Kippur (Day of Atonement). On both of these a ram's horn, the *shofar*, is blown at certain points of the service. We had one shofar with us, whose owner demanded 300 cigarettes as rental. Finally he accepted a tin of sardines, and the *shofar* made the rounds of the improvised synagogues. In the Polish compound next to ours the slave labourers stopped to listen and pray, until the German guards chased them back to work with curses and blows. Some memoirs claim that a *shofar* and a Torah were exchanged between the Dutch compound and ours, with the guard nicknamed 'Popeye' or 'Mizrahi' acting as carrier, but I suspect that this was one of the many myths camp life was apt to produce.

The most fervent celebrations took place on the two days of Rosh Hashana. Each of the different congregations or political parties had its own improvised synagogue and makeshift tables set for a communal meal in one or other corner of the huts. On the first day a 'very striking' sermon by Rabbi Adolf Silberstein produced many tears and a general sense of good will and solidarity, but an 'extremely weak, long-winded' sermon by Rabbi Tibor Fettmann, which came soon after, spoiled the atmosphere. When the power was suddenly cut off, Kolb made a speech in the dark, calling for a 'struggle against human wickedness and our own bad deeds'. This was followed by a poetry recital and singing, which lasted until 'midnight in the clear starry night'. At the same time, in another room, Rabbi Salamon Strasser, 82 years old, cried throughout his sermon, and his whole congregation cried with him. On the second day the festivities were disrupted by a roll call lasting one and a half hours, but after a 'quiet celebration with the Chalutz pioneers' Kolb was able to look back on 'an extremely beautiful evening'.[63] Even the author of 'Deportation to Bergen-Belsen' for once adopts a more serene tone, emphasising the joyous aspects of the festival, while not forgetting the pain that never left us for long: 'On those days the whole camp was united, reconciled and harmonious, all the disagreements were settled, we celebrated and we mourned together.'[64]

The weekly celebrations of the Sabbath – either on Friday evenings or on Saturdays – showed up the divided nature of the group. The deepest divisions were those between the Orthodox and the Neologues, the Zionists and the non-Zionists, the assimilated and the traditionalists, although there were many overlaps between them. As my father kept his distance from these events I have no clear personal memories of them. But three examples from the recollections of others may give an impression of the diversity of approaches.

Ester Jungreis, the daughter of a rabbi, recalls a quiet orthodox celebration within the family, when her father

> would gather us around in the middle of the night so that no one would find out and he would start to sing very softly, *shalom alechem* [peace be with you], and he would make *kiddush* [blessing]. And it was very, very beautiful. And my father would take from his rations, every day, a small little piece and he would put it away for shabbos so that we would know that it was shabbos.[65]

In contrast, Kolb reports a 'socialist celebration' of the Hashomer Hatzair party one week after our arrival in Bergen-Belsen, when 'prayers', 'speeches' and 'singing till late at night, even dancing' introduced 'a beautiful Sabbath behind barbed wire'. A German guard threatened to bring 'a machine gun next time', but the occasion was repeated, albeit in a lower key, in subsequent weeks.[66] Kolb recognises that the festivities of both the secular and the religious groupings could create a sense of 'freedom in spite of the fence'.[67] However, for those who belonged to neither side he has less understanding. A boisterous gathering of assimilated women strikes him as decadent: 'A café atmosphere with music, Hungarian songs, marches, shrieking, shouting. A completely different world from that in the chalutz-pioneers' hut.'[68] He fails to realise that this raucous entertainment was yet another attempt to overcome our desolation.

Four of the major Jewish rites of passage – circumcision, Bar Mitzvah, marriage and funeral – also took place while we were in the camp. The first boy to be circumcised was born during one air raid and the ritual was carried out during another, with many spectators watching spellbound as the child was symbolically admitted to the covenant with God in one of the most God-forsaken places created by men. When the second boy was about to be circumcised a few weeks later, the fierce guard we called 'Betar' interrupted the proceedings. When he was told what was happening, he commanded: 'This is a holy action – carry on.'[69]

Several boys, reaching their thirteenth birthday, celebrated their Bar Mitzvah. The ceremonies, which include reading and commenting on a passage from the Torah in front of the congregation and making an after-dinner speech, were held in one or other of the temporary synagogues. Some of them were again witnessed by more or less benignly curious guards. Yehuda Blum was one of the boys. In his speech he quoted the formula 'Next year in Jerusalem' and, unlikely as this prophecy seemed, it turned out to be true for many members of the group.[70]

While no wedding took place in the camp, a young couple from Kolozsvár got engaged about three weeks after our arrival. Given our situation, I do not know whether this was a deliberate, defiant act of faith in the future or a quixotic gesture that could have ended just as easily in death as in marriage after liberation.

The first of several funerals was that of Eva Breslauer on 9 August. Depressed since the trauma of Linz, when she had been among those women forcibly shaved, she died of pneumonia at the age of seventeen. She was washed and dressed in white, as the tradition demands, and a large crowd gathered to say farewell to her. It was sobering to see that her coffin was removed by the cart that normally collected the rubbish, but everybody was profoundly moved. Two weeks later, when a ten-month old child and a woman of sixty-seven died, Kolb noted in his diary: 'The emotions are much less strong than with Breslauer.'[71]

In keeping with the large religious cohorts, there were many rabbis in our group, representing all persuasions from the Reformed to the ultra-Orthodox. The most distinguished was the Chassidic rabbi of Szatmár, Joel or Jajlis Teitelbaum. Although he owed his life to Kasztner's Zionist enterprise, he hated Zionism and after liberation emigrated to the US rather than Palestine. I remember him as a distant but compelling figure, surrounded by a few dozen devoted followers, who did all they could to shield him from the hardships of Bergen-Belsen. They had arrived with a large chest full of kosher food and a cook of their own, who was allowed to prepare the rabbi's meals in the camp kitchen, even though he lived mainly on bread and jacket potatoes. When our leadership required all the men in the group to shave their beards, either to reduce the hiding places for lice or to avoid provoking the Germans, he could keep his, although he had to wear a scarf round his face, as if he had a toothache. He was in the habit of using the latrine during roll calls, so that we had to wait longer in the cold before the guards decided that none of us had escaped. His disciples kept themselves to themselves and assumed a superior attitude, which did not endear them to the rest. But he had a unique charisma that nobody could deny. In Yehuda Blum's words, 'he was no ordinary human being, whether you liked him or not'.[72]

I might add that when my father had hard decisions to make, often about my own upbringing, he used to ask Teitelbaum for advice. This could suggest that he felt in need of spiritual guidance, but he also used to ask Szondi for advice on the same matters. Being neither religious nor a believer in psychology, he probably thought it wise to leave nothing to chance.

The Orthodox venerated Teitelbaum like a saint. Perhaps his most salient feature was the calm confidence he derived from his faith. While most of us lost heart at some point or other, he seemed to know that no real harm would ultimately come to him, and he radiated this feeling to those around him. Jacob Gross, one of his most devout followers, explains: 'His spirit was not sagging. He was always invigorating and giving courage to us . . . he was always smiling and telling us that things will be all right . . . God will help us.'[73]

A cynic might say that Teitelbaum had reason to be calm and confident, as he was one of the most privileged individuals in our relatively privileged group. But he had truly uncommon inner resources and an overpowering magnetism. His behaviour at Simchat

Torah, the festival celebrating the sacred scroll, is remembered by many with astonishment. Even Kolb was impressed. He praises the procession of children bearing the Torah round the compound, and he dismisses the official picnic laid on by Fischer for the upper echelons as a 'characteristically lukewarm bourgeois event'. When he comes to Teitelbaum's performance he acknowledges the infectious spiritual rapture he is witnessing: 'The mood is ecstatic. The rabbi dances round the room. The Chassidim sing and clap until they are totally exhausted. Many look on, as if they were in the theatre. At 8 o'clock the lights go out. The singing and dancing continue. It ends by candlelight.'[74]

The Orthodox sometimes found themselves in a strange dilemma about the food we were given. It was typical of either the irrationality or the hypocrisy of the Nazi system that part of our daily soup was supposed to be kosher. Some of the containers had a letter K painted on them and generally contained vegetables without any meat. This satisfied the conscience of most of the Orthodox, although Teitelbaum for one never touched it. But from time to time there were bits of meat in a 'kosher' container, probably because the K had been painted on it in error. When this happened some of the Orthodox went without lunch, while others, more happily than realistically, thanked their lucky stars for being given kosher meat. As for the sausages or black pudding we sometimes received, the Orthodox adults either bartered them or fed them to their children. Since children needed proper nourishment even more than adults, the religious rules allowed them to eat these forbidden delicacies, but some felt so guilty that they could hardly swallow.

The barbed-wire disease

For all our privileges and our efforts to maintain a civilised existence, our five-month stay in Bergen-Belsen was marked by steady physical and emotional decline. A constant source of misery was our isolation. We were surrounded by people in other compounds, but any communication with them was strictly forbidden. Some surreptitious contacts were made all the same. Patients or doctors attending the clinic in the Dutch compound and bearers collecting our meals in the camp kitchen managed to exchange a few words with other inmates. On the walls of the shower unit written messages were left from time to time. Hurried conversations took place and notes, food or cigarettes were handed through the barbed wire. However, these contacts did little to alleviate our sense of being cut off from the rest of humanity.

We were not supposed to obtain any information about current affairs either, but again a certain amount trickled through. Some of the guards, whether out of kindness or in exchange for cigarettes, told us the news or gave us scraps of newspaper, mainly the Nazi daily *Völkischer Beobachter*. From time to time we received post from friends and relations, although it took a long time to arrive and said little in order to pass censorship. When we heard about Horthy's 7 July ban on deportations, many of us began to believe that we had delivered ourselves unnecessarily into the hands of the Germans. Reports about the 20 July attempt on Hitler's life and the advances of the Allied armies gave us hope, but also made us fearful of possible fighting around the camp. Szálasi's coup of 15 October led us to wonder whether we were not better off in a German concentration camp than in Hungary under Arrow Cross rule. The adults were constantly speculating about what might be happening in the world outside, but the unreliable mixture of fact, rumour and fantasy that circulated brought more disappointment than comfort.

A tantalising reminder of another world came from the sky. As the war progressed, larger and larger formations of Allied aircraft flew over the camp to bomb Hannover and other German cities. Their slow, steady drone that must have seemed so ominous to the Germans was most welcome to our ears. If the planes came at night we would watch the distant sky lit up by explosions as we crowded round the small windows of the hut, with the guards outside furiously gesturing us to go back to our bunks. I was constantly being pushed out of the way by the adults, but usually managed to see enough of the spectacle to be excited and happy. If the planes came by day they dropped thousands of silvery ribbons, which I and other children collected greedily without realising that their practical purpose was to scramble the German radar system. To the adults these bombing raids held out a promise of survival and freedom, and I shared their elation. But when the raids were over and the planes had returned to their bases we felt as miserable as before.

While a spell of sunshine or an encouraging rumour could raise our spirits, as time passed without any sign of our early release, hunger, cold, illness, frustration and fear took their toll. In July, only a fortnight after our arrival in Bergen-Belsen, Kolb noted the demoralising effect of lice and scabies on our self-respect: 'Despair spreads over how we could come down so low in so little time.'[75] Early in August he complained: 'Not much cleanliness, no order and no system, phlegmatic flouting of camp commands.'[76] In the first week of October he noted our continuing decline, putting special emphasis on frictions between individuals, antisocial behaviour and deteriorating health:

> People's nervous state and moral behaviour are deteriorating more and more. Tension near breaking point, loud arguments and insults over a bunk, the stove, the positioning of a lamp and a spoonful of jam. Everything gets stolen – people don't even regard stealing as a sin . . . The majority are ill, wasted, hungry and nervous.[77]

In mid-October Kolb wrote about what he called 'barbed-wire disease . . . nervous excitement, distrust, quarrelling, depression, the decay of moral inhibitions'. The possible causes, physical or emotional, that he mentions are 'the great weight loss, about 10–15 kilograms per person, an increase in thyroid function, the eternal hunger, the uncertainty, the constant togetherness, the total absence of privacy (instead, no collective but a painful loss of individuality in the mass), sexual disorder etc.'[78]

The lack of privacy – even in our bunks, not to mention the communal latrine – was most upsetting to some: 'If you wanted to cry you could only do so at night and even then you were assisted by at least fifty of the hundred and fifty sleeping and snoring inhabitants of the hut who had heard you and woken up.'[79] The close proximity in which we were forced to live with each other produced aggression. There were more and more arguments as everybody became 'irritable, quarrelsome and nervous, parents with their children, friends among themselves and even strangers between them.'[80] Far from encouraging selflessness and consideration, the inhuman conditions made us more anti-social: 'The camp just brought out the worst in people. People stole and people lied and manipulated – things that people under normal circumstances don't do.'[81] The constant pressure made us lash out against our fellow-sufferers: 'When people are in good moods, they are friends with each other. But when things start getting really bad, people start to get nasty with each other.'[82] Nor was the anger confined to individuals. There were also conflicts between – and within – the different political, religious or social factions. Socialists quarrelled with capitalists, fundamentalists with atheists, young *chalutzim* with old bourgeois, the left-wing Hashomer Hatzair with the right-wing Betar or the Orthodox Mizrahi, the smaller but more powerful contingent from Kolozsvár with the larger but less influential one from Budapest. The Neologues regarded the Orthodox as uncouth fanatics, while the Orthodox condemned the Neologues as godless apostates. The Zionists considered the non-Zionists as traitors, while the non-Zionists denounced the Zionists as chauvinistic bullies. These arguments aroused huge passions and fallings-out, which were often followed by formal reconciliations and more arguments.

Morale was also battered by events in the compounds surrounding us. More and more wretched captives were being moved to Bergen-Belsen from other camps. In September 3,000 Hungarian women arrived from Auschwitz, worn out, starving, in convict clothes and with numbers tattooed on their arms. They were first put up in the Tent Camp, where they slept on the ground without mattresses or blankets. They had no latrines, no medical provisions and hardly any water. One of our gynaecologists, Vali Stark, was detailed to examine them and carry out some abortions. She was not allowed to talk to them, but managed to exchange some information, which was supplemented by other surreptitious methods. Their stories upset us deeply. I did not discover until after the war that my cousins Helén and Goldi were in this group.

Unlike our guards, those of the Star Camp next to us had no orders to spare the inmates, and we witnessed a great deal of abuse. In Miriam Buck's words 'People were being beaten and kicked day after day. It was a terrible feeling to stand by helplessly, watching old women receiving blows in the face because they couldn't bear standing for hours during roll calls.'[83] I would like to think that we were still able to pity others being treated in this way, but it was only natural for us to be afraid of our own future, as Judy Jacobs admitted: 'What we saw made our spirits sag because we thought, "this is what we are going to look like, this is what is going to happen."'[84]

By mid-November the external conditions had become extremely depressing. Darkness fell before 5 pm, it rained constantly, the wind hardly ever dropped, and the temperature was only a degree or two above freezing. We were starving, our clothes and shoes were soaked during the *Zählappell*, and even the healthiest among us were suffering from stomach problems or flu. Our hopes of liberation were rapidly fading. We tried to spend as much time as possible lying passively in our bunks, but this made our apathy and despondency even worse. Miriam Buck noted: 'The inactivity as such is degrading'.[85]

The emotional limbo in which we lived is poignantly illustrated by two small incidents reported by Kolb. In the wash room he overhears a woman saying: 'I think of my earlier life only as a vanished dream, all its contours are fading in front of my eyes.' Walking with his wife Edit in the icy wind up and down the compound, reviving old memories, he muses of those not in captivity: 'Everybody else has a present, while the past and the future are irrational; we have a past and I also regard the future as a reality, but we truly have no present.'[86] Eliezer Cohen's prevailing mood of 'boredom mixed with fear of death'[87] must have been shared by many. Edit Goldstein, without either belittling or exaggerating the ordeal, puts the suffering to which she and the rest of us were subjected fairly in perspective: 'What I went through wasn't Auschwitz, but it was a very profound humiliation.'[88] Finally, the letter writer known as Willy recalls our lives in the camp with such accuracy and force that I want to quote him at some length:

> The provisions we had brought with us were running out, and the food that came from the camp kitchen became less and less and worse and worse. People grew thin like shadows, and the smokers suffered in addition owing to lack of tobacco. I was in a hut with intellectuals. There were dozens of doctors with all kinds of specialisms, professors, literary men, civil engineers and the like. Nevertheless, the cleanliness of the bodies as well as of the hut revealed a shameful lack of the most elementary sense of hygiene I would never have thought possible. The air in the hut became unbearable. Staying outside was impossible because it was raining constantly or almost constantly. In addition, I myself, who set such great store at the cleanliness of my body and my bunk etc, discovered that I had had crab lice for weeks. We had a dermatologist in the women's hut, who soon cured me with simple disinfectants. But an inner disgust remained with me. Disgust with myself, with the hut, with the food, and particularly with the people . . . When I received the food – it was rubbish – the smell alone irritated me so much that I couldn't

force it down . . . When I came into the hut and smelled the urine, the exhalations, the dirt and the decay, my stomach turned over. I vomited again and again . . . My wife sacrificed herself in vain, selling her starvation rations umpteen times in order to barter milk, tins and bread for me . . . I had become too weak to rise from my bunk, and in the many, many hours I had to lie in the stinking, noisy dump, my thoughts were with my mother, about whose fate I knew nothing, and I was tortured by self-reproach for failing to look after her enough and to bring her with me.[89]

As time passed the children were increasingly adopting bad habits. The adults tried to keep us in order by organising activities – academic, religious, political – but these gradually atrophied. Kolb notes that the 'children suffer from the nervousness of their parents, but they in turn make their parents nervous'.[90] He attributes their 'loutish behaviour' to 'wrong education' and 'bad example'. Attempts to make them greet adults, be still from time to time, and realise that 'a minimal education and politeness are compulsory for them too' failed.[91] A group of Polish orphans was particularly rough. Some had already spent years in camps, others had witnessed all kinds of atrocities. As a result they were brutalised and full of hatred against everybody and everything. Ági Hendell analyses the way the adults' own behaviour deprived the children of role models and objects of respect:

We were just observing the grown up people, how fast they lost their composure, their humanity. Everything that we were told that grown up people know it all and they are wise and we have to listen to them, it kind of evaporated in Bergen-Belsen because grown up people weren't behaving too nice . . . Lots of them who were held as exemplary citizens, like lawyers and businessmen, they were not behaving the way we children expected them to behave.'[92]

Yehuda Blum sums up: 'We didn't know how to handle this situation of our parents completely losing authority.'[93]

In the early stages we played traditional games in a more or less disciplined manner, but eventually we tired of them. I remember lying in my bunk a lot of the time, daydreaming about food, about Palestine, later about Switzerland. Kolb watched his little daughter and her friends reenact the history of our group, beginning with the departure from Budapest, prominently featuring the *Zählappell* and petering out with other scenes of Bergen-Belsen without arriving at a conclusive ending. For boys there was another, somewhat unorthodox, game that I may even have invented myself. On good days people used to sit in the sun with their backs against the outside wall of the latrine. On the other side of the wall was the urinal, and we tried to pee over the top to give the sunbathers a shower. I do not remember whether we ever succeeded, but it was fun while it lasted.

Perhaps we inevitably became neglected children. But it is possible that we bore the hardships better than the adults, mainly because we were not aware of the desperate reality of our situation. I myself remember being afraid, but also feeling part of an adventure, of which being afraid may itself have been a part. And of course I was with my father and at the age of eleven could still believe – however wrongly – that he was protecting me.

Our gradual decline was briefly interrupted by an exciting event in August.

The August group

As soon as we had arrived in Bergen-Belsen we started dreaming of liberation and wondering what, if any, progress Kasztner was making with the SS in Budapest. In our impatience we read hopeful messages into insignificant events. One day a German soldier took away the card index with our names. Another day the German commander entered our compound with two civilians and told Fischer that we would soon be leaving. As a result everybody was feverishly trying to establish some entitlement, seeking patronage and hoping to be allowed to leave before everybody else. But time passed and nothing happened.

Suddenly, on the afternoon of 16 August, we were summoned to a second roll call. The news spread: 'Krumey's here. We're leaving.' It was true, up to a point. Hermann Krumey had really arrived and was facing us, flanked by a few other SS officers and some of our own leaders, with a list in his hand. Miklós Speter, Fischer's deputy, read out the list, which ended much sooner than we would have wanted. It contained the names of about 300 lucky individuals who were to leave for Switzerland.

It is not entirely clear how the list had been prepared. According to Kasztner's report, it had originally been compiled at the RSHA in Berlin and contained 500 names, mainly of children and old people, with only a few men fit to bear arms. A number of recommendations by Kasztner had been taken on board, but the total had then been reduced by Eichmann himself to 300. Kasztner's and Brand's families had to stay in Bergen-Belsen as hostages.[94] Many names on the list started with A or B, but on the whole there seem to have been no clear selection criteria. In some cases children were separated from parents, wives from husbands. The anonymous author of 'Deportation to Bergen-Belsen' claims that one of the leaders removed sixteen people from the original list and substituted his own relatives for them.[95]

A pandemonium of joy and fury followed the announcement. Krumey was mobbed by hundreds begging to be added to the list. László Devecseri and his wife Boris implored him to let their family go because their baby son Tamás was gravely ill with dysentery: Krumey agreed, but the grandparents had to stay behind. William Stern's father also asked Krumey, but when he listed thirty family members, Krumey hit him in the face and refused. Thanks to the laxness of the Germans' method of identification, several people on

the list could be replaced with others. The different political groupings, notably the young pioneers, had their own priorities – e.g. children, pregnant women or activists with special merits – and some
of their members who had originally been listed withdrew, either
voluntarily or on instructions from their leaders, in favour of others
who took their place and their identity. There were admirable
instances of self-sacrifice and there were also bitter arguments.
Finally, with Krumey's consent, the original 300 had been increased
to 318.

As the lucky ones were packing, the rest of us stood by, envying
them. Some left their food, cigarettes, medicines and clothes for those
who had to stay behind. Others took everything they possessed with
them. There were more arguments, more reconciliations and more
exchanges of places. Those about to leave stopped being apologetic
and hiding their happiness, while those who were to stay behind soon
began to wish them on their way.

Finally, in the early afternoon on 18 August, the 318 stepped out
of the gate and marched away along the same road that had brought
all of us to the camp six weeks before. We learnt later that they spent
two and a half days in cattle trucks, before crossing the Swiss border
at Basel on 21 August. They were put up for three weeks in the
vacant Bellevue Hotel in Montreux, and then transferred to nearby
Les Avants. In November most of them were dispersed to various
refugee homes in Switzerland, while some with money of their own
were able to move into private accommodation.

When the 318 had gone the rest of us were both relieved and
devastated. Yehuda Blum, for one, remembers being left behind as
'one of the most traumatic experiences' of his life: 'I had a sense of
having been somehow sentenced to death.'[96] I made a nuisance of
myself by continually asking my father why we had not been selected.
Before Krumey left Bergen-Belsen he promised that we too would
be going in a matter of weeks. This gave us hope, but as time passed
without further news we felt worse and worse. Miriam Buck recalls:

'We were apathetic, restless, thirteen hundred disappointed people clinging despite bad experiences, lies and deceits, to the only thing left to them, hope.'[97] David Kohn, aged twelve, noted: 'Krumey promised that a second transport would leave in 2 weeks and then six weeks later the whole camp. But 2 weeks, 4 weeks, 6 weeks have gone and the promise has remained a promise. People are terribly depressed.'[98] I kept telling myself to be patient and was sometimes literally shaking with impatience and impotent anger.

Nevertheless, the promise of more departures galvanised us into further planning. The leadership compiled lists and priorities amid 'constant pushing and jockeying for special favours'.[99] Debates in political or religious organisations, for instance about the respective merits of loyalty to a party and usefulness to Palestine as the decisive factor for selection, soon degenerated into slanging matches. When Fischer issued guidelines specifying categories and numbers, even more arguments followed both within and between the different echelons of the administration and among the people in general. All this poisoned the atmosphere for many weeks, but ironically proved a complete waste of time because in the end we all left together in December.

One source of our misery, among many, was not knowing how Kasztner's negotiations were progressing. The few messages he managed to send included two letters, one to his father-in-law and one to his wife.[100] In the first letter, written in German on 2 August and delivered by Krumey, he informs Fischer that 'it has been decided for the time being to allow about 500 of you to continue your journey to Spain'. He explains that 'it is the delicate task of the camp leadership to compile the list' and that 'rather than choosing the individuals from here, we prefer to indicate the guidelines you should use'. The guidelines were as follows:

For the young *chalutzim*, the Orthodox and the people from Kolozsvár a quota corresponding to their numbers must be

(*Left*) Ladislaus Löb, aged five, with parents Izsó and Jolán Löb.

(*Below*) Aged nine, with toy dog.

(*Below*) Jolán Löb, 1940.

(*Right*) Izsó and Jolán Löb with two relatives, 1931.

Rezsö Kasztner, 1947.

Rezsö Kasztner
with wife Bogyó and
baby Zsuzsi, 1945.

From left
to right:
Otto Komoly,
Hansi Brand,
Rezsö Kasztner,
Peretz Revesz,
Zvi Goldfarb,
1944.

Shmuel Tamir

Joel Brand

Hansi Brand

Benjamin Halevi

Adolf Eichmann

Kurt Becher

Dieter Wisceleny

Hermann Krumey

Irma Grese, Josef Kramer

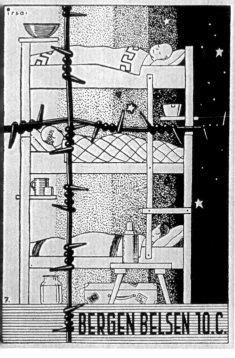

Bedtime, by István Irsai

Rations, by István Irsai

Béla Zsolt

Leopold Szondi

Joel Tietelbaum

Dezsö Ernster

Bergen-Belsen after liberation. Huts 9 and 10 are visible in the background

Hut 11

Izsó Löb (*right*) and Ladislaus Löb
(*above*) on arrival in Switzerland

Rezsö Kasztner, with his
daughter Zsuzsi, aged eleven.

secured. This also applies to the Zionists. You should not forget
those who have contributed to the supply of food and equipment of the transport and whose share must also be guaranteed ... Families with small children receive preferential
treatment.

There seems to be no evidence that such a list was actually prepared
by our own leaders. However, Kasztner's letter lists a number of
specific individuals or families who should be included, and some of
these finally made the journey while others did not. The closing para-
graph contains a coded reference to Kasztner's recent arrest and a
vaguely encouraging message to those of us who are to stay in Bergen-
Belsen: 'I have recently returned from a 9-day excursion, by the way
I am in good health. I hope to hear the same about you. Please give
my regards to all our friends and tell them that we hope that it will
soon be their turn.'

The second letter, written in Hungarian to Kasztner's wife and
dated 11 August, reflects the ups and downs he experienced
throughout the ordeal of negotiating with Eichmann. He is disappointed by the turn of events that took us to Bergen-Belsen instead
of Spain: 'I myself never imagined that your journey would be like
this, and I regret that it has turned out this way.' He is clearly not
anticipating Eichmann's decision to detain his family in Bergen-Belsen
as hostages, when he reassures Bogyó: 'I reckon that in a week's time
you will not be in that camp any longer.' And he strikes a note of
confidence in the future of those of us who will not be included in
the first transport to leave the camp: 'Unfortunately it hasn't been
possible to ensure everybody's departure, but you must reassure
everybody: it is only a question of waiting one's turn. The authorities that decide your fate have categorically declared that your transport will leave in one way or another. These authorities have never
disappointed us. I hope that it will soon also be the turn of the second
part.'

Such letters could occasionally alleviate our sense of isolation, even though the hopes they roused could easily prove false. The 500 had been reduced to 318 and the turn of the rest of us came later than Kasztner had expected.

CHAPTER 9

A Hard Bargain

The interim agreement

While we were struggling to come to terms with the shock of arriving in Bergen-Belsen, the Jews of Budapest were granted a brief stay of execution. In late June and early July Pope Pius XII and King Gustav V of Sweden appealed personally to the regent, Horthy, to stop the deportations, and on 26 June President Roosevelt threatened harsh reprisals if they did not cease forthwith. On 2 July Budapest suffered the heaviest Allied bombing raid of the war, and on 7 July Horthy finally gave a direct order for the deportations to cease. The hate campaign continued, but 200,000 Jews in Budapest were spared that particular ordeal, although many of them were to die in other ways.

The Germans, and the Hungarian mob, wanted the deportations to resume on 5 August, but Horthy refused. The next starting date, agreed between the Germans and the Sztójay government, would have been 25 August. However, the representatives of Sweden, Portugal, Spain, Switzerland and the Vatican demanded a 'definitive end' to this 'inhumanely implemented process'[1] and on 24 August Horthy informed the German ambassador Veesenmayer that the Jews could only be relocated within Hungary. The next day the Hungarian

government formally advised the ambassador of the ban on deportations. In the small hours of the same day a cable from Himmler
ordered Winkelmann, the commander of the German security units
in Hungary, to stop all the preparations. It is not certain what made
Himmler give this order. One factor may have been the progress of
the negotiations between Kasztner, Becher and Mayer at the Swiss
border. This was claimed by Kasztner and Becher, and if true it was
indeed a major triumph.

Another factor was the defection of Romania from the Axis to the
Soviets on 23 August. On the evening of 25 August Wisliceny
summoned Kasztner and told him: 'You have won. The staff is pulling
out.'[2] He explained that the Judenkommando had been ordered to
leave Budapest because Himmler wished to avoid any further ill-
treatment of Jews that might inflame anti-German feelings and push
Hungary into following the Romanian example. But Eichmann did
not leave Hungary altogether. He stayed in the country, waiting for
an opportunity to restart the deportations. He did not have to wait
long.

For a few weeks, a new Hungarian government under a new prime
minister, Géza Lakatos, pursued a more moderately anti-Semitic line.
The halt in the deportations had taken the edge off the worst persecution. Although Jews were still being seized and tortured or killed,
there were no wholesale murders. This respite came to a terrible end
with the Arrow Cross coup of 15 October.

While we were agonising over the Auspitz–Auschwitz conundrum
in the siding at Mosonmagyaróvár, Kasztner called on Eichmann to
demand an explanation for our delay. Eichmann claimed that our
group had grown too large for Strasshof and he had cabled instructions for the train to take us to another 'privileged camp', called
Auspitz, but as Auspitz too was unsuitable he had redirected us to
Bergen-Belsen. It was true that the advance of the Allies in France
had made it impossible for us to travel to Spain as agreed, but given
Eichmann's notorious untruthfulness, he may well have intended both

the delay at Mosonmagyaróvár and our subsequent captivity in Bergen-Belsen to provide him with further opportunities for blackmail and extortion. It was at this time that Becher was gradually replacing Eichmann as the chief SS negotiator. Although he was a dubious ally, Kurt Becher played an indispensable part in Kasztner's successful operations.[3]

Nearly two months after Joel Brand's start on his ill-fated 'goods for blood' mission, on 5 July, the Vaada in Budapest at last received the 'interim agreement' from Istanbul. Describing themselves as the Authorised Representatives of the Jewish Agency, Barlas, Brand and two others promised that the difficulties in obtaining the merchandise the Germans demanded would be resolved as soon as the Jewish side was convinced of the seriousness of the German offer. While awaiting the definitive agreement, they undertook to pay the Germans one million Swiss francs monthly for the cessation of the deportations, 400,000 US dollars for each convoy of 1,000 persons allowed to emigrate to Palestine, and one million US dollars for each convoy of 1,000 persons allowed to emigrate to other countries. They also promised the Germans one half of any food, clothing and medicines they would be allowed to deliver to ghettos and camps.

Kasztner used this blatantly false document to convince Eichmann and Becher that 'our friends abroad' were ready to agree a large deal. He attributed Brand's failure to obtain the trucks primarily to the fact that the Jews who should have served as 'exchange objects' had been sent by Eichmann to Auschwitz and gassed. He floated the idea of a German representative meeting senior Jewish officials on neutral ground to negotiate the fate not only of the Hungarian Jews but of all the Jews in German hands. He stressed that, for such negotiations to succeed, the Germans would have to supply a 'proof of good will' by allowing our Bergen-Belsen group to leave for a neutral country, and he added that there was 'no prospect of success if the Jews of Budapest were deported in the meantime'.[4]

Having obtained Himmler's approval, Becher began to make preparations for a meeting in Lisbon with Joseph J. Schwartz, the Joint's representative in Europe, and Eliahu Dobkin, a member of the executive of the Jewish Agency. However, Eichmann was determined to forge ahead with the 'final solution'. On 17 July he told Kasztner that unless Brand returned from Istanbul forthwith, we would be taken from Bergen-Belsen to Auschwitz and 'put through the mill', i.e. gassed immediately. Biss remembers Kasztner, whom he 'had never yet seen weep', saying to him 'with tears in his eyes, that all was now lost'.[5] A slightly earlier letter to Nathan Schwalb in Geneva confirms Kasztner's growing despair:

> The dream of the great plan is over; hundreds of thousands went to Auschwitz unaware till the last moment of what it was all about and what was happening. We, who did know, tried to act against it, but after three and a half months of bitter fighting I must say that it was more like watching the unfolding of a tragedy and its unstoppable progress, without our being able to do anything to prevent it . . . The speed of the collapse was so savage that . . . actions of succour and rescue could not keep up with it; even thoughts were too slow; I cannot give you a picture of the annihilation or of its impact; I could only feel it.[6]

But Kasztner was not a man to give in to despair. He soon recovered his energy and rejoined the battle. In July and August a series of meetings took place between him and various SS officers. Some of these are recorded in a number of diary notes he dictated to his secretary immediately after they had occurred. Since they were intended to assist his own memory, there is no reason to doubt their truthfulness. As one watches him bargaining for human lives with a gang of ruthless mass murderers, one is amazed at his ability to appear calm and confident on the surface, while he must have been boiling with fear, frustration and loathing within.

The first meeting between Kasztner and Becher to be recorded in the notes took place on 15 July, probably in Becher's office rather than Eichmann's headquarters. It opened with Becher's remark: 'Now we are meeting in neutral territory.' Kasztner replied: 'For me there's no neutral territory here, there's only enemy territory here.' He then complained that the entire Jewish population of the Hungarian provinces had been deported and at least 300,000 exterminated, despite Eichmann's and Wisliceny's assurances that there would be no ghettoisation or deportation and that all would be 'kept on ice' pending the outcome of negotiations. He warned Becher that a high-level meeting in Lisbon would be worthwhile only if the exterminations were halted immediately. He then demanded our release: 'A prolonged stay of a group of 1,600 in Bergen-Belsen certainly won't help the discussions abroad.' An argument followed, with each side accusing the other of failure to deliver. Becher promised to discuss our fate with Himmler, but wondered whether Kasztner would lose his interest in a deal once his family was safe. Kasztner assured him that he was not guided by 'personal and family reasons'.[7]

Such exchanges are typical of Kasztner's ambivalent relationship with Becher. Each tried to bluff, deceive and exploit the other, but as time passed, a degree of intimacy, not to say friendship, seems to have developed between them. Kasztner came to see Becher as an ally against Eichmann, although he knew that Becher could exert absolute power over him at any time he felt like it. Becher, for his part, was prepared to extort from the Jews all that he could – either by threats, blackmail and deception or by promises and concessions – but in order to survive he had to show results to Himmler, and for that purpose he needed Kasztner. If Kasztner was aware of any war crimes Becher might have committed before he came to Hungary, he had to ignore them for the sake of his own rescue enterprise.

Soon after that conversation with Becher, Kasztner was kidnapped. As he was walking home from Kolumbusz Street on 18 July, he was stopped by two civilians who introduced themselves, in German with a Hungarian accent, as Eichmann's messengers and asked him to follow them. When he declined he was dragged into a car by three other civilians, who spoke Hungarian. Blindfolded and handcuffed, he was driven to the gendarmerie station of Gödöllő 30 kilometres from Budapest. There he was questioned for three hours about the Vaada's connections with the SS and the ransom that had been paid for us. He was held for four days in a stuffy store room, before he was taken to the gendarmerie inspectorate in Ungvár (today Uzhgorod in the Ukraine), where Captain Leo Lulay, adjutant of László Ferenczy, the head of the Hungarian gendarmerie, again questioned him about the deal with the Germans, the origin of the monies paid, and whether he was an American spy. Both Lulay and Ferenczy were executed for their crimes soon after the war.

According to a later statement by Lulay, Ferenczy had ordered him to kill Kasztner if he refused to divulge everything about his negotiations with the Germans. Kasztner agreed to cooperate, but Lulay had the impression that he was 'not entirely sincere.'[8] It is not clear how much Kasztner told Lulay, but five days later he was driven back to Budapest and questioned personally by Ferenczy, who ordered him not to tell Eichmann who had abducted him. At his next meeting with Eichmann Kasztner claimed that he knew nothing because he had been blindfolded all the time, and Eichmann did not pursue the matter any further. On his way back from Ungvár Kasztner had been deeply distressed by the signs of the recent deportations:

We travelled via Subcarpathia – once an area with the densest Jewish population in Hungary – through deserted towns and abandoned villages. Everywhere we were reminded, by closed offices, workshops and shops with Jewish signs, and silent syna-gogues, of the Jewish life that had been extinguished here.[9]

Kasztner saw Becher again on 2 August. Becher reported that Himmler was still prepared to allow Jews to emigrate in exchange for goods and had also given permission for 500 members of our group to leave Bergen-Belsen for a neutral country, with the rest soon to follow. Eichmann angrily acknowledged Himmler's order, but warned that he would not authorise any departure before the date of the first meeting between Becher and the 'representatives of world Jewry'[10] had been fixed.

Kasztner was to instruct József Fischer to distribute the 500 places in accordance with the Vaada's earlier guidelines. As we have seen, Kasztner did this immediately by means of the letter Krumey delivered to Fischer when he came to Bergen-Belsen to release a reduced contingent of 318 later in August. Eichmann added that the rest of us could in principle follow within a few weeks, but only if Brand returned from Istanbul. 'I'm not in the habit of letting Jews emigrate by German courier aircraft',[11] he said to Kasztner. In fact Eichmann was determined to complete the deportation of all the Hungarian Jews, including the Jews of Budapest, by 15 September, as he had promised, and therefore did all he could to break his agreements with Kasztner and to evade Himmler's orders.

The ransom for our group was handled by Eichmann as deviously as everything else. The accounts were to be agreed between Biss, for the Vaada, and Obersturmführer (lieutenant) Karl Grabau, for the SS. The crucial issue was the rate of exchange for the millions of pengős and valuables already delivered to the Germans. The Vaada insisted that the 1,000 dollars per head had been paid when Kasztner, Offenbach and Hansi Brand handed over the three full suitcases to Klages on 20 June. Becher denied this and demanded further payments in 'goods'. The Vaada responded by 'a Swiss bluff', presenting Becher with a letter of credit for the price of 30 tractors, which they claimed had been delivered, but which in the event never left Switzerland. Two truckloads of sheepskins from Bratislava were also certified as awaiting collection, but when an emissary from Berlin came looking for them months later, there were none. The Vaada did deliver 15,000 kilograms of stale coffee lying in Budapest free port and paid for by the Joint. Hansi Brand recalls: 'The deliveries of goods reached Becher in part and were in part promised, and on that basis negotiations continued with Eichmann to release Jews.'[12]

Although the ransom had in fact been paid, Eichmann refused permission for us to leave Bergen-Belsen. As Kasztner wrily puts it, he suddenly developed a 'concern' for our lives. By now the Allies were approaching Paris and the German railway lines were continually being bombed. Eichmann asked Kasztner: 'What if the train is hit by a British or American bomb or if it gets stuck on the way? Or do you think the Reich has nothing else to do now than protect Jews?'[13] Kasztner thought it most likely that Eichmann wanted to hold us in order to extort a larger ransom from Jewish organisations, although it was also possible that, having received the ransom, he was toying with the idea of blowing up our train and blaming it on Allied bombs. At any rate he told Eichmann that the Vaada would take responsibility for whatever happened and he suggested that instead of trying to get to Spain through France we might undertake the safer journey to Switzerland.

During Kasztner's detention Schwartz had abandoned the idea of a meeting with Becher in Lisbon, because as an American citizen he was forbidden to communicate with Germans. Becher, for his part, decided not to go because he had been warned about a possible British attempt to take him hostage in neutral territory. At this point Saly Mayer – to whom Schwartz had referred Kasztner for any further negotiations – came fully into the picture.

As the representative of the American Jewish Joint Distribution Committee in Switzerland, Mayer had been authorised by the World Refugee Board to engage in discussions in order to gain time for the Jews, but he was forbidden to make any financial or political commitments. By 1944 the Joint had placed 6.5 million dollars at his disposal, of which 3.8 million were earmarked for refugees in Switzerland and 2.7 million for European Jews in need of assistance. He had no funds for ransom payments and was expressly required by the Joint to temporise and try to extract concessions from the Germans without giving them anything in return.

The cooperation between Mayer and Kasztner was far from smooth. To a considerable extent their disagreements were due to a personality clash. While Mayer objected to Kasztner's recklessness and negligence, Kasztner considered Mayer narrow-minded and lacking in understanding or compassion. Mayer was an upright Swiss citizen and orthodox Jew, with an abrasive manner and a stubborn, petulant streak. Lacking finesse, inclined to lecture and moralise, he was not ideally suited to a task that required diplomacy, imagination, flexibility, bravado and downright crookedness in a good cause. Nevertheless, given the constraints under which he had to work, he scored some very real successes. While Kasztner was frustrated by Mayer's refusal to make extravagant promises to the Nazis, the representative of the World Refugee Board in Switzerland, Roswell McClelland, praised Mayer's masterly delaying technique of 'talking, promising, cajoling, intimating, threatening', and 'dangling goods and money'[14] before the Nazis, when he had almost nothing to deliver. While Kasztner claimed that more Jews could have been saved if Mayer had been more adventurous, it is possible that any more blatantly unrealistic promises would have been counter-productive. The truth is that Mayer played a more positive part than Kasztner was able or willing to recognise. Yehuda Bauer, the outstanding historian of rescue deals between Jews and Nazis, is probably right in saying that whatever was achieved 'would have been inconceivable without Mayer's delaying tactics, although Kasztner and Biss, who exploited every opening, also played a key role.'[15]

When Becher's meeting with Schwartz in Lisbon had fallen through, Kasztner made arrangements for him to travel to the Swiss border to meet Mayer instead. On 12 July – by which time there were no Jews left in the Hungarian provinces – he asked Becher to confirm that the 200,000 Jews in Budapest were safe from deportation. Becher answered: 'Until we finish our talks, there will be peace in the city. If the talks have a negative outcome, the situation in the city could turn critical.'[16] Therefore, given the unlikelihood of obtaining the goods demanded by the Germans, Kasztner's only chance of preserving 'peace in the city' was dragging out the negotiations as long as he could. If the Germans were to spare the lives of as many Jews as possible until the end of the war, they had to believe that a large deal could be made either with world Jewry or with the Allies. And if the Allies were to give the Germans this impression, they had to be shown that the Germans were prepared to let Jews live at a price. Our release from Bergen-Belsen would be such a signal and a decisive first step towards saving much larger numbers still alive. Kasztner desperately tried to persuade Saly Mayer to cooperate in misleading Becher, but Mayer had his own instructions and his own way of doing things, and they were not what Kasztner expected.

At least promise

As early as 25 April the Vaada had informed Mayer of its negotiations with Wisliceny, describing the increasingly precarious situation of the Jews in Hungary and asking the Joint for 2 million dollars in case of an agreement. On 4 May Mayer had answered that 'the Germans would have to provide clear proof that they are improving, in particular stopping the deportations from France'. Kasztner writes bitterly: 'In other words: if we taught the naughty Nazis better manners he would be prepared to help.' Somewhat simplistically, he accuses Mayer and the Jews in the free world of failing to hasten to the aid of those in the hands of the Germans because of a lack of empathy and solidarity: 'They were over there, we were here; they were not directly concerned, we were immediately affected. They were moralising, we were afraid of dying. They had pity and thought they were powerless. We wanted to live and believed that it must be possible to save us.'[17] A few weeks later a series of meetings between Kasztner, Mayer, Becher and some others began, which could be called a grotesque farce had their background not been so tragic. Meanwhile Eichmann, having left Budapest, was biding his time in the country.

The first meeting was scheduled for 21 August. As Mayer had been unable to obtain a Swiss entry visa for Becher, it was to be held at the border between Germany and Switzerland. Kasztner's diary note of a conversation with Klages on 18 August vividly reflects the mixed feelings of despondency and determination with which he was looking ahead to the occasion and which he experienced much of the time. He lists the formidable obstacles he is facing. Owing to the Allied advances in France, 'the Spanish line is now out of the question'; Switzerland 'will not admit a large number of Jews'; and there is no way 'merchandise from overseas can be brought here'. This leaves little hope, but he is determined to continue the fight, come what may: 'However great the difficulties, this agreement must be brought about because there is no other way.'[18]

On 19 August Kasztner and Becher set out from Budapest, together with Becher's adjutant SS Hauptsturmführer Max Grüson and Wilhelm Billitz, a converted Jew and director of the Manfred Weiss conglomerate, which Becher had misappropriated from its owners, the Weiss family. When they arrived at their hotel in Bregenz on 20 August, they were joined by Krumey, who had just visited Bergen-Belsen to oversee the departure of the first contingent of our group. He reported that Eichmann had reduced the permitted number from 500 to 300 and given express orders for Kasztner's and Brand's relations to stay behind. With Krumey's permission 318 had left the camp on 18 August and arrived in Basel three days later. Despite the infinitesimal number in comparison to the millions who perished, it was a momentous event, as Kasztner writes:

At least the first step had been taken. 318 people were free. They were the first – not only from the KZ Bergen-Belsen but from the large mass of the Jewish people languishing under the

Hitlerian yoke – to cross the border of a neutral state as a substantial organised group before the eyes of the whole world.[19]

By coincidence, the first meeting between Mayer and Becher also took place on 21 August at the German–Swiss border – to be precise, on a bridge across the Rhine between the Austrian town of Höchst and the Swiss town of St Margrethen. Mayer had brought two advisers with him. They were Marcus Wyler, his lawyer, and Pierre Bigar, a representative of the Swiss Federation of Jewish Communities. Becher and his party were not allowed to enter Swiss territory. Mayer declined Becher's invitation to join him in the German customs office. It was not an auspicious start and Kasztner became increasingly worried as the talks progressed.

Becher introduced himself as Himmler's representative, authorised to discuss issues relating to Jews in German hands with representatives of the Allies and 'world Jewry', in order to seek an agreement based on 'economic considerations'. In particular the fate of the Jews facing deportation from Budapest depended on what sacrifice the Allies and world Jewry would be willing to make for them. He then asked whether Mayer was prepared to accept the German offer of a million Jewish lives in exchange for 10,000 trucks. Mayer replied that he had come to the meeting solely as the representative of the Swiss Support Fund for Refugees and knew nothing about a German offer, although he would contact the appropriate authorities. He added that 'the deportation of Budapest's Jews in itself would be no disaster, but the Germans should at last stop the damned gassing'. Becher undertook to ensure that Himmler stopped the gassing and he pointed out that the Germans had already proved their good will by allowing 318 members of our group to leave Bergen-Belsen for Switzerland. He promised that the rest of us would soon follow, and asked what Mayer could offer him in exchange. When Mayer suggested 'money', although the Joint had forbidden him to make any commitment, Becher demanded 'goods'. When

Mayer appealed to humanity, Becher replied: 'I can't negotiate on this basis.'[20] When Mayer reiterated that he would contact the appropriate authorities, Becher angrily accused Kasztner of bringing him to the Swiss border under false pretences. Billitz saved the situation by suggesting that both parties needed time for reflection, and Becher agreed to meet again a week later. What happened subsequently is highly controversial.

On 25 August Becher cabled Himmler a detailed report. As he put it, Mayer had recognised the seriousness of the German offer thanks to 'the fact that at that very moment three hundred items were crossing the border'. It is hard to tell whether by describing human beings as 'items' he was expressing his own contempt for Jews or echoing Himmler's. Accepting that it is impossible to obtain trucks from the Western Allies, he recommended that the Germans should demand other commodities, such as 'chrome, nickel, ball bearings, survey instruments, tool manufacturing machines, wolfram, aluminium, etc.', which could be supplied by neutral states. He listed the next steps to be taken: '(a) To secure authorization and cover by the supreme American authority for implementation in principle; (b) The total amount of foreign currency which must be found in order to carry out the arrangement; (c) The creation of an overall pattern for the supply programme; (d) Specification of the merchandise which can be supplied immediately.' He quoted the Jewish side's warning: 'If further deportations to the Reich were now carried out, the deciding authority will not regard the negotiations as serious, and hence they would fail.' And he ended with: 'I humbly request permission to continue the negotiations, in accordance with this information.'[21] Himmler's brief reply, dated 26 August, closed with the words: 'I instruct and permit you to continue the negotiations in accordance with your information.'[22]

After the war, in American captivity, Becher claimed that Himmler had decided to halt the deportations from Budapest in response to his progress at the Swiss border.[23] This is often disputed. Himmler's cable ordering Winkelmann to stop the preparations was sent at 3 am on 25 August. At 11.15 am on the same day the German ambassador in Budapest, also by cable, asked foreign minister Ribbentrop for confirmation of Himmler's order, which he duly received by the same method.[24] Becher cabled his report to Himmler at 6.10 pm on 25 August. Thus Himmler's ban on the deportations preceded Becher's report by several hours. However, Becher could have seen or telephoned Himmler at some point between 21 and 25 August, in which case his cable could have been a confirmation of what he had agreed with Kasztner and put to Himmler by word of mouth. The strongest advocate of this hypothesis is Yehuda Bauer, who concludes: 'It would appear that these talks, initiated and promoted by Kasztner, were the direct cause of the rescue of the Jews of Budapest.'[25] The opponents of Becher's claim argue that Himmler's concern was not to expedite the deal with Kasztner but either to forestall more hostility to Germans in Hungary or to improve his own image in the eyes of the neutrals and the Allies. However, this does not preclude the possibility that Becher's report – and therefore Kasztner's proposition – also contributed to the ban on the deportations.

Over the next few weeks Kasztner pressed Becher 'almost daily' to free our group from Bergen-Belsen, but Becher refused to recommend this to Himmler in the absence of a satisfactory reply from Switzerland about the larger issue. To set things in motion, Kasztner suggested that the Germans allow us to continue our journey and in addition to let 2,500 more Jews emigrate from Budapest for a ransom of 100 dollars per head. Becher forwarded the suggestion to his chief and received the following cable: 'The opposite side must be crazy. One Jew's entry into America costs a thousand dollars. One Jew's departure from Europe also costs a thousand dollars. – Himmler.'[26]

Early in September Kasztner and Grüson met Mayer and his advisers several times on the bridge at St Margrethen, while Becher was waiting for news in nearby Bregenz. Mayer consistently refused to give any of the assurances Kasztner tried to elicit from him. Kasztner was infuriated by these prevarications, although as a delaying tactic they had their merits. Becher had almost certainly realised that Kasztner was leading him on, but he needed a sign of progress, however specious, to show to Himmler. On one occasion Mayer reported that the American authorities had instructed him not to say 'no' to the German proposals. When Kasztner asked whether this implied the possibility of a positive response, Wyler answered on behalf of his client: 'No. We're only instructed not to say no.' Grüson intervened: 'Herr Mayer, I ask you, please give this promise. Otherwise my boss Kurt Becher won't be able to do anything for the Jews and the gassings will go on. At least promise! It's only words! You'll have time to keep the promise. And by then many things can happen.' Mayer answered: 'I promise only as much as I can keep.'[27] In fact he occasionally promised more than he could keep, but he did so more cautiously than Kasztner, with his cavalier ways, could appreciate.

When Becher heard what had happened he said: 'I'm sorry, but I can't do more for the Jews than Herr Saly Mayer is willing to do.' It would take a clear 'yes' by cable from Mayer to persuade him to return to the negotiations, which would have to be on Swiss territory rather than on a bridge, and for which he would insist on a Swiss visa. By now Kasztner too had lost any belief in a positive agreement and was only hoping to gain time: 'So long as Himmler did not budge from the commercial basis and the West persisted in rejection and distrust, these negotiations could at most be about both parties trying to bluff each other.'[28]

In late August, there had been an uprising against the Germans in Slovakia. This gave Eichmann an excuse to start planning the deportation of the 23,000 Jews still left there. Kasztner asked Becher to intervene with Himmler, but Becher declined in view of the lack of progress at the Swiss border, although he agreed to reconsider if he received an unambiguous commitment from Mayer. Despite many telegrams from Kasztner, it took Mayer until late September to reply that he was ready to open an account for the Nazis in a Swiss bank. On 28 or 29 September Kasztner met Mayer and Wyler again at the Swiss border. This time Kasztner was accompanied by Sturmbannführer Herbert Kettlitz, who had replaced Grüson. Mayer agreed to promise Becher money in order to save the Slovak Jews. Kasztner advised Becher that the Joint would pay 15 million Swiss francs provided '1. The operation against the Slovak Jews ceases; 2. No deportation of Budapest Jews takes place; 3. The rest of the Bergen-Belsen group is allowed to leave Germany forthwith.'[29]

Around this time Kasztner began to believe that our release was approaching. Two of his letters written on 6 October,[30] one to his wife and one to his father-in-law, reflect his frustration at Eichmann's procrastination but also his hopes for an early end to our captivity. In the letter to Fischer he explains: 'We have been repeatedly assured that you would leave sooner or later, since we had fulfilled our obligations. But when your departure was linked to the broader negotiations, the date of your departure was postponed.' He mentions a plan for 'a further transport of 200' to follow the 318 who left in August, which would have included Fischer's family, but which 'didn't leave because in the meantime the idea of dealing with the whole group had arisen'. Referring to Mayer by the code name 'Uncle', he ends on an optimistic note as he announces our impending liberation in a roundabout way so as to deceive the censor: 'The negotiations with Uncle have now reached a decisive stage. The delegation which is to conclude the contract will probably travel to Uncle in the middle or at the end of next week. There is the most serious prospect of the contract finally being wrapped up.' Unfortunately the prospect receded and we had to spend two more months in Bergen-Belsen as autumn hardened its grip on Lüneburg Heath.

To his wife, of course, Kasztner writes in a more personal tone. He is concerned for her 'frail health', but he urges her to keep up the morale of everybody else: 'You have taken care of your physical and emotional condition, and you'll continue to do so for the near future and also make sure that the family and the whole company don't lose their confidence. In my absence that is your primary task and duty.' He expects a decision about our release to be made 'in the course of next week', but he also has plans in case of failure: 'If counter to all expectations your departure proves impossible I will join you.' Joining her – and us all – could well have meant death, and Kasztner seemed prepared to follow that path. In a postscript to his mother and brother, he adds: 'In my thoughts I am with Mummy, Ernő and the whole transport, for whose fate I carry the gravest responsibility that can be placed on any man.' Kasztner may have been a gambler, but he was genuinely committed to the task he had taken on.

A serious result

The lull in the persecution of Hungary's Jews ended with Horthy's announcement of a ceasefire on the Russian front on 15 October. Ferenc Szálasi, the leader of the ultra-fascist Arrow Cross party, with German panzer units ready to assist him, deposed the regent and declared himself prime minister and head of state. With the appointment of Emil Kovarcz as minister for mobilisation and Gábor Vajna as minister for internal affairs, two of the most ferocious anti-Semites found themselves in charge of Jewish affairs. The regime of terror which followed was to claim tens of thousands of victims.

Two days after the coup, on 17 October, Eichmann reappeared in Budapest. He was drunk, as so often by that time, when he summoned Kasztner to Becher's office: 'Well, you see, I'm back!' he gloated and continued briskly:

The Jews of Budapest will be evacuated, this time on foot. We need our transport for other things now. But if you provide us with the appropriate number of trucks we could use those for the evacuation. Or perhaps that doesn't suit you? You're afraid, what? But don't give me your American fairy tales any more. Now we'll be working, smartly and at the double! Right?[31]

While Eichmann was determined to destroy the remaining Jews in Budapest, Becher tried hard to obtain Himmler's approval for further deals. On 25 October, after a lengthy exchange of telegrams with Mayer, Kasztner was able to present Becher and Kettlitz with Swiss entry visas. On 2 November Becher arrived in Zürich and announced that Himmler had given his approval for our group to leave Bergen-Belsen. At a meeting in the Hotel Walhalla in St Gallen on 4 November, he explained that Himmler was prepared to negotiate about the possibility of releasing further groups from German concentration camps to Switzerland and of awarding certain categories of Jews the status of privileged foreigners, civilian internees or prisoners of war, to be looked after by the Red Cross. In return, Himmler insisted on the 'immediate delivery of the earmarked goods'.[32] Becher, for his part, is thought to have offered to let hundreds of thousands of Jews emigrate – albeit not to Palestine – for 20 million Swiss francs, to be paid within two or three weeks.[33]

On 5 November an extraordinary meeting took place in the Hotel Savoy Baur-en-Ville in Zurich. Counter to the Allies' ban on any contacts with Nazi officials, Becher, in the presence of Kasztner and Mayer, was introduced to Roswell McClelland, the representative of the US War Refugee Board in Switzerland. The WRB in Budapest was working with the Swiss mission and the Red Cross to assist Jews in hiding, and also helped to publicise the horrors of Auschwitz through diplomatic and propaganda channels. One of McClelland's specific tasks was obtaining State Department licences for the Joint to transfer funds to Hungary for relief and rescue operations. With a slight stretch of the imagination, Becher was able to inform Himmler that he had broken through the Allies' refusal to negotiate with Germans and was discussing business with a powerful US official.

Kasztner, for his part, hoped that the apparent involvement of a high-ranking US authority might induce Himmler to make significant concessions to the Jews. Mistakenly calling McClelland a Quaker, he describes the encounter in the hotel as follows:

> The War Refugee Board could hardly have sent a more worthy representative: McClelland, the Quaker, a humanitarian par excellence, a sober, supremely cultured diplomat, who was aware of the European Jewish tragedy in all its details. On the other side Becher, concerned for the prestige of the Third Reich, representative of a mechanised mentality, attached to a lost cause but searching for something that he did not yet dare to articulate.[34]

Becher had obtained Himmler's prior approval for the meeting. To what extent McClelland was acting on orders from above, or on his own initiative, is not certain. In any case he explained that he was prepared to authorise the Joint to deposit 20 million francs (5 million dollars) in Switzerland, which the Third Reich could use to buy goods, subject to export permits by the Swiss authorities, which he would expedite. In return he demanded that the Germans put an end to the persecution and respect the 'lives of all civilians in German hands, regardless of race, religion or nationality'.[35] Becher undertook to transmit McClelland's proposal to Himmler. Kettlitz was to remain in Switzerland to buy the goods.

Mayer showed Becher a telegram, signed by the US secretary of state, Cordell Hull, to the effect that the State Department had given the Joint permission to transfer 5 million dollars to Switzerland for rescue operations under supervision of the War Refugee Board. What he did not tell Becher was that it could be spent only with the consent of the US government. McClelland, for his part, cabled a summary of the discussions to the WRB and the State Department on 16 November, and five days later received the reply: 'No funds from any source should be used to carry out such a proposal.'[36] Kasztner himself called the proposal 'the 20 million franc bluff'.[37]

In his testimony in the Eichmann trial Becher later claimed that he had never been taken in by the Jewish tricks: he had gone along with the deception because he considered it the only way to obtain concessions for the victims from Himmler. Becher may indeed have suspected that the Jewish side was bluffing, but it was hardly the humanitarian desire to save Jews that made him cooperate. With the Soviets rapidly advancing on Budapest, he must have realised that the war was lost and begun to fear for his own life. As Kasztner suggests, the encounter with McLelland, coupled with Mayer's deceptive offer, allowed Becher to dream either of pulling off a spectacular diplomatic stunt at the last moment or at least of saving himself from the approaching debacle:

> Now he could report to Himmler that he had suceeded in making personal contact with a special representative of Roosevelt. Attached to this contact were vague and unarticulated hopes, secret desires for a political rapprochement and a possible personal alibi, which became the more intense, the worse the Third Reich fared on the battlefield.[38]

Mayer hoped that the promise of 20 million francs would persuade the Germans to place the concentration camps under Red Cross protection until the final collapse of the Reich. Kasztner wanted to use the apparent involvement of a high US authority to extract even more far-reaching concessions from Himmler. After the meeting with McClelland he prepared a list of demands, which he presented to Becher as they were about to leave Switzerland. They included a total ban on the deportation of Jews still surviving in Budapest and Slovakia, prisoner-of-war status for all Jews in German hands, access for the Red Cross to all concentration camps, and the release of our group and others from Bergen-Belsen. After a heated debate Becher agreed to recommend to Himmler that men under sixteen and over fifty years of age and women under sixteen and over forty, as well as the seriously ill, should be exempt from deportation from Budapest. This was a lot less than Kasztner wanted, but if Himmler agreed, it would save the most vulnerable.

As soon as they reached German soil, Becher took Kasztner's German 'foreigner's passport' away. The Germans had granted Kasztner all his apparent privileges – exemption from the yellow star, freedom of movement, protection from the Hungarian authorities and, most astonishingly, permission for repeated journeys to Switzerland – only in order to make him a more efficient tool in their own hands, and Becher's gesture was a reminder that he was still entirely at their mercy. Nevertheless, during the long car journey back to Budapest, Becher spoke to him as to an equal. In particular he tried to defend Himmler. He called the Reichsführer-SS a 'kind-hearted man and no mass murderer',[39] who had been forced into taking various anti-Jewish measures he had never intended. In addition, he referred to intrigues being conducted against himself by Kaltenbrunner and the Gestapo; he must also have thought of Eichmann, who did all he could to undermine his operations and his position as a favourite of Himmler. At the end of the journey Becher assured Kasztner that, as a result of meeting McClelland, he would advise Himmler to order a stop to the extermination of all the Jews in German hands. He further confirmed that the only Jews deported from Budapest would be men and women capable of hard labour.

They arrived back in Budapest on 8 November. On the same day Eichmann began herding the Jews of the city into the Ujlaki brick-yard in the suburb of Óbuda in order to be sent to Austria on the notorious 'death marches'. Kasztner appealed to Becher, and on the following day Eichmann released the children, the old and the sick. The remaining 30,000, of whom 70 per cent were women, were forced to march to the Austrian border, 180 kilometres away. For six or seven days they marched, in rain and snow, without food and

adequate clothing, spending the nights in the open, and harassed by
SS soldiers and Arrow Cross activists. Thousands died of exhaustion, hundreds were shot when they could walk no further. On 13
November Eichmann ordered the deportation from Budapest of all
children above ten years of age. Kasztner warned Becher, who phoned
Eichmann and threatened to send a telegram to Himmler if he did
not stop 'meddling' with his enterprise. Eichmann withdrew the order
and for a few days the marches were suspended.

After the war Becher claimed almost all the credit for the cessation of the marches. He maintained that Himmler's order was the
result of a protest he and Winkelmann, the police chief, had lodged,
and that it was he who had inspired a similar protest by
Obergruppenführer Hans Jüttner. However, the representatives of
the Red Cross, the Vatican and the neutral countries also urged Szálasi
to stop the marches. The contribution of Kasztner and Becher may
have been significant, but was not the only attempt to improve the
lot of the marchers.

On 21 November Eichmann tried to persuade Kasztner to help
him round up between 65,000 and 70,000 more Jews to be sent to
Austria. When Kasztner refused, Eichmann warned him: 'The Reich
has committed itself not to do in any more Jews. But where's the
return? The Americans are only trying to gain time . . . I'm prepared
to respect your agreement with Becher but only as long as I don't
find that the other side is bluffing.' With his usual audacity Kasztner
replied: 'The Americans are fully informed. They know about Slovakia,
they know about the forced marches. They are the ones who would
have the right to regard all the concessions in the Jewish question
offered by Germany as bluff.'[40] The marches were resumed a few
days later and lasted until early December. All the Vaada could do
was to supply the victims with some food and medicines. The total
of men, women and children forced to undergo this ordeal was 76,000.
Almost 20,000 of them died.

In Switzerland negotiations were stalling. On 18 November Becher received a telegram from Kettlitz reporting no progress after several days of negotiations with Mayer: 'Money not yet received. Continuously new objections. Am convinced that no compliance intended or possible because complete volume unavailable.'[41] Becher was furious. He warned Kasztner that Himmler would probably break off the negotiations at once if he did not receive a positive response about the 20 million francs, and he asked Kasztner to cable Mayer to that effect. The next day he flew to Berlin to see Himmler. Without awaiting a reply from Mayer, Kasztner sent him the following – totally untrue – phone message: 'I am instructed to repeat that the 20 million francs are available. The delay is due exclusively to financial technicalities. Saly Mayer and his superiors are working day and night to overcome the final difficulties. The assumption that no payment is intended has no foundation whatsoever.'[42]

By now Becher no longer believed Kasztner's promises, but he had to act as if he still did. At this late stage in the game, admitting to Himmler that he had let the Jews trick him might well have cost him his life. On the other hand, if the purpose of the negotiations was to polish up his – and possibly Himmler's – image as a saviour of Jews, adopting Kasztner's bluff was the wisest course. As Yehuda Bauer writes, for Kasztner Becher was the only means of 'reaching Himmler and alleviating the lot of the remaining Jews' and for Becher Kasztner had become 'a kind of walking life insurance'.[43]

On 27 November a new telegram arrived from Kettlitz: 'Have been unable to speak to Saly Mayer for ten days. Denies himself on the phone. Stay in Switzerland pointless. Please recall me.'[44] At their next meeting Kasztner and Becher were joined by Eichmann, who gloated: 'Well, I could see all this coming. I warned Becher countless times not to let himself be led by the nose.' He issued Kasztner with an ultimatum: 'Send a cable to Switzerland to have the matter sorted out. If I don't have your positive reply within 48 hours I'll have the whole Jewish filth of Budapest liquidated.'[45] All Kasztner could say was that there must be a misunderstanding. Billitz, who was also present, suggested that Kasztner should travel to the Swiss border to see Mayer. Becher immediately agreed, as did eventually Eichmann, extending his deadline for a positive reply by cable to 2 December and warning of further actions against the Jews in Budapest if it was not met. Eichmann then announced that our group was to leave Bergen-Belsen soon, but threatened to detain Kasztner's relatives to ensure that he did not try to escape. Kasztner refused to travel to the Swiss border unless they were allowed to leave with the rest of us. Finally Eichmann grudgingly accepted his promise to return under all circumstances: 'Brand assured me of the same thing . . . But listen carefully, if you stay abroad too there'll be no mercy. Your Jews will be taught a lesson.'[46]

All this time Kasztner had continued to pester Becher for our release from Bergen-Belsen. Although Becher had told Kasztner that permission had already been granted on 24 October, there was no movement. In mid-November Krumey cabled from Vienna that our departure had been postponed to between 28 and 30 November because of 'transport problems', meaning further blackmail attempts by the Nazis. In response to Kasztner's request Becher gave him permission to send the following message to Bogyó through the SS special service: 'Dr Kasztner sends his love to his wife and informs her that the group will soon be leaving. He hopes to see her soon.' The message was delivered to her on 18 November by the German camp commander, Adolf Haas, who added his own regards. 'The effect of the telegram on the group, which had already given up all hope of leaving, can easily be imagined', Kasztner writes.[47]

On 26 November Becher returned from Himmler's headquarters, beaming. 'I've won all along the line,' he announced to Kasztner. He reported that a memorandum he had submitted to Himmler had resulted in the following orders: the extermination of Jews was to cease and the gas chambers were to be dismantled forthwith; Jews working in the Reich were to receive the same rations as 'workers from the East'; Jewish patients were to be admitted to hospital, if necessary together with 'Aryans'; the forced marches from Budapest were to stop. Becher himself had delivered the orders to Kaltenbrunner with Himmler's instructions to forward them to all the commanders of concentration camps and Gestapo units. He said to Kasztner: 'Now I hope Mr McClelland will appreciate Himmler's cooperation. Twenty million francs is a ridiculous amount in comparison to what I have achieved.'[48] Again, in the absence of conclusive evidence it is difficult to assess the veracity of Becher's assertions.

On 28 November Kasztner and Billitz left Budapest by car together with SS Hauptsturmführer Erich Krell, one of Becher's adjutants. Krell had strict orders to cable Becher by 2 December whether or not Mayer had delivered the 20 million francs. As the departure of our group from Bergen-Belsen was imminent he also had orders to detain us if the money had not been delivered. On 29 November the three men arrived at the border to find that Mayer had waited for two hours and then returned to St Gallen. Kettlitz reported that not only was the payment still outstanding, but he had also been ordered to leave Switzerland within 24 hours. Against the background of these unresolved issues, on 1 December, the SS Border Commissariat in Bregenz was informed by cable from the Reichssicherheitshauptamt (RSHA) that we were due to leave Bergen-Belsen on 4 December and reach the Swiss border two days later, when we were to be allowed to leave Germany without any difficulties.

Ironically, it was also on 1 December that Mayer told Kasztner in a hotel in St Margrethen that there could be no question of the 20 million francs being deposited. At the most, Mayer himself might be able to raise 4 million, contrary to the instructions of both Swiss and American authorities. He offered to withdraw from the negotiations and hand them over to the Red Cross, but Kasztner persuaded him to carry on. Returning to Bregenz, he explained to Krell and Kettlitz that a truthful telegram to Becher would play into Eichmann's hands, whereas it was their duty to help Becher gain time. He assured them that the problems with the Allies were only temporary and had been triggered by the resumption of deportations in Slovakia, the forced marches from Budapest and the delay in releasing our group from Bergen-Belsen. Upon our release, the mood on the other side would immediately change and the money become available. In the interim Krell and Kettlitz must cover Becher's back. Krell said: 'So you want us to send a false cable to Budapest? I'd be happy to agree with you. But do you realise that we're putting our own heads in the noose?'[49] Finally he cabled Becher that initially 5 million francs were being deposited, and that the prolonged confinement of our group in Bergen-Belsen had caused new difficulties with the Allies.

On 4 December Becher 'provisionally' noted Krell's report and confirmed that the lives of the Jews who had meanwhile been ghettoised in Budapest would be respected. However, if the outstanding 15 million francs were not deposited 'the situation would become untenable'. Krell and Kettlitz now demanded proof from Kasztner that the 5 million francs had actually been deposited. On 5 December, in St Margrethen, Mayer told Krell that Kettlitz had earlier presented him with a 48-hour ultimatum. He had informed his superiors, who were not willing to engage in a 'mechanical' discussion, but the question of the 5 million francs would be 'investigated'.[50]

After this frustrating meeting Kasztner returned to Bregenz to await the arrival of our train, for we had indeed left Bergen-Belsen on 4 December, as announced in the RSHA's cable of 1 December. While waiting, he wrote to his friend Hillel Danzig, who had reached Switzerland with the August group. It is a moving letter, but also important for the insight it gives on Kasztner's hopes and plans. Showing more emotion than usual, he confesses: 'I hardly dare to think of the moment when I see my loved ones again.' More practically, he reports that the 'boss' – who must be Himmler – has accepted the 'advance payment' and is awaiting further developments. Looking ahead to his next meeting with Saly Mayer and his own 'companion' – probably Becher – he fervently asks: 'Wouldn't it be possible *now* to save everything and everybody?' He lists Chaim

Weizmann, Rabbi Steven Wise and the Jewish World Congress as possible allies, and he urges Danzig and Nathan Schwalb to make every effort to move the deal forward, 'now that a *serious* result is at last appearing'.[51] Reading this letter, one cannot doubt that he was trying to save far more lives than those of his own relatives and friends or our so-called 'VIP group'.

On 6 December, still holding his breath in Bregenz, Kasztner wrote a letter to his wife Bogyó, which gives an intimate impression of his feelings while he was struggling to save us:

> It's five months since I last saw you. I've had a busy life with enough worries, problems and work. All the same, I constantly saw Bergen-Belsen before me. I tried to imagine the camp and not you because you were least of all born for it ... When Hannover was bombed, when the western offensive got close to you, I constantly thought of you. I was tortured by the idea that the group could be hurt. The possibility of something happening to you was unbearable. I regretted letting you go a hundred times.

He pays her a great compliment for her behaviour in the camp: 'I know how strong you can be in a difficult situation. I've heard that on the journey and in the camp you surpassed yourself. Take care of that other Bogyó, the real one.' Using the Hebrew term for 'going up', which was the common expression for 'emigrating to Palestine', he urges her to think of going as soon as possible, although in the event they stayed in Switzerland for two and a half years after the war: 'Go on Aliyah. We've had enough of Europe.'[52] Bearing in mind the circumstances in which the letter was written, one will hardly blame him for idealising both Bogyó and Palestine.

Towards 7 pm on 6 December, then, our train arrived in Bregenz. We were accompanied by Hermann Krumey. Meanwhile in St Margrethen an argument had developed between Krell and Kettlitz.

The cause, according to Kasztner, was Saly Mayer's failure to produce proof that the 5 million francs had been deposited for Becher. In addition, Krell was contesting Kasztner's valuation of the assets already given to Becher for our ransom. It is possible that at this late stage Eichmann also threw in a threat to send us to Auschwitz. In any case, Krell was in favour of allowing us to continue our journey to Switzerland, while Kettlitz was against. Eventually they told Kasztner that we could go.

At 9 pm we left for Lustenau, where we were transferred to a warm and brightly lit Swiss train. József Fischer and Kasztner jointly signed a receipt for the 'delivery of 1,368 Jews'.[53] The figure was inaccurate – 1,368 in December plus 318 in August adds up to 1,686. As I will explain later, the correct total was about 1,670. But when our train crossed the bridge over the Rhine into Switzerland shortly after midnight, none of us felt like counting.

After our departure Kasztner and Krell retired to the customs office in Lustenau to agree the final accounts of our ransom. The debate about the value of the Hungarian and foreign currencies, jewellery, gold and other valuables, which had been handed over to the SS five months earlier, continued. On the Vaada side Endre Biss, Shulem Offenbach and a Jewish jeweller had valued them at 7.2 million Swiss francs. On the SS side Grüson and two German jewellery experts valued them at 3.2 million Swiss francs. While the Jewish estimate would have more than covered the ransom for our group, the Germans had reduced theirs by another million francs, which enabled them to make further demands. Kasztner calculated that the Vaada was entitled to 400 more lives. Krell maintained that the Vaada still owed the SS 65,000 dollars. This was how things were left when they returned to Bregenz in the small hours.

Eichmann had suspected that Kasztner might decide to stay in Switzerland with his family, but he was wrong. Kasztner returned to German captivity in order to continue his rescue efforts. One can imagine how tempted he must have been to choose safety and comfort in a free country rather than hardship, humiliation and the constant threat of death under a monstrous dictatorship. But he remained firm in spite of Bogyó's requests that he join her. What he wrote to her three weeks after her arrival in Switzerland remained valid until the end of the war four months later: 'Be good and strong. You know that at the moment it isn't possible to do anything other than what I am doing.'[54]

CHAPTER 10

From Bergen-Belsen to Switzerland

On tenterhooks

The departure of the first group of 318 from Bergen-Belsen in August 1944 was followed by rumours that we too would leave soon, but none of these materialised. We examined and re-examined trivial events – Fischer being summoned to the camp commander, three important-looking Germans visiting our compound, a soldier collecting the card index with our names – as possible signs of our impending deliverance, but nothing happened. Some letters from Kasztner aroused great expectations, but offered no immediate comfort. As September and October passed, our hopes rose and faded almost daily as we hovered between extremes of optimism and despair.

Early in November the rumours intensified for a while, but when no further news came and our questions were answered by the German guards with 'icy silence or a cruel smile', as Miriam Buck put it, our mental and physical condition declined rapidly: 'The relapse into despair was terrible, there was more and more illness, the whole camp was a big hospital.'[1]

On 13 November Krumey appeared in our compound. He was accompanied by another SS officer and a civilian. I still do not know who they were, but one of them was heard asking Jenő László, a member of our internal governing body, how we were getting on. László answered that we were well, except for the cold. The German replied: 'Never mind, in a fortnight you'll be in Switzerland.'[2] More formally, the visitors informed our leaders that we would be leaving in 8–10 days' time for the same destination as the first 318. Later, the SS officer nicknamed Cut Mouth said to Fischer, in the past tense, as if bidding farewell: 'There were some mistakes, but on the whole we were satisfied with all of you.'[3] Fischer returned the compliment.

On 18 November camp commander Haas gave Fischer a message for Bogyó Kasztner: 'Tell her that her husband is sending his love and I am also sending her my regards. Within two weeks she'll be together with her husband.' Fischer asked: 'Is Kasztner coming here?' Haas replied: 'No, she is going to her husband.' Fischer's next words are reported differently by different people. Depending on whom one believes, he asked either 'And what about the others?' or 'And what about me?' In any case Haas replied: 'The others too, all are leaving.' This raised our spirits to the high level of 13 November: 'The same scene again, within seconds the whole camp is on its feet, loud jubilation',[4] Jenő Kolb wrote in his diary. But not for long. Although the rumours continued for the next few days, we heard nothing definite. Kolb noted on 22 November: 'People's mood is at point zero. They have done the worst to us. Instead of leaving us to our lethargy . . . the news has upset our lives, made feelings run high, and now everybody has plunged again to the depths.'[5]

However, by 23 November our mood had once more improved dramatically when a number of parcels containing food, warm clothes, cigarettes and chocolate were delivered for Kasztner's, Brand's and Offenbach's relatives. This was taken as a good omen and things began to look even better the next day with the arrival of 88 letters to various recipients. Two of the letters were from Kasztner, one to Fischer and one to Bogyó, both dated 18 November.

In his letter to Fischer Kasztner announced that the moment of our departure seemed to have arrived. We 'should already have been moved on at the end of October, but because of transport problems this has become possible only at the end of this month'. He explained that we would have to stay in Switzerland until the end of the war, as travel to Palestine had become impossible, but by 'transport problems' he really meant Eichmann's blackmail attempts. The letter to Bogyó is shorter and more personal. Although Kasztner restrained his feelings because he knew that the censor would read everything, we see the tough adversary of the SS here as a devoted husband, son and brother:

> I have been with you in my thoughts day and night. I know how difficult it has been for you to hold on, with your health and your nerves. I hope you have been strong enough . . . You are now about to leave. I'll go with you, perhaps not only in my thoughts . . . Wait for me and don't forget what you promised me. Kiss my mother and brother for me.[6]

It is particularly moving to read about his idea of joining Bogyó in Switzerland, bearing in mind that once he had seen us all to safety he went back to the horrors of Germany to try to save others.

On receipt of Kasztner's letter Fischer swiftly convened an extraordinary meeting of the governing body in order to start planning our journey. Now the rumours had a Pullman train standing ready for our departure and our last meal being cooked in the camp kitchen. 'Everybody is excited, there are no pessimists in the camp',[7] Kolb remarks with dry irony.

On 25 November a miracle seemed to have happened. From the Red Cross in Geneva we received some 60 cases containing food, medicines, vitamins and in particular 1,300 boxes of a product called 'Starkosan'. This was a chocolate powder with added vitamins and nutrients. I have never forgotten the pleasure of stuffing myself with it and was delighted to find my own childhood memory confirmed so eloquently by Kolb's adult diary:

> For the first time in five months a cultured flavour: chocolate! Old people and children are truly becoming drunk on it; they are eating it with spoons, dry, on bread, with butter, with water, with jam, mixed with glucose etc. There has been a change in people. Cheerful, calm faces, chattiness, an optimistic mood . . . and by the time it's dark the Starkosan, of which one is supposed to take three dessert spoonfuls daily, is finished in most cases.[8]

To this day, when survivors from our group get together, sooner or later somebody begins to rave about 'Starkosan'. It was one of the most enjoyable signs that our fortunes were to take a turn for the better, although we needed more than one outbreak of gluttony to recover from five months of hunger.

The Germans were no less amazed by these riches than we were, and promptly demanded a share. On 27 November the camp commander, calling our leader 'dear Fischer', asked him to leave the medicines behind for the other inmates when we left. Fischer promised to do so, adding that what was left of the medicines we had originally brought with us would also be placed at the commander's disposal.

But although the commander's request was seen as an encouraging sign, Fischer could only report that we would at best be leaving 'next week'.[9] Our elation gave way to deep gloom. It only took one day for Kolb to note: 'The mood has dropped from the crest to the trough of the wave. The Starkosan has run out. No news about our departure, many patients with headache and upset stomachs. The bath, I thought I had seen it for the last time, now I'm here again with the skeletons.'[10] And three days later he wrote only four words: 'Waiting. Hope is dying.'[11]

At this low point, on 3 December early in the morning, we were woken by the sudden announcement that we were leaving on the next day. This was followed by what Shoshana Hasson describes as 'total hysteria'.[12] In chaotic haste we got our luggage ready and by midday we had dragged it to the camp gate to be checked, as ordered. It was pouring with rain. Halfway through the checking we were told to return to our compound with the lighter pieces, leaving the heavy stuff at the gate. Some documents, photos and tools were confiscated. For me, things could have ended in disaster at that point. In an act of bravado I slipped a small bottle of vitamin tablets through the barbed wire to one of the emaciated figures in the Dutch compound next to ours. As soon as I had done this I thought that a guard had seen me. I rushed back to the hut in a panic and hid under the bunks until it became clear that no guard was coming after me. I shall never know whether a guard had seen me in reality or only in my imagination.

Although I was too young to appreciate fully what was happening, I remember sharing the emotional ups and downs with the rest of the group as we swung from hope to despair in quick succession. I remember, too, the shock we all felt when a number of people were removed from our compound and transferred to other parts of the camp to remain in German captivity.

On 18 November, when commander Haas first advised Fischer of our imminent departure, Andreas Kassowicz, his wife and their three children had been taken to the Neutrals' Camp, which held South American and Spanish inmates. The reason was that on arrival Kassowicz had declared himself and his family Romanian nationals and the Germans had decided to retain them for an exchange against ethnic Germans from Romania. The exchange never happened. I have mentioned that my own father had agonised, given our Transylvanian background, whether or not to call ourselves Romanian, and finally decided to be Hungarian like everybody else. Had he followed Kassowitz's example, it is unlikely that either he, with his war wound, or I, aged eleven, would have lived to see the end of the war. Kassowicz died a few days after liberation, although his family survived.

Two other families suffered an equally ironic fate. Eugen Kertész and Alexander Weiss had discovered that their daughters, who had been deported to Auschwitz, were now in the Women's Camp in Bergen-Belsen. When we received our marching orders, they begged Kramer, the new camp commander, to allow their daughters to join our group, pretending that they had met by chance on the way to the showers. To punish them for their illicit communication, Kramer transferred the parents to the Star Camp, while the daughters remained in the Women's Camp. Kertész died before liberation, Weiss and Mrs Kertész soon after.

Eight more people were likewise separated from the rest of us and moved to the Star Camp. They were Joel Brand's mother, his sister and some other relatives. They had to stay behind to satisfy Eichmann's desire to take revenge for Brand's failure in Istanbul. Most of them survived, but Brand's mother died a few days after being liberated.

This brings me back to the question of numbers. Although several lists were compiled during and after our captivity, none of them is accurate. Kasztner himself claims that 1,684 of us left Budapest on 30 June.[13] As I have already said, nobody knows exactly how many were on the train when it pulled out of Rákosrendező marshalling yard and how many got on or off before it reached the Austrian border, but 1,684 was the most likely number on our arrival in Bergen-Belsen.[14] It is generally accepted that 318 left for Switzerland in August. When the rest of us arrived at the Swiss border in December, Kasztner and Fischer signed a receipt for 1,368. This makes a total of 1,686. The seventeen unfortunates who were left behind seem to be included in the receipt, although it is not clear how three deaths and eight births reported by Kasztner fit into the equation.[15] One list prepared subsequently in Switzerland seems more trustworthy than most. It contains the names of 1,351 arrivals in December, and if 318 are added for August, this makes 1,669. Without regarding this figure as absolutely correct, I would say that Kasztner's Bergen-Belsen operation saved about 1,670 lives.

During the night after the announcement of our departure none of us got much sleep. We could hardly believe that our ordeal was about to end, but our sense of relief was overwhelming. Although we did not quite trust our good luck, the camp already felt like an almost distant memory. We naturally pitied everybody who had to stay behind, but were too happy to resist the urge to celebrate our release even before it had taken place. When the leaders began to distribute our food reserves, we pounced on them as if we would never eat again. As we counted the minutes until the dawn of our liberation, all attempts at keeping silence, order and cleanliness were abandoned. Kolb reports 'a lot of singing, a huge amount of rubbish and feverish waiting'.[16]

Saved

On the morning of 4 December Krumey appeared again, accompanied by Kramer and some other SS officers. For a while we saw them chatting with Fischer and Bogyó Kasztner. Eventually the arrangements for our departure were formally announced. Small children and old or sick people would be taken to the train by lorry, together with our heavy luggage. The rest of us, with our light luggage, would walk. When some 600 hands were raised requesting transport, it transpired that there were only fifty seats, many of which were promptly occupied by our leaders. At 1 pm we were finally on our way back to the Bergen-Hohne platform, where we had arrived five months earlier. In our condition it took us two or three hours to cover the distance of six or seven kilometres, and some of the weakest even longer. Children were crying as they tried to catch up with their parents, from whom they had been separated while waiting for non-existent transport. Parents were anxiously calling for children they had expected to have overtaken them in the lorries. My feet were aching from the stiff wooden soles that must have cost my father a fortune in cigarettes. The guards were shouting and the dogs barking at us, as they had done before. But we did not mind. We were going to Switzerland.

Our euphoria was short-lived. The five or six hours we spent on that platform waiting for our train proved to be one of our most uncomfortable experiences. I have my own clear memories of the ordeal, but David Kohn's notes recreate the same details with the added flavour of having been written down soon after the event by a child of twelve:

We arrived at 5 o'clock. We sat down and waited. It started raining, then it stopped, then it started again. It went on like that till it was dark. One air raid warning after the other. We were soaked and frozen to the bones. Meanwhile we were looking for our luggage. We waited till 11 pm when the train arrived. They were passenger carriages. We got a third-class carriage, but there were also second-class ones. People swooped on the train. There were punch-ups. There were accidents. Some fell under the carriages, but nothing happened to them beyond the fright. The train started with difficulty. Once it was moving they started distributing food. We were given jam, sugar, margarine, bread. We were in clover.[17]

I too remember the endless wait in the atrocious weather, the panic over the air raids, the search in the dark for the heavy luggage that had been dumped willy-nilly on the platform, the battles for seats once the train arrived. What I did not know at the time was that our leaders had snatched the most comfortable coach from its rightful passengers, as Kolb remarks drily: 'There is no coach number 9. The Klal party, who had been allocated coach 9, has no coach, because the leadership has simply occupied number 9 – first class, Pullman.'[18]

When we finally left after midnight we were, in Miriam Buck's words, 'too tired to be happy'.[19] The Germans had issued each of us

500 grams of bread, 30 grams of margarine, 150 grams of dried meat, 20 grams of jam and 500 grams of tinned meat. In addition, our leaders had distributed some more of our own reserves. After starving for five months we all ate greedily, with dire consequences. Béla Zsolt describes some episodes of this journey in the unfinished second part of *Nine Suitcases*. He exaggerates only slightly when he writes: 'On the train everybody overstuffed himself, and everybody had diarrhoea . . . Now that we were on our way to freedom, we vomited all over the express train's corridors and the toilets were dreadful.'[20] He shrewdly interprets this 'collective coprophilia' not merely as a physiological necessity, but also as a 'revolt against the strict discipline we had been forced to observe in this respect behind the barbed wire'.[21]

Our train crossed Germany from north to south at a slow rate, often stopped by air raids or diverted either because of bomb damage or in order to give priority to transports of soldiers. From time to time we turned east and people became nervous. To quote Zsolt again, we were beginning to believe our neighbours in the Dutch compound, 'who rightly envied and hated' us for leaving without them and who had tried to cheer themselves up by assuring us gloomily that we would be taken 'towards the Russian front, to dig trenches, build bunkers, or be annihilated'.[22] When we turned south again, the relief all round was almost tangible, and in the compartments of the young pioneers there was laughter and singing.

Although the passenger coaches were poles apart from the cattle trucks, as time passed we felt more and more uncomfortable. Twenty or more of us were crammed into compartments designed for eight passengers. In the hours of darkness we had to turn off all lights in case of air attacks. The lack of air and the heat of the bodies became overpowering. We were not given anything to drink and at one point I became extremely thirsty. When we stopped at a large station my father got out to look for some water. I watched through the window as a soldier, who might have been all of sixteen years old, hit him in the face before ordering him back on the train. I think we were in Göttingen, one of Germany's great university towns. But on another occasion, while the train was standing somewhere near a farm, boys in Hitler Youth uniforms gave us apples. I spent much of the journey daydreaming, while pretty villages with red and white half-timbered houses and forbidding cities full of blackened ruins sped past the window. People muffled in shapeless coats and scarves scampered to and fro, shoulders hunched up against the cold. Although it was winter no smoke rose from chimneys.

On 6 December we found ourselves surrounded by mountains. The countryside was covered in snow. In the early evening we reached Lindau. From a pitch-dark Germany we stared across Lake Constance at the lights of Switzerland. A few months before, the Swiss authorities had lifted the blackout with the soberly practical intention of avoiding any Allied bombing of their territory, but to us the sight seemed like a symbolic fairy-tale. A little later we stopped at the station of Lustenau in Austria, where we were met by Krumey and Kasztner. There was a delay of several hours, which I now know was the result of continuing extortion attempts by the Germans. Then we changed into a Swiss train, and at 1 am on 7 December we arrived in St Margrethen in Switzerland. We had escaped from the Nazis.

In St Margrethen we were received by friendly Swiss soldiers, members of the Women's Auxiliary Corps and Red Cross personnel. They distributed chocolate and newspapers: we had almost forgotten what those things were like. Kolb records a conversation with the first Swiss officer to enter his compartment. The extraordinary situation and the profound emotions of the participants may account for the formality of the exchange:

'You are now in Switzerland.' 'Thank God.' 'We know that you've been through a lot and we hope that you'll recover here.' 'And we thank freedom-loving Switzerland for letting us in.' 'But that's only natural.' A wonderfully humane rationality. All are touched.[23]

The next stop was in nearby St Gallen, where we got off the train and walked to an army barracks. Some sick members of the group were immediately taken to hospital. In the middle of the night, after the darkness of Bergen-Belsen, we were amazed to see brightly lit streets, illuminated shop windows and stylish cars still on the move or parked along the pavements. Some passers-by actually greeted us. Miriam Buck catches our mood perfectly: 'In the small hours of 7 December I was stumbling in an endless herd of human beings from St Gallen station towards the barracks . . . What I saw was a strange contrast: a peaceful small town in a picturesque situation and we in it, ragged, emaciated . . . For all of us this town will remain the epitome of true humanity.'[24] Sadly, the Swiss did not always treat Jewish refugees so hospitably, but we in the Kasztner group owe them a great debt of gratitude.

When we reached the barracks and looked in through the windows, we could see tables set with tablecloths and proper plates, glasses and cutlery. In the approaching dawn we were given a supper of 'cheese, soup, potatoes, bread, apples – the first things with a European flavour,' as Kolb exclaims.[25] We were also given cigarettes and Kolb saw a new life starting when he threw a butt away rather than keeping the last crumbs for recycling.

I wish I could say that we all sat down in an orderly fashion and ate our meal politely. Unfortunately, after five months in Bergen-Belsen, most of us were too far gone for such refinements. The table manners observed by Tibor Bielik were an outward sign of our dehumanisation:

There were bowls, empty bowls, with a spoon, a knife and fork and in each bowl was a slice of white bread. And like animals people rushed to those bowls, picked up one piece of bread and as much as they could gather forgetting that they are taking somebody else's bread . . . I mean they were normal people, intelligent people, prominent people, and in this crowd now that we are all liberated, we are free, we just got out of a train from Germany, we were committing these acts of – what do I call this? . . . You stop being a human . . . the animal part takes over.[26]

After this meal we were directed to a large, heated gymnasium, where we were able to stretch out under warm blankets on comfortable mattresses without bedbugs, lice or fleas. I had not slept so well for a long time. In the morning the luxuries continued. After a hot shower we were given comfortable, warm clothes and, for the children, toys. But I think it was also here that our fingerprints were taken and we were photographed with a number round our necks.

On the fourth day we boarded another train – again one for human beings, not cattle – and crossed Switzerland from north-east to south-west. This journey ended in Caux, 700 metres above Montreux on Lake Geneva. Because of the war there were no tourists in Switzerland and many hotels served as havens for refugees. We were distributed between two of them. The Orthodox minority was housed in the Regina, the non-religious majority in the Esplanade. Both were over-crowded and unheated, and we were not allowed to leave the prem-ises. But there was no *Zählappell*, no watch towers, no latrines and no SS. The soldiers who guarded us were friendly, the food was edible, the scenery breathtaking. We were alive and we could look forward to freedom and rehabilitation.

Again the euphoria was short-lived. Our joy at having survived was soon overcome by our memories of the persecution, our uncer-tainty about the fate of the relatives and friends we had left behind, our gradual discovery of exactly what had happened in Auschwitz, our fear of the future. There were psychosomatic illnesses, nervous breakdowns and suicides. I had my share of nightmares, but during the day led an adventurous life exploring the hidden corners of the Esplanade, frightening the pants off my father by climbing the turrets on the roof, watching rubbish come down the chutes until a Red Cross nurse stopped me, and, on a rare outing to Montreux, receiving a gift from heaven in the form of a small purse on the pavement with one franc inside, the exact price of the unaffordable object of my dreams: a banana. So much for a child who was trying hard to remain one after five months of Belsen. As for the adults, Miriam Buck's words eloqently convey the trauma, anticlimax and disappointment that cast a dark shadow over a lucky escape:

> These stories from the privileged camp contain no horrors, nothing about sealed wagons, gas chambers and children's corpses. Nevertheless the 'camp experience' weighs heavily on me . . . I don't know why the eighteen hundred of us out of six million deserved the great favour of fate to go to a 'privileged camp' and, even more importantly, to escape from it . . . We are chilled to the bone not only by what we have lived through but also by what we have been spared . . . Life, freedom, hope, everything that we have been given, tastes so bitter because we have nobody to rejoice in it with us . . . That is why our joy is blighted, our freedom worthless, our hope bereft of wings to soar.'[27]

Soon after the end of the war the US and Swiss authorities decided to transfer us to a camp of the United Nations Relief and Rehabilitation Agency in Philippeville, Algeria. We noisily protested. Dezső Hermann, who had become group leader when József Fischer was permitted to leave Caux before the rest of us, wrote to Churchill, to the new US president, Harry Truman, and to other influential figures. I do not think he got many replies. The next suggested venue was Tunisia and there were rumours that the authorities intended to use force. We held more stormy meetings in the great dining room of the Esplanade, with rousing speeches, cheering and booing, and me firing a cap pistol at the appropriate moments. As far as I know, no further attempts were made to move us against our will. In August 1945 a group of 700, led by Fischer, left for Palestine via Italy. About

180 returned to Hungary. Some emigrated to the United States and other countries overseas. Some settled in Switzerland.

I could have gone to Palestine on an early transport, but my father was unable to obtain an immigration permit from the British authorities, and we were terrified of being separated after what we had been through together. He consulted Teitelbaum and Szondi, both of whom, for rather different reasons, advised him not to let me go. He persuaded a relief organisation to cough up the modest fee needed to send me to the Ecole d'Humanité, a boarding school based on unusually progressive ideas and situated in one of the most beautiful regions of the Alps, where I spent two happy years without hearing one anti-Semitic remark. Then, as my father gradually established himself in business, I attended grammar school, followed by university, in Zurich. After the twelve statutory years of residence, having been investigated by three different police forces and grilled on Swiss democracy by a panel of politicians, we were granted Swiss citizenship. It was then that my father married David Kohn's mother, who had gone to Palestine and moved back to Switzerland to join us. David studied medicine in Zurich and became a highly respected geriatric specialist in Israel. I worked for a while as a school teacher and journalist before I came to Britain to teach German – of all things – at the University of Sussex for one year. That was in 1963 and I am still there.

CHAPTER 11

Rescuing the Camps

Work with small details

Our release from Bergen-Belsen seemed to prove that the Germans were prepared to spare Jews for the right price, and Kasztner was determined to continue his rescue efforts, at the risk of his own life. While bringing 1,670 Jews to Switzerland out of a Nazi concentration camp was a highly dramatic event, from now on he tried to prevent the extermination of much larger numbers, but in a less conspicuous way.[1] By his own account he and Becher carried out a number of rescue missions on an extremely large scale, but since most of the relevant documents were destroyed it is difficult to tell the extent to which the survival of many thousands was due to their efforts or to other factors.

On 8 December, the day after we crossed the Swiss border, Kasztner met Krell and Kettlitz again in Bregenz, while Becher was waiting for news in Budapest. He persuaded them to cable Becher that 5 million francs had been deposited in Switzerland and the outstanding 15 million were being processed. In the belief that the 5 million francs were actually in the bank, Becher insisted that the 'balance' of 15 million be deposited forthwith. He also demanded delivery of a number of trucks promised by Kasztner earlier in

exchange for the safety of the Kolumbusz Street camp. The trucks
– fifteen according to Kasztner, thirty according to Biss[2] – should
have been supplied by Alois Steger, a Sudeten German businessman
living in Bratislava, who agreed, for a handsome bribe, to inform
Becher that they were ready for delivery in Slovakia. When Becher
eventually tried to collect them he found that they had been confiscated by the Wehrmacht.

About this time word got round that the Arrow Cross intended
to liquidate the Budapest ghetto with its 80,000–100,000 inhabitants.
Kasztner and Biss later claimed that it was their intervention through
Becher that actually prevented this massacre. Not surprisingly, Becher
concurred. According to his 1961 statement, it was at his request
that Himmler had told a reluctant Eichmann to ensure that no further
atrocities were committed against the Jews. In fact we cannot be at
all sure what happened. Kasztner and Biss may have overestimated
both the immediacy of the danger and their own role in averting it.
Becher, for his part, was hardly the most reliable witness. But although
individual rampages by Arrow Cross gangs continued to cost many
lives before the Soviets finally captured the city in February 1945,
the liquidation of the ghetto of Budapest was one war crime that did
not take place.

While Kasztner was trying to save Jews through Becher's influence
on Himmler, Otto Komoly, Hansi Brand and Biss, in extremely difficult and dangerous conditions, did all they could to help the victims
of the Arrow Cross terror. They supplied food, bought with Joint
money on the black market, to the ghetto, set up children's homes
and hid fugitives. They often cooperated with representatives of neutral
countries, Red Cross personnel, and young Zionist pioneers, who also
undertook daring rescue missions of their own. Komoly probably
saved between 5,000 and 6,000 children before he was arrested by
the Hungarian secret police on 1 January 1945 and never seen again.

The most successful operations were those of the Swedish diplomat
Raoul Wallenberg, the Swiss consul Charles Lutz and the Chief

Delegate of the Swiss Red Cross Friedrich Born. They are credited with saving the lives of some 100,000, 60,000, and 15,000 Jews respectively, by freeing them from arrest, giving them shelter in 'protected houses' recognised by the Hungarian and German authorities as having extraterritorial status, or issuing passes that declared them to be under the protection of Sweden, Switzerland or the Red Cross. In many cases the rescuers were able to present their protégés as prospective emigrants, on the basis of entry permits to Palestine sent to Hungary by the Istanbul Vaada and by Zionist organisations in Switzerland. In other cases they issued unauthorised documents, which nevertheless often achieved their purpose. In these enterprises an important part was played by the head of the Budapest Palestine Office, Miklós (or Moshe) Krausz, who had taken refuge in the building of the Swiss legation. Kasztner's claim that the activities of the Palestine Office and the Vaada 'complemented each other'[3] is justified up to a point, but most of the time cooperation between the two bodies was hampered by bitter personal rivalry and hatred between the two leaders.

While large numbers of people were saved by such actions, one group was less lucky. After our departure for Bergen-Belsen about 3,500 Jews took refuge in the Kolumbusz Street camp, which was no longer guarded by the SS but officially protected by the International Red Cross. The inmates organised a self-defence force and got hold of some weapons against possible attacks. On the night of 2 December an Arrow Cross gang tried to steal the food stocks of the camp. Two of the thugs were killed by the defence force and the others fled. The Hungarian police then occupied the premises. The camp leader, József Moskowitz, the physician, Dr Rafael, and Rafael's son, aged seventeen, were executed in retaliation for their 'resistance'. Men and women capable of work were transferred to Germany and the rest confined to the ghetto.

On 10 December Kasztner sent a message to the Vaada in Budapest that no monies could be expected from Mayer. One day later Becher demanded an immediate confirmation that the 15 million had been deposited. At that point Joseph Schwartz, the European director of the Joint, was about to travel to Switzerland, and Kasztner persuaded Kettlitz to cable Becher that he was coming expressly to deposit the 15 million.

From 20 December Kasztner conducted a series of discussions with Schwartz, Mayer and Nathan Schwalb in Switzerland. His main purpose was to secure Schwartz's assistance in another bluff. If US regulations did not allow any actual payments 'the Germans could at least be *shown* the money that they would never get'.[4] With great difficulty, Kasztner got Mayer to write a letter promising that the 20 million would be deposited by the time of the next meeting at the border.

Matters became even more complicated for Kasztner when two Orthodox brothers, Elias and Yitzhak Sternbuch, launched their own rescue operation with the help of the former Swiss Federal Councillor (cabinet minister) Jean-Marie Musy, who had good personal relations with Himmler. The scheme was supported by Walter Schellenberg, the deputy leader of the RSHA, and the role of intermediary was performed by a Swiss businessman called Curt Trümpy. On 21 December the brothers asked Kasztner to ditch Mayer and to advise Becher to work with them on the release of some 1,200 Jews from Theresienstadt. Kasztner refused. He suggested instead that they join forces with him and focus on large-scale rescues with the assistance of Mayer and the prestige of the Joint behind them. He explained that the aim of any promise to the SS had to be the rescue of those Jews who were at the 'most endangered point' at any one time. Currently the inmates of the Budapest ghetto and the concentration camps in German-held territories were in the most acute danger. While 'a transport of Jews arriving abroad was more spectacular', what really mattered was 'the gruelling, difficult work with small details which consisted in preventing the annihilation of the largest number of Jews wherever they happened to be'.[5]

Such a statement may seem odd coming from Kasztner two weeks after he had accomplished the spectacular release of our group from Bergen-Belsen to Switzerland. On the one hand, his objections to the brothers' plan suggest a desire to be in sole command. On the other hand, they are consistent with what he had said right from the start: that our rescue was meant to be only the first stage of a process which he hoped would save a much larger number of lives. The brothers declined Kasztner's offer, but they were soon to cause him trouble.

Kasztner left Bregenz on 28 December. As the Soviet forces had completed the encirclement of Budapest on the previous day, he stopped in Vienna, where he was to be based for three months in the Grand Hotel. Becher and Eichmann had left Budapest a few days earlier under heavy shelling. Eichmann stayed in Berlin until the collapse of the Third Reich. After a spell in Austria he went into hiding in Argentina, before being kidnapped and taken to Israel, where he was put on trial and executed in 1961. Becher spent the last months of the war travelling between Berlin, Vienna, Hamburg and various concentration camps. After three years in American captivity he was freed and became one of Germany's richest businessmen. Wisliceny and Krumey had decamped from Budapest to Vienna. Wisliceny was eventually tried and executed in Czechoslovakia, while Krumey was arrested and released several times before being finally sentenced to life imprisonment.

On 7 January the Joint transferred 20 million francs to Mayer, but Becher was still kept in the dark about the ban on any part of this sum being spent without the approval of the US government. On 11 January Becher returned to Vienna from Berlin after a visit to Himmler, who had promoted him to Standartenführer (colonel). He reported that Himmler had been shocked to hear about the delays in payment, given the clear agreement reached with McClelland. A fierce argument followed. Kasztner complained about Eichmann's constant failures to respect Becher's undertakings and even Himmler's orders. He urged Becher to ensure that the Budapest ghetto was not harmed at the last moment before the fall of the city to the Soviets. Becher assured him: 'The Reichsführer has told me that he would refrain from any retaliatory measures of any kind.'[6] He then complained of certain SS figures who had earlier advised him to steer clear of any rescue attempts, but who were now trying to discredit him and to gatecrash his enterprise. A fortnight later he became even more explicit, when he gave Kasztner permission for Red Cross representatives to visit labour camps with supplies of food and clothes, but warned him: 'You must be very careful not to make the matter too conspicuous. You know how much Kaltenbrunner would like to compromise me in one way or another.'[7] By this time Becher was treating Kasztner more and more as his equal. As for Eichmann, it had long been clear that he was doing all he could to undermine Becher's efforts and to circumvent Himmler's explicit orders, driven partly by professional jealousy and partly by his dogged determination not to leave a single Jew alive in Hungary.

Meanwhile the Sternbuch brothers had continued their operation. As Becher nervously reported on 29 January, his enemies in the RSHA had told Himmler that unlike the Joint and McClelland, who were bluffing, Musy could deliver goods, money and propaganda in exchange for further transports of Jews to Switzerland. To reassure Himmler, Becher ordered Kasztner to travel to the Swiss border for yet another meeting with Mayer. Krell and Kettlitz were to travel with him and after the meeting Krell was to cable Becher unequivocally as to whether Mayer had receipts for the deposit of 5 and 15 million francs, whether these amounts were held at the unlimited disposal of Becher, and whether Mayer was prepared to obtain a visa for Becher to continue the negotiations in Switzerland.

At the meeting which followed Mayer promised to produce a copy of a letter stating that 20 million Swiss francs had been deposited at a Swiss bank at the joint disposal of himself and McClelland, earmarked for negotiations with Becher. Krell demanded that the money be placed expressly at the disposal of Becher. The next meeting was fixed for the afternoon of 2 February. In the morning a message arrived: 'Saly Mayer is busy with family matters.'[8] After an impasse lasting three days, Krell received an official phone call from Berlin ordering him to break off the negotiations. This was followed by a call from Becher himself, announcing from Himmler's headquarters that 1,000 Jews had been dispatched to Switzerland as a sign of good will. These were in fact the 1,200 Jews whose release from Theresienstadt Musy had agreed with Himmler on behalf of the Sternbuch brothers.

On 11 February yet another meeting took place between Kasztner, Becher, Krell and Mayer, this time in the St Margrethen customs office rather than on the bridge over the Rhine. Mayer showed Becher the promised letter about the deposit of 20 million francs, but explained that Swiss neutrality did not allow the money to be placed at a German's disposal. Becher demanded a meeting with McClelland. Mayer promised and Becher returned to Vienna. But the meeting could not be arranged, possibly because the phone lines had been destroyed by military action.

Two letters Kasztner wrote to Bogyó from Vienna around this time give an illuminating insight into his state of mind.[9] In the first, dated 1 February, he complains of 'loneliness and isolation' and confesses that he would like to 'rest a while', but he tries to cheer her – and himself – up: 'Dear Bogyó, don't worry about me; I still believe in my luck and I only weaken when I think of you.' In the second, dated 11 February, he is calmer and more detached: 'We are past the dramatic part and I try to do things with less internal emotion and trembling.' His sense of anti-climax is a predictable reaction to the completion of a nerve-racking assignment, but his use of the bridge metaphor reveals the gambler and adventurer in his make-up: 'My work now is almost becoming dull and commonplace. It's as if the bidding is over, and Jean can finish the rubber.' However, despite his world-weariness, Kasztner is clear that he still has a mission to fulfil: 'Unfortunately, while the game is only about part scores . . . the grand slam means life.' Therefore he has no intention of abandoning his self-appointed task and he is all the more determined to persevere because he has been promised 'greater personal safety' than 'in the past'. This was a veiled hint that Becher, facing the inevitable defeat of Germany, would make a concerted effort to secure his own alibi by protecting him.

In March Kasztner embarked on several lines of rescue. Becher refused to help him free a number of prominent Hungarian anti-fascists, both Jewish and Christian, from Mauthausen. But, in return for the promise of a delivery of textiles and edible oil, Kasztner received Becher's permission to compile a list of 50 Slovak Jews hiding in Bratislava to be taken to Switzerland. It was in a Bratislava street that Kasztner had the misfortune of running into the Hungarian gendarmerie chief, Ferenczy. When he reached his hotel two armed Hungarians in SS uniforms pounced on him. They frogmarched him into the lobby, where Ferenczy was waiting. Ferenczy bawled: 'You're coming with me.' 'Where?' Kasztner asked. 'I'm taking you in my car, you'll see where.' 'Lieutenant-Colonel, you have no right to do this,' Kasztner said in a raised voice. Ferenczy rasped: 'Shut up, I know who you are.' Kasztner shouted for help as loud as he could. A knot of people had gathered in the lobby, including two German officers. Ferenczy explained to them: 'I know him well. This man is an American-Jewish spy.' When Kasztner showed the German officers his passport Ferenczy gave up and left. Kasztner then went to his room, hid the Swiss francs he had brought with him to buy merchandise, and destroyed some sensitive notes. As soon as he had done that, five agents from the staff of Hauptsturmführer Alois Brunner, the SS officer in charge of the annihilation of the last Jews remaining in Slovakia, burst into the room, and the following exchange took place:

'Are you Dr Kasztner?'

'Yes.'

'Under what name are you staying here?'

'What kind of question is that? Under my own, of course.'

'Are you a Jew?'

'I am not regarded as a Jew.'

'Are you circumcised?'

'Yes, but I'm still not regarded as a Jew.'

'Well – by our laws you are a Jew. You're coming with us.'[10]

Kasztner was taken to SS headquarters, where Brunner's deputy inspected his documents before taking them to Josef Witiska, the Gestapo chief. Witiska was aware of Kasztner's connections with Becher, and within an hour Kasztner was free. He had been reported to Brunner's office by Ferenczy.

This incident ended with 28 Jews, who had been hiding in Bratislava, being transported by lorry to Vienna. In addition, Becher allowed a number of Hungarian Jews working in Vienna to join them, and on 19 April a group of 68 arrived in Switzerland. They included Dov Weissmandel, who in the previous autumn had managed to escape from a train bound for Auschwitz and go underground. They did not include Gizi Fleischmann, his partner in the 'Europa-Plan' negotiations with Wisliceny. She too was put on a train to Auschwitz and specially selected to be murdered on arrival.

The great moment

As the defeat of the Third Reich was approaching, Himmler came under increasing pressure to cease the killings. On 29 March Becher had some momentous news to report to Kasztner. In a recent conversation Himmler had assured him that no more Jews would be murdered and all the camps would be handed over to the Allies intact. The Sternbuch–Musy operation had caused a violent argument between Hitler and Himmler. Hitler had ordered an immediate stop to all negotiations, but Himmler had stood his ground. Himmler's new approach was also confirmed to Kasztner by Krumey. Visiting Vienna on an inspection tour of the defences against the Red Army, Himmler was asked by the local Gestapo chief what was to happen to the Jews of the region. According to Krumey, he replied: 'They mustn't be touched in any circumstances.'[11]

A week later, on 6 April, the German retreat before the Soviets was in full swing. Becher and Krumey received Kasztner in their billet in a medieval castle near the small town of Spitz on the Danube. Becher told Kasztner with a flourish:

Now your 'great moment' has come. I have just seen Himmler. I submitted to him a comprehensive proposition about improving the treatment of both the Jewish prisoners and the political prisoners in general, according to our earlier discussions. Himmler accepted my proposals and appointed me Reich Special Commissioner for the affairs of all Jewish and political prisoners. Now I would like to visit all the larger concentration camps together with you and Krumey, and take the necessary steps on the spot. After the first trip we'll go to the Swiss border to discuss the details with McClelland.

Becher showed Kasztner a document signed by Himmler: 'To SS Standartenführer Kurt Becher. In view of the difficult situation with regard to sanitation and housing I appoint you Reich Special Commissioner for all concentration camps.' Becher explained that Himmler had agreed to a reorganisation of the concentration-camp system 'in a humane spirit' and was prepared to forgo any financial reward either from the Jews or from the Allies. The Ministry of Economic Affairs would reimburse the Vaada for all earlier payments or use the funds to improve conditions in the camps.[12]

This was the beginning of Kasztner's last major enterprise. Both he and Becher maintain that it was Becher who persuaded Himmler to order the peaceful surrender of the concentration camps to the Allies, and they also claim credit for ensuring that the order was carried out in several camps. In fact Himmler had given the order in response to intercessions from many different quarters: the vice-president of the Swedish Red Cross Count Folke Bernadotte, the World Jewish Congress representative Norbert Masur, Himmler's own physician Felix Kersten and many others advised him to spare the last surviving victims. As for the execution of the order, Kasztner and Becher indeed visited several concentration camps during the chaotic final weeks of the war, but the extent to which the surrender of the camps may or may not have been due to their efforts is hard to assess.

They first went to Bergen-Belsen. On 10 April Becher, in his Berlin apartment, told Kasztner that he had once more advised Himmler to hand over the concentration camps to the Allies without a fight. While Kasztner waited in Becher's Mercedes, Becher and Krumey called on Eichmann in his office to make sure that he did not sabotage the orders. When Eichmann came out of the building two hours later he pretended not to see Kasztner. Becher and Kasztner immediately left Berlin, arriving in Bergen-Belsen at 5.30 pm. Commander Kramer, 'coldly and indifferently', informed them about the terrible conditions in the camp. In early February there had been 89,000 inmates. Now 53,000 were alive. Most deaths had been caused by starvation or typhus, but that was 'not his fault'.[13] Kasztner suggested that the only way to end the horror was to hand the camp over to the approaching British forces.

On 11 April Becher phoned Himmler, who authorised him to arrange an immediate surrender. This time Kramer showed Kasztner and Becher round part of the camp. They saw thousands of 'living skeletons', although they were kept out of the areas with the dead bodies. The Wehrmacht commander, Colonel Karl Harries, initially refused to capitulate, but Becher, after a visit to the high command of the Army Group North, announced that he had prevailed and the offer was on its way to the British. On 12 April, while inspecting the camp of Hamburg-Obergamme, he received a message that a British staff officer had arrived in Bergen-Belsen to negotiate the surrender of the camp. When he told Himmler on the phone that he was about to leave for Bergen-Belsen his boss rapped him over the knuckles: 'That's not your business, Becher. Kindly leave the capitulation to the Wehrmacht.'[14] The camp was finally handed over to the British on 15 April.

Most of these accounts appear in Kasztner's own retrospective report and there is a dearth of hard evidence to support them. However, in some cases he made notes almost as the events themselves were taking place. While the later report was calculated to justify his own actions, these spontaneous notes enhance his credibility. An instructive example is a letter he wrote late on 11 April in Hamburg, where he was spending the nights between his visits to Bergen-Belsen. A brief passage which seems to confirm that Becher – whose first name also served as a code name in Kasztner's correspondence – played an important part in saving the surviving inmates from falling victim to a battle at the last moment:

> Kurt's suggestions were received with little enthusiasm. But Kurt had obtained the agreement of the army group commander, and by 8 pm the decision had been made: the whole complex was declared a neutral zone and would be surrendered to the Allies without a fight. A colonel was delegated to deliver this decision to the Allies.[15]

Elsewhere in the same letter he writes that Becher made arrangements for Buchenwald to be surrendered with 30,000–40,000 inmates on terms similar to those for Bergen-Belsen.

On 13 April, as they were driving back to Berlin, Becher made a blatant attempt to build up his alibi. 'If we were to lose this damned war after all, I hope the Allies will have enough insight to appreciate my efforts and achievements,' he said to Kasztner. With even more nerve, he put in a good word for Himmler, who was finding himself in a 'delicate' position 'as a result of the measures he had taken in the interests of the Jews and political prisoners'. The good word for Himmler was followed by a bad one for Mayer, which proves that Becher was aware of the subterfuges on the Jewish side, although it does not indicate when his suspicions had begun: 'If Mr Saly Mayer had behaved differently, if at least he hadn't been economical with promises, we could have achieved more.'[16] It is true that Mayer was not as good at bluffing and cheating as Kasztner would have liked him to be, but whether a more devious approach would have wrested greater concessions from the Nazi criminals is far from certain.

When Becher and Kasztner arrived in Berlin they discovered that, despite Himmler's orders, substantial numbers of inmates had been dragged from some camps to others to prevent them being liberated by the Allies. For example, a few days before the surrender of Buchenwald the commander had sent a contingent of 22,000 to Flossenbürg and Dachau. Becher told Kasztner that at his request Himmler had undertaken to cable the commanders of all the camps, forbidding the evacuation or liquidation of the inmates.

To ensure the peaceful surrender of the camps, Becher decided to travel to Mauthausen and Flossenbürg. Kasztner, together with Krumey and Hunsche, managed to get to Theresienstadt on 16 April despite attacks from low-flying British aircraft. Rabbi Benjamin Murmelstein, the 'Judenältester' appointed by the Germans, was directed to give them a guided tour of the sanitised 'model ghetto', which had already hoodwinked the Red Cross in June 1944. Meeting some of the inmates, Kasztner assured them that they would soon be free. Krumey delivered Himmler's order for the command of the camp and its 32,000 surviving prisoners to be transferred to the Red Cross. This was eventually done on 5 May, three days before Soviet forces took over.

Becher turned up in Mauthausen on 27 April. He apparently countermanded the commander's orders to blow up 22,000 slave labourers in an underground ammunition plant, although to what extent the final surrender of the camp to the Americans on 5 May was due to his efforts is not clear. In any case he had another, more personal, assignment to fulfil here. One of Kasztner's closest associates, Moshe Schweiger, had been arrested by the Gestapo and interned in Mauthausen soon after the German invasion of Hungary. One day before the liberation of the camp by the US army, Becher freed him. As we shall see, his reasons were not entirely humanitarian.

Kasztner, for his part, travelled once more to Switzerland. On 20 April he was in Geneva, trying to obtain the agreement of McClelland, Mayer and Schwalb for another meeting with Becher at the border. However, he was told that in view of the Allied advances such a meeting was no longer necessary.

On the previous day Kasztner had called on our group in our haven in Caux, where he received an enthusiastic welcome. On behalf of both the Orthodox minority in the Hotel Regina and the non-religious majority in the Hotel Esplanade, he was given a purpose-made certificate with symbolic drawings tracing the crucial stages of our journey from Kolozsvár, via Budapest, Mosonmagyaróvár, Linz and Bergen-Belsen, to St Gallen and Caux. According to the Hebrew text – in which Kasztner's first name is also given in Hebrew – '1685 saved Jews' pray God to bless our 'noble rescuer and protector, Dr Israel Kasztner', who had 'fought his miraculous and heroic battle to deliver us from the bloodthirsty enemy at the risk of his own life and with true self-sacrifice.'[17] It was one of Kasztner's happiest moments. There were many unhappy ones to follow.

CHAPTER 12

Post-war Projects

Struggles for recognition

The end of the war naturally meant the end of the rescue operations, but by no means the end of Kasztner's story. In late April 1945, shortly before Germany finally surrendered, he and his wife Bogyó had moved into the Sergy boarding house in Geneva, which remained his base until he emigrated to Palestine in December 1947. Between 1945 and 1948 he made several journeys to London and Nuremberg, where he assisted the Military Tribunal with information, conducted interviews and wrote articles. His living expenses were met by the Palestine Office, the Jewish Agency and the war crimes courts. His only child, Zsuzsi, was born on 26 December 1945. In a letter to a relative in Palestine he called her 'the only clean and bright spot' in his inner state of malaise.[1] To his friend Dezső Hermann he confided that 'being a father is not a role but a state of mind, an inexplicably good feeling' and he described 'the little girl with slit-eyes like a Japanese' as 'a solid, durable piece of work, the most successful of all my creations'.[2]

But fatherhood was not enough to lift his spirits. In the words of Yechiam Weitz, the most knowledgeable observer of his life after the war, 'both mentally and physically, Kasztner was a shadow of his former self'.[3] To Joel Brand, who met him in Geneva in May 1946, he seemed 'grey not only in his features but also in his thoughts'.[4] After the excitements of confronting the SS, his new activities seemed mundane and boring. He was distressed by arguments with Bogyó, who understandably resented his earlier affair with Hansi Brand. He had expected to be thanked and celebrated, but was plagued instead by innuendo, rumour and open accusation of grave malpractice during the Holocaust. He felt frustrated, disillusioned and bitter.

Kasztner's accusers were a mixed bunch: they included his personal or ideological enemies, survivors who had lost relatives or had themselves suffered in the camps, and even some members of our Bergen-Belsen group. The hate campaigns were often carried on anonymously, which he found particularly exasperating. In an angry letter to Eliahu Dobkin he objected to people 'playing behind the scenes' and demanded that any 'misunderstandings . . . be clarified', any 'suspicions be expressed out loud' and any 'complaints be formulated with precision'.[5] Dobkin flatly, but untruthfully, denied the existence of any complaints or suspicions, and the backbiting continued.

Kasztner felt deeply wronged. As he wrote to Hermann, he believed that he had been 'tripped up' by the leaders of the Yishuv (the Jewish community in Palestine) because they 'did not appreciate the results we achieved as much as we, knowing the facts, imagined'.[6] Similarly, writing to his friend Walter Eliezer, he blamed the hostility he was experiencing on 'the difference in understanding resulting from the difference of experiences'[7] between the Jews in Europe and the Jews in Palestine during the Holocaust. Ben Gurion and Sharett had been too busy creating the state of Israel to think of saving Jews in Europe, while other members of the Jewish Agency, such as Dobkin or Yitzhak Gruenbaum, had first ignored and then deliberately used the survivors as pawns in their own internal politics. Even before the foundation of the Jewish state – and a dozen years before his own death – Kasztner recognised a dichotomy that was to become one of the major rifts in Israeli society and a crucial factor in his own tragedy. But there was more. In addition to his grievance against the Yishuv leaders, Kasztner claimed that Saly Mayer, the Joint, the Sternbuch brothers and the orthodox Aguda movement were trying to usurp the credit due to his own work. All this may have been slightly paranoid, but he was also becoming the victim of real misrepresentation and malice.

Kasztner defended himself by issuing a series of statements, boasting about his wartime activities, aggressively demanding recognition, and overreacting to any actual or imagined belittlement. One of the first retrospectives of this kind is a four-page letter to members of the Jewish Agency, written in August 1945.[8] Reflecting on the 'moral justification and political appropriateness' of the Vaada's work, Kasztner affirms that the paramount aim was 'Hazalah, i.e. saving human lives'. He then lists the successes that 'must be attributed above all to our efforts': the release of the Bergen-Belsen group; the survival of the Strasshof contingent; the prevention of deportations from Budapest; the exemption of children and old people from the foot marches to Austria; the rescue of the Budapest ghetto from the Arrow Cross; Himmler's order for the cessation of all exterminations; the liberation of Jews hiding in Bratislava; and the peaceful surrender of Bergen-Belsen and Theresienstadt to the Allies.

In the years that followed, Kasztner was to repeat the list many times. There are slight variations in detail between the different versions, but the substance remains the same. As he put it with deserved pride in a letter to Walter Eliezer: 'What we did in and from Budapest is unique in the history of the catastrophe.'[9] He may have exaggerated his own contribution to wider developments, but it seems clear that he was trying to accomplish a vast mission, of which rescuing our group of 1,670 was only a small part. While all his dreams were not fulfilled, his far-reaching intentions are confirmed, for example, by a letter to Aryeh Tartakower of the World Jewish Congress, in which he points out that 'in 1944, the year in which more than a million Jews were gassed, there were chances of a large-scale rescue'.[10]

In the autumn of 1946 Kasztner became embroiled in a particularly heated argument. On 4 October the Joint issued a press release which gave fulsome praise to Saly Mayer for saving Hungarian Jews, without once mentioning Kasztner. Kasztner was furious. In a letter to Mayer he rebutted every item in the release, claiming all the credit for the Vaada, or rather, for himself. He issued statements to the same effect in various newspapers. He urged the World Jewish Congress, the Jewish Agency and the Joint itself to put the record straight. In December he received a half-hearted apology from the Joint's executive secretary, Moses A. Leavitt, and its vice-chairman, J. C. Hyman, who blamed the errors on a report by the World Refugee Board representative Roswell McLelland. One particular sentence may have struck Kasztner as a pointed put-down, although it contained an obvious truth: 'No organisation can claim for itself that it alone did the work.'[11] About the same time he blew his own trumpet again in a 'Memorandum',[12] probably intended for the Jewish Agency, in which he reiterates the outcome of his agreements with Becher: the release of the Bergen-Belsen group, the redirection of the Strasshof group, the rescue of the Budapest ghetto, the surrender of Bergen-Belsen, Mauthausen, Neuengamme and Theresienstadt.

The most damaging attack in that period came from Kasztner's old rival, Moshe Krausz. In the summer of 1945 Krausz had been removed as head of the Budapest Palestine Office after a Jewish Agency inquiry into his slapdash and confrontational work habits. He was acquitted because of lack of evidence, but as a counter-attack he wrote a report for the commission of inquiry, praising his own rescue efforts and denigrating those of Kasztner. He claimed that Kasztner had not only missed opportunities of saving many more Jews while concentrating on the release of the Bergen-Belsen group, but had also misused funds earmarked for rescue actions, sacrificed Hungarian Jewry for his personal safety and hampered Krausz's own large-scale operations. At Kasztner's request, a court of honour was set up on the fringe of the 22nd Zionist Congress in Basel in 1946 to examine Krausz's complaints. Two meetings ended without a decision, as there had not been enough time to gather evidence. A second court, also requested by Kasztner, never materialised.[13] Looking further ahead, after the introduction of the Nazi and Nazi Collaborators (Punishment) Law of 1950 in Israel, Kasztner was questioned by the police, but no charges were brought. His wish to refute the rumours and to achieve the recognition he craved was his main reason for writing his *Bericht* and presenting it to the 22nd Zionist Congress. The report has been criticised for its inclination to 'self-vindicating analysis' and 'self-aggrandisation'.[14] Nor did it succeed in silencing Kasztner's enemies. Nevertheless, handled with care, it is an invaluable record of an extraordinary undertaking.

The slurs were many and varied, but their ultimate message was that Kasztner had collaborated with the Nazi murderers for his own profit. It was a horrendous charge and Kasztner did all he could to defend himself. Naturally, he was not an objective witness, but there is at least one account by an observer who was able to judge Kasztner's work from close quarters without having an axe to grind. It is part of the report submitted by Roswell McClelland to his superiors at the World Refugee Board in August 1945, soon after the events in question. While McCelland's balance sheet is in many respects a mirror image of Kasztner's own, it has the advantage of being clear, terse and sympathetic, but without obvious bias. Kasztner's major successes, as McClelland sees them, were:

1) The bringing to Switzerland of two groups of Jews from Hungary, via the concentration camp of Bergen-Belsen, on August 21, 1944 (318 persons) and on December 6 1944 (1355 persons)

2) The avoidance of the deportation of upwards of 200,000 Jews remaining in Budapest on August 25, 1944

3) The exemption . . . of elderly and sick persons and children . . . from the forced evacuation on foot of Jews from Budapest in November 1944

4) The diverting of transports of some 17,000 Hungarian Jews
to Austria rather than to Auschwitz in June 1944

5) Tacit SS agreement that the International Committee of the
Red Cross be permitted in Budapest and environs to shelter
some 3000 Jewish children in homes under the Committee's
protection (August through December 1944)

6) Facilities for the procurement and distribution of foodstuffs
and clothing to some 7000 Jews in labor camps of the Vienna
region (January 1945)

7) The release and arrival in Switzerland of 69 prominent Jews
formerly from Slovakia and Hungary on April 18, 1945.[15]

There are a few small inaccuracies in the list, and it is doubtful
that Kasztner's impact was really as great as McClelland suggests.
However, McClelland is cautious enough to ignore the surrender
of the concentration camps, where Kasztner's influence is perhaps
most debatable, and he takes care to point out that Kasztner's negotiations with Mayer and Becher were not 'exclusively and solely
responsible for the above-mentioned results' before concluding that
they had 'undoubtedly contributed in very large measure to their
attainment'.[16]

Later in the same year McClelland intervened in the dispute about
Kasztner's and Mayer's respective merits. In a letter addressed to
Kasztner himself he refers to the 'indispensable and highly important
role' Kasztner had played 'with Mr Saly Mayer, Kurt Becher . . . and
a few others' in the 'prolonged and difficult negotiations' at the Swiss
border. He gives Kasztner the highest praise:

Had it not been for your original initiative in Budapest in estab-
lishing the necessary contact and 'working agreement' and for
your constant mediatory action throughout (in enemy-occupied
territory, it might be added) it is difficult to imagine that these
negotiations could have taken place at all, or at least that they

could have produced any where near as successful results as they did.[17]

Some of the worst accusations were levelled jointly against Kasztner and our Bergen-Belsen group. Understandably, but less than fairly, both he and we were blamed for surviving while millions died. McClelland, for one, firmly took the side of the living. To an unnamed recipient he writes that neither 'those who organized the departure' nor 'the participants of these transports' can be 'held responsible for the fact that they and not other Jews were saved'. Rather than criticising Kasztner for failing to do the impossible, he pays tribute to what he accomplished in Bergen-Belsen in August and December 1944: 'In view of the desperate circumstances prevailing at that time, and the mentality of the Nazi leaders involved, the very fact of bringing these two groups safely to Switzerland was to be considered as an achievement of great importance.'[18]

Unfortunately, many saw it differently, and before long the voices speaking up for Kasztner were to be drowned by howls of defamation.

Affidavits

Kasztner's vociferous praise of his own achievements went hand in hand with three projects, which occupied a great deal of his time and energy and required numerous journeys to Nuremberg between 1945 and 1948. He intended to recover the property stolen from Hungarian Jews by the SS, to hunt down Eichmann, and to bring the Grand Mufti of Jerusalem, Mohammad Amin al-Husseini, to justice for collaborating with the Nazis in exchange for their undertaking not to allow any Jews to emigrate to Palestine. It was in connection with these projects that he submitted a number of affidavits to various war crime tribunals about four SS officers who had been stationed in Hungary. The officers were Dieter Wisliceny, Hans Jüttner, Hermann Krumey and Kurt Becher. The statements reveal a spectacular change in Kasztner's attitude, with the later ones being surprisingly favourable to notorious Nazis.

Wisliceny first appears in completely negative terms. In 1945 Kasztner attributes any good he may have done purely to self-interest: 'He believed that by keeping me alive and by making some concessions in the campaign against the Jews he might have a defence witness when he and his organisation will have to account for their atrocities.'[19] By 1948 he has become 'the first SS officer who obtained concessions, however minor, that breached the principle of total annihilation which was then in effect'.[20] Kasztner does not seem to realise that the temporary suspension of the deportation in Slovakia had nothing to do with Wisliceny or the bribe he had taken from Weissmandel and Fleischmann for allegedly bringing it about.

Jüttner receives a brief but positive mention in 1948. Kasztner credits him with protests against the murderous treatment of tens of thousands of Jews forced to march from Budapest to Austria in the autumn of 1944. In conclusion Kasztner notes that 'the "Death March" was halted', against Eichmann's protests, 'following the intervention of Becher and Jüttner with H. Himmler'.[21]

The affidavit for Krumey was preceded by a number of letters. In December 1945 Krumey's wife asked Kasztner to help her husband, who was being held in a British prisoner of war camp. Initially Kasztner refused, but eventually he assured her: 'I am prepared at any time to put into writing to what extent your husband assisted us in our rescue enterprise, sometimes at considerable personal risk.'[22] To Krumey himself he promised that he would try to help him regain his freedom and 'start a new life on a new foundation'.[23] In the affidavit, which followed in May 1948, he states that Krumey helped to save 29 Jews in Bratislava and 'counteracted . . . orders which aimed at the annihilation of about 30,000 inmates' in Theresienstadt. With reference to the 15,000 Hungarian Jews in Strasshof, he praises Krumey's 'remarkable good will towards those whose life or death depended to a great extent upon the way he understood and implemented his orders'. Not forgetting his own role, Kasztner adds that his 'proposals to Krumey aimed at alleviating the plight of this special group' were always met 'with full understanding and sympathy on his part'.[24]

Becher figures in two affidavits, apart from the one shared with Jüttner. The first, given in September 1945, deals mainly with the persecution and extermination of Hungarian Jewry, and Becher's part in it is relatively small. As with Wisliceny, Kasztner finds a selfish motivation behind his show of benevolence: 'SS Standartenführer Becher took me under his wings in order to establish an eventual alibi for himself. He was anxious to demonstrate after the fall of 1944 that he disapproved the deportations and exterminations and endeavoured consistently to furnish me with evidence that he tried to save the Jews.'[25]

The second affidavit, dated 14 August 1947, could almost have been written by a different person. It is entirely devoted to Becher and has nothing but praise for him. Once again Kasztner, with slightly different numbers, lists the rescue missions he carried out with Becher's help: the release of the '1,685' from Bergen-Belsen; Himmler's suspension of the exterminations in the autumn of 1944; the prevention of the Arrow Cross massacre of 85,000 residents of the Budapest ghetto; the survival of 55,000 inmates in Bergen-Belsen, 12,000 in Neuengamme and 30,000 in Theresienstadt. He then describes Becher's behaviour in the most flattering terms:

> There can be no doubt that Becher was one of the few SS leaders who had the courage to take a stand against the programme of extermination of the Jews and who tried to save human lives . . . Becher did everything he could, given his position, to save innocent human lives from the blind, murderous rampage of the Nazi leadership. For this reason I never for a minute doubted Kurt Becher's good intentions, even if the form and basis of our negotiations may have been of an objectionable nature . . . In my

opinion, when his case is judged by Allied or German authorities, Kurt Becher deserves the fullest possible consideration.

He ends his impressive eulogy for Becher with a list of equally impressive titles for himself:

> I make this statement not only in my name but also on behalf of the Jewish Agency and the World Jewish Congress. Signed, Dr Rudolf Kasztner, Delegate of the Jewish Agency in Geneva. Former Chairman of the Zionist Organisation in Hungary, 1943–1945. Representative of the Joint Distribution Committee in Budapest.[26]

Ten years later this affidavit sealed Kasztner's tragic fate.

Becher

There is no doubt that Kurt Becher helped Kasztner save thousands of Jews. He was also a Nazi with a dubious history.

Kurt Alexander Becher was born in Hamburg in 1909. After working as an employee in a corn-trading company, he joined the SS in 1934 and the National Socialist Party in 1937. From 1940 he served in the Waffen-SS in Poland and the Ukraine starting as an Unterführer (corporal) and rapidly rising through the ranks to Standartenführer (colonel). In 1944 he was appointed as Himmler's Special Representative in Budapest, and in 1945 as Special Commissioner for All Concentration Camps. From 1945 to 1948 he was in US captivity, suspected of being a war criminal, but not charged. In 1948 he was cleared by a German denazification court. In 1949 he resumed corn-trading in Bremen and by 1960 he was a multimillionaire. He died in Hamburg in 1995.

By most accounts Becher was a good-looking, suave rogue, an unscrupulous operator and slippery double-dealer, a passionate horseman and a passionate social climber. His most sympathetic character witness is Kasztner's daughter Zsuzsi. She met him when he was eighty-six, and was charmed by the 'handsome, attractive, charismatic . . . ladies' man'. Stressing that there is no proof of his participation in the 'final solution', she says: 'Becher was really keen on helping my father save as many Jews as possible.'[27] A similar judgement is recorded by Endre Biss. Discounting the possibility of any wrongdoing, he claims that Becher saved 'several tens of thousands' from death in order 'to atone, in part, for the crimes that had been committed in the name of all his fellow-countrymen'.[28]

Most other observers paint a very dark picture. In 1961–2 the Swiss journalist Kurt Emmenegger published a series of articles designed to demonstrate that Becher was not just an 'extortionist and robber', but a 'Nazi criminal who, through unscrupulous lies, distortions and smart combinations of half-truths, managed like no other to avoid his punishment and even to present himself as a benefactor'. His seemingly humanitarian actions were motivated by his search for 'goods in exchange for human beings, and a great alibi for himself and his Reichsführer'.[29] Resorting to the SS techniques of 'terror and blackmail,' he committed 'theft, robbery, extortion' and 'perjury'. But his worst crime – from which he was trying to divert attention by posing as a great 'Jew saver' – was 'participation in mass murder'.[30]

In the 'Kasztner trial' the judges anticipated Emmenegger's view. They branded Becher a war criminal who had used Eichmann's deportations to strip the Jews of everything they had. District Court judge Benjamin Halevi found that 'Becher's extortion machine could not have functioned without Eichmann's murder machine'. The five judges of the Supreme Court similarly decided that 'the extermination made the extortion more effective'.[31] Kasztner himself drily remarked: 'The interaction between the different branches of the SS was exemplary: the Judenkommando did the killing, the Economic Section collected the money.'[32]

Among the historians who wrote about Becher, Yehuda Bauer is perhaps the most judicious. He calls Becher an 'opportunist Nazi' who may have taken part in mass exterminations but who also rescued masses: 'Becher was a killer probably, a murderer probably, a robber and blackmailer most certainly – and a saviour of maybe hundreds of thousands of Jews.' But Bauer's last word is one of unequivocal condemnation: 'He saved those lives to benefit himself in the long run.'[33]

Becher's wartime activities break down into two separate phases. In Poland and the Ukraine he had been deployed in close proximity to mass murders. In Hungary he engaged in large-scale extortion but also in substantial rescue enterprises. Not the man to pass up an opportunity either to enrich himself or to secure his own survival, Becher employed whatever method was most convenient at any one time.

Between 1940 and 1943 he served in various cavalry units of the Waffen-SS, also known as Death's Head units. These units were designed to carry out police reinforcement duties behind the front line in occupied territories. They undertook 'punitive expeditions' and 'clean-up operations', killing partisans, innocent civilians and, above all, Jews. Their leaders enjoyed a life of luxury and debauchery based on corruption, extortion and robbery, gaining Himmler's approval in the process. One of the most prominent perpetrators was Becher's superior Hermann Fegelein, who later became Hitler's brother-in-law.

In July 1941 Becher's unit was operating in the Pripyat marshes in the Ukraine, with Himmler's orders to exterminate the 'racially and humanly inferior' inhabitants of the region. Fegelein added that communist functionaries were to be hanged in public, suspicious civilians shot, and Jews ghettoised, gunned down or driven into the swamps to drown. About 14,000 Jews died. In August Becher was appointed aide-de-camp to Fegelein. He later claimed that he had never taken part in – or even heard of – the killing campaigns. This is not easy to believe, because shortly before his appointment he had been a platoon sergeant in a cavalry regiment which was 'cleansing' the marshes, and after his appointment his duties included transmitting operational commands and reports on the outcome. Nor is it easy to reconcile his claim that he had sabotaged Himmler's orders with the letter of January 1943 from Himmler commending him for his 'intrepid struggle against subhumanity'. Emmenegger, for one, suspects that Becher had been 'not only an accessory, but an active participant in the annihilation of tens of thousands of Jewish men, women and children'.[34]

Becher arrived in Hungary soon after the occupation of 19 March 1944 as head of the SS 'economic staff', with his subordinates Max Grüson, Herbert Kettlitz and Karl Grabau. Officially he was supposed to be buying military equipment and horses for the SS, but he held secret special powers from Himmler. His main job turned out to be the expropriation of Jews for the benefit of the SS, an opportunity he used also to line his own pockets. He had direct access to Himmler and often tried to enlist his help against Eichmann, with whom he either cooperated or competed, depending on what his own interests demanded at any one time. He rose highest in Himmler's favour by acquiring the Manfred Weiss industrial empire for the SS.

The Manfred Weiss Corporation was Hungary's largest industrial complex, owned by an extended family of Jews, converts and non-Jews. By a combination of intimidation, coercion, blackmail and false promises Becher maneouvred the owners into handing their majority shareholding over to the SS, with him in charge. He also moved into one of the most luxurious Weiss villas with his mistress, Countess Hermine von Platen. In exchange, nine members of the Weiss clan were flown to Switzerland and 32 to Portugal in June 1944. Five were detained in Vienna as hostages to ensure that the truth behind the fake deal remained hidden. The brunt of Becher's machinations was borne by Dr Ferenc Chorin, the head of the Corporation, and Dr Vilmos (Wilhelm) Billitz, one of the senior directors, who was subsequently involved in the deal that saved our lives. Becher later claimed that his prime objective had been to preserve the corporation for the owners, but this did not prevent him transporting all its movable assets to Germany as the Soviet Army advanced towards Budapest.

Having appropriated the Manfred Weiss Corporation, Becher dreamt up more methods of extortion. With his adjutants he set up workshops in which Budapest's best-known artisans produced luxury goods for the SS in return for protective passes but without any wages. In addition, there were the 50 or so rich people he included in the Bergen-Belsen group and who paid him personally a handsome bribe on top of the 1,000 dollars per head he was already receiving for the SS from the Vaada.

In October 1944 Becher was appointed head of the joint Hungarian–German 'evacuation unit', whose task it was to move strategically important goods out of the approaching Soviet army's reach. Under his command some 1,200 trains, 370 ships, and 63,000 cars and trucks carried steel, raw materials, machinery and other cargo to Austria and Germany. Some of these were integrated into the German war industry, but there is some evidence that he was planning to use the rest to set up large industrial installations of his own after the war. In addition, he seized the cash and gold holdings of Hungarian banks and stripped several museums of their works of art.

As the end of the Third Reich approached, Becher needed to solve two interrelated problems: how to cover up his involvement in any Nazi crimes and what to do with the ransom he had received from the Vaada for the Bergen-Belsen group, which was still in his possession. This was where Moshe Schweiger came in. In 1944 Schweiger had been deported from Hungary to Mauthausen. By 1945, starving and exhausted, he was close to death. On 27 April he was summoned to the commander, in whose office a civilian he did not know told him in a whisper that he would 'do something for him'. He was moved to more comfortable quarters, fed and given civilian clothes instead of his prison uniform. On 4 May he was taken by car to the small town of Waldsee on the Danube. There he met the civilian again, who turned out to be Becher and who explained that he had freed him from Mauthausen as a 'personal present for Dr Kasztner'. They travelled to a hunting lodge near Weissenbach in the Salzkammergut region, where Becher and his staff had taken up residence. On the way Becher praised Himmler: 'When you personally meet the Reichsführer you will see what a wonderful person he is.'[35]

On 8 May – incidentally, VE Day and my twelfth birthday – Schweiger wrote a detailed letter to 'all military and civilian authorities of the Allied occupation powers'. Describing himself as a member of the 'Council of Jewish Agency for Palestine' and of the 'Central Committee of the Zionist-Socialist World Association Ichud', he explained that Becher had 'applied himself for a long time to preserving and saving mainly Jewish persons'. For good measure, he added that Becher and his staff – each listed by name – had 'initiated and carried out the really practical rescue work with unstinting personal commitment'.[36] The letter was clearly written under Becher's influence.

A few days later Becher brought Schweiger two suitcases, opening them to reveal six steel boxes which in their turn held twenty-eight bags full of valuables. He explained that this was the complete ransom for our Bergen-Belsen group, which he had promised to return to Kasztner. He then disposed of the six boxes and replaced the bags in the suitcases. He asked Schweiger to take the suitcases to Switzerland, but on 24 May Schweiger, afraid of being accused of looting, gave them for safe keeping to a Jewish captain in the US counter-intelligence unit, CIC 215, who forwarded them to his own superiors.

In October Schweiger joined Kasztner in Geneva. Together they informed the Jewish Agency that assets estimated to be worth 8 million Swiss francs, or 2 million US dollars, had been recovered. They petitioned the US authorities to hand the assets over to the Jewish Agency. In a letter to CIC 215, they described them as 'gold,

cigarette boxes, watches, jewels as well as Napoleons, gold, and platinum' and 'money in pengő', plus 'dollars and gold coins which were
sent to us by the Waad in Istanbul'.[37] This time they valued the collection at 8.7 million Swiss francs. The Joint's general secretary Leavitt,
for his part, pressed the US Secretary of State for the return of the
assets, but got no satisfaction.

On 24 May, under a bed in the hunting lodge at Weissenbach, the
CIC found a much larger hoard of gold, platinum, jewellery, money
and gold teeth, which must have come from a concentration camp;
and in late June five Hungarian Jews, who had travelled with Becher
to the Salzkammergut, delivered a further consignment to the CIC.
The US authorities treated both these finds and the suitcases delivered by Schweiger as 'abandoned property'. Becher was never interrogated about them. At some point in 1946 everything was deposited
in two banks in Salzburg.

Under pressure from the Joint, the US State Department eventually decided to surrender the assets received from Schweiger to the
Jewish Agency. In March 1947 two representatives of the Jewish
Agency, Dagobert Arian and Meir Benzion Meiry, withdrew twenty-
eight bags from the Austrian banks and took them to Switzerland.
When the contents finally arrived in Palestine they proved to be
worth only about 65,000 dollars instead of 2 million, as they should
have been according to the Vaada's original valuation. Becher claimed
that he had returned the entire ransom to Schweiger. Kasztner
supported Becher. Arian maintained that Becher must have spirited
most of it away and misled Schweiger about the value of what he
had left behind. The historian Ronald Zweig mentions two possible
causes of the shortfall – 'inflation and the Hungarian currency reform'
and the inevitable 'loss of value when precious personal possessions
are lumped together' as booty[38] – but he adds that these could account
only for part of the discrepancy. As to the rest, we shall probably
never know for certain what happened.

Soon after leaving Schweiger with the suitcases, Becher was

captured on 12 May by Austrian freedom fighters and handed over
to the US forces. He spent the next six months in the internment
camps of Natternberg and Oberursel. When he was sent to Budapest
to testify in a trial of Hungarian fascists he was terrified of falling
into Soviet hands, but was eventually returned to the US authorities.
In January 1946 he was interrogated for two weeks by CIC Captain
Richard A. Gutman, who suspected him of being a war criminal but
did not have enough evidence to start proceedings. In the same year
Becher was 'wanted by the United States for murder' and in the next
by the Allies for 'torture committed in Budapest and Mauthausen'.
A Hungarian request for his extradition had been rejected by the
Americans, who planned to prosecute him in connection with events
in Mauthausen, but by the time that trial began in 1948 they had
lost interest in him. During his interrogations all the signs that he
might have been involved in atrocities before his deployment to
Hungary were ignored. In 1952 the Swiss police refused his application for an entry permit, and in 1961 the Attorney General of
Israel ruled that if he ever set foot on Israeli soil he would be put in
the dock. In the 1960s a Munich tribunal charged Becher with partic-
ipating in the massacre of Jews in the Pripyat swamps, and as late
as 1982 he stood accused of murder by a court in Bremen. Both
cases were discontinued owing to lack of evidence.

    The most important investigation of Becher from Kasztner's
point of view took place in the German IV Denazification Court
in Nuremberg. The Hamburg Criminal Police had assessed Becher
as 'a convinced, vain and ambitious Nazi, who would break his
promises whenever this was to his advantage', but could supply no
proof of any 'criminal activities'.[39] With the help of his mistress and
his lawyer, Becher rustled up some 50 written testimonials from
business partners and former SS associates intent on whitewashing
his character. In these fabrications he appears as an honest man,
who was always prepared to help people in need regardless of their
nationality or race, who risked his own life protecting Jews, and

who received no material rewards for his humanitarian labours. The decisive affidavit was the one submitted by Kasztner on 14 August 1947.

Shortly before writing the affidavit, Kasztner visited Becher in prison and took an active part in an interrogation conducted by the US intelligence officer Curt Ponger. Ponger's minutes show that at some points he actually put words into Becher's mouth. In particular, with many heavy hints, he got Becher to 'remember' saving the Budapest ghetto with up to 100,000 inmates in December 1944. According to this doubtful recollection, the commander of the German garrison, Karl Pfeffer-Wildenbruch, had cabled Himmler for advice with regard to the Arrow Cross decision to liquidate the ghetto and the Nazi custom of leaving no living Jews behind when they retreated. Himmler had consulted Becher, who had replied: 'Naturally, nothing must happen to the Jews.'[40] Himmler had then issued the orders that saved the ghetto.

Becher was released early in 1948. According to the head of the US investigation department, Walter H. Rapp, the cancellation of the Americans' plan to prosecute Becher was 'solely the result of Kasztner's pleadings' and Kasztner's 'affidavit regarding Becher was the main if not the sole reason' for their 'decision to free him'.[41] In July 1948 Kasztner himself described the outcome of his efforts in a letter to Eliezer Kaplan, the treasurer of the Jewish Agency, as follows: 'Kurt Becher was a former SS colonel and served during the rescue enterprise as liaison officer between me and Himmler. He was released from the Nuremberg prison by the Allied occupation forces as a result of my personal intervention.'[42] He was to pay dearly for this boast.

After the war Becher took every opportunity to present himself as a saviour of Jews. From 1945 to 1948, while in US captivity, in informal conversations as well as formal statements, he claimed credit for persuading Himmler to issue a number of orders which saved many thousands. Some of his most colourful assertions are found in his testimony in the trial of Eichmann in 1961. As the Israeli authorities had refused to grant him safe conduct, he declined an invitation to Jerusalem. Instead he answered a number of written questions before a judge in Bremen. Lacking evidence, it is difficult to disentangle the truth from the exaggerations, distortions and lies to which he resorts to clear himself at the expense of Eichmann. He claims that the assets he had extorted from the Vaada had enabled him 'to reason with Himmler on the basis of contributions by the Jews'. The bogus trucks-for-lives negotiations had given him an opportunity to intervene on behalf of the Jews, even when he 'saw quite clearly that this was not meant as a serious proposal'. He is at his most hypocritical when he explains why he deceived Himmler, although he knew that the Vaada was bluffing: 'My efforts to protect Jewish and politically persecuted persons were the reason why I pretended that I wished to carry out these business deals, because I considered them to be the only chance of obtaining concessions for these people from Himmler.'[43]

Becher's account of his operations reads like a mirror image of Kasztner's report, but the self-glorifying slant is all his own. He is probably telling the truth when he declares that the Bergen-Belsen group was released because he had 'insisted time and again to Himmler that this transport must continue'. His other stories are best taken with a pinch of salt. About the outcome of his talks with Saly Mayer on 21 August 1944 he writes: 'Immediately after I made my report, Himmler ordered that deportations of Jews from Hungary be halted.' In October or November he allegedly 'managed to get Himmler to issue' the directive that put an end to the Holocaust: 'With immediate effect, I prohibit any annihilation of Jews, and on the contrary, I order that weak and sick persons be looked after.' He claims that the 'stoppage of transporting Jews to Austria by foot marches' in November was 'another result of my efforts with Himmler', and that it was he who induced Himmler to repeat his ban on deportations to a reluctant Eichmann in December: 'If until now you have exterminated Jews, from now on, if I order you, as I do now, you must be a fosterer of Jews.' Finally, he chalks up the peaceful surrender of several concentration camps and their 250,000 surviving inmates to the Allies in the spring of 1945 as yet another success of his manipulation of Himmler: 'The measures I carried out in the last weeks of the War to protect the lives of the inmates of concentration camps are also to be considered as a result of this attitude on the part of Himmler which I managed to bring about.' It is likely that Becher's influence on Himmler really did play a part in all these events but, as suggested earlier, he was probably only one player among many.

The most repulsive aspect of Becher's testimonies is his insistence that in his deals with the Hungarian Jews he had been guided exclusively by humanitarian motives. Leaving aside what he may or may not have done behind the eastern front, his extortions in Hungary went far beyond anything he needed to camouflage the rescue operations. Kasztner reports numerous instances of Becher's threats and bullying. Although Eichmann is anything but a reliable witness, he may be telling the truth about Becher urging him to speed up the deportations in order to create a 'nervous climate' which would make it easier to rob the Jews 'more elegantly and speedily'.[44] Becher saved a large number of Jews, but by no means for the noble reasons he invented to justify his far from noble actions.

CHAPTER 13

The Trial

Setting the stage

It was not until December 1947 that Kasztner finally emigrated to Palestine with his wife and child. He had found Europe a more convenient base for his attempts to recover Jewish property stolen by the Germans and his pursuit of Eichmann, and he wanted to clear his name of all accusations before arriving in his new country as a hero. At first things looked promising. The press gave him a 'really warm welcome'. The Mapai, or Labour, leadership was considering him for an important appointment. He had a 'very friendly' conversation with Ben Gurion, and the Jewish Agency supported his participation in the Nuremberg trials more warmly than he had expected.[1] He was penniless and had to borrow money from his brother-in-law Pesach Rudik for a one-bedroom flat in Tel Aviv, but when some friends organised a whip-round he was able to move into more comfortable accommodation, first in Amsterdam Street and then at 6 Emanuel Street, which was to be his last address.

Although Kasztner never became wealthy, he soon rose to a high-ranking position in the Mapai administration. From 1949 he served as director of public relations in the Ministry of Supplies, the Ministry of Transport and the Ministry of Commerce and Industry, each time following in the wake of the peripatetic minister, Dov Joseph. He also worked as editor of the Hungarian-language paper *Új Kelet* and as head of Hungarian broadcasts on Kol Yisrael state radio. He narrowly missed being elected to the Israeli Parliament (the Knesset) on two occasions. In 1949 Mapai won with 46 seats, but he was 59th on the list of candidates. In 1951, when Mapai won with 45 seats, he was 53rd.

Then a seemingly ludicrous slur escalated into a court battle that not only destroyed Kasztner himself but also shook the state of Israel to its very foundations. In fact, the 'Kasztner trial', as it is inaccurately called, proved to be the most sensational and controversial ever to take place in Israel, not even excepting that of Adolf Eichmann.

What made the 'Kasztner trial' so significant was that it forced Israelis to confront the Holocaust and its impact on themselves in public and for the first time. In the process, one of the deepest unspoken divisions in Israeli society turned into open conflict. Briefly, the Jews who had settled in Palestine before the war and watched the Holocaust from a safe distance felt impatient with the Jews of Europe who had allowed the Nazis to drive them 'like lambs to the slaughter' while the survivors from Europe, in their turn, struggled to get over the loss of their loved ones and their own sufferings. In addition, there was guilt – on one side for failing to give help when it was needed, on the other side for surviving when so many died. As the trauma was brought to the surface, the political parties, pressure groups and individuals with vested interests – gleefully accompanied by the razzmatazz of the press – proceeded to stir it up with a vengeance. The result, in Yechiam Weitz's words, was an explosive mix of 'genuine guilt feelings juxtaposed with a manipulative and cynical exploitation of these emotions for political purposes and personal gain.'[2]

The chain of unfortunate events was set in motion by one Malkiel Gruenwald, a Hungarian Jew aged seventy-two and an active member of the Orthodox Mizrahi movement, who had emigrated to Palestine from Vienna two years before the war. A former journalist, he now owned a small hotel in Jerusalem. His son had died in the Israeli War of Independence in 1948. His daughter, who had belonged to the Lehi Group, or Stern Gang, later committed suicide. He had lost the rest of his family in the Holocaust. His favourite pastime was writing, mimeographing and personally distributing a series of pamphlets called 'Letters to my Friends in the Mizrahi', attacking a wide range of public figures and policies, rooting out real or imagined crimes and corruption, preferably on the part of Mapai. Tom Segev describes Gruenwald's writings as 'an angry brew of political commentary that revived forgotten conflicts, old grudges and all kinds of dusty scandals.'[3] He was disliked for his cantankerousness, but as a rule not taken seriously. Kasztner was the target of his 17th newsletter, published in the summer of 1952.

Gruenwald was not one for understatement. He starts his invective at top volume:

> My dear friends, the stench of a carcass fills my nostrils! This will be the choicest funeral! Dr Rudoph Kastner must be liquidated! For three years I have been waiting for the moment to unmask this careerist who grew fat on Hitler's lootings and murders. Because of his criminal machinations and collaborations with the Nazis I consider him implicated in the murder of our beloved brothers.[4]

He goes on to assert that Kasztner 'saved no fewer than fifty-two of his own relatives', while 'hundreds of other Jews – most of whom had converted to Christianity – bought their rescue from Kasztner by paying millions!' Leaving 'thousands of senior Zionists' to die, Kasztner had 'saved the members of Mapai' and 'people with connections', making 'a fortune in the process'. He had helped Becher evade justice in order to make sure that his fellow-criminal would not 'reveal to the international court their deals and their joint acts of robbery.'[5]

Initially nobody took much notice of Gruenwald's diatribe. But libelling a high-ranking government official was tantamount to libelling the state, and an election was looming on the horizon. Chaim Cohn, who was both Attorney-General and Minister of Justice in the Mapai government, filed charges of criminal defamation against Gruenwald. Kasztner was to be the chief witness for the prosecution. Cohn expected an easy victory. Had he foreseen the real outcome he might well have listened to the voices that advised him to let sleeping dogs lie.

Kasztner himself was in two minds. He asked Cohn not to proceed with the case. Ten years after his death his widow Bogyó said in an interview: 'Rezső did not want the trial, but he was in an impossible situation . . . He was told he had to agree to the government's submission of a libel suit on his behalf or resign from his position . . . I told him, "Resign!" But he answered that he had no choice.'[6] At the same time a part of him wanted to fight. Urged by his friend Dezső Hermann, he was only too willing to seize this 'chance to become part of history'[7]. Bogyó's cousin Rivka Bar-Yosef thought that he saw the case as a means of 'restoring to him the status of hero and saint'.[8] According to his brother-in-law Pesach Rudik, he expected to walk out of the court as a national hero. Weitz believes that, for all his apprehension, 'his adventurous spirit and his craving to be in the limelight got the upper hand. He saw the trial as an opportunity to escape the drab comfort of his job as spokesman of a government ministry and to attain the position he deserved.'[9] The indictment was filed on 25 May 1953 under 'Criminal case No. 124/53'. The trial opened in the Jerusalem District Court on 1 January 1954.

The judge was Benjamin Halevi, a German-born Israeli in his forties. A few months earlier, in a military tribunal, he had pronounced exceptionally harsh sentences on fifteen young militants charged with terrorism. The sentences were followed by an outcry from the Right, who accused Halevi of trying to ingratiate himself with the Mapai leadership. In December 1953 he was passed over in the appointments to the Supreme Court. In an unusual move he approached Prime Minister Ben Gurion and threatened to resign as district judge, but was persuaded to continue. In 1954 he was passed over again. In 1961 he was to serve on the panel of three judges who tried Adolf Eichmann, and two years later to be appointed, finally, to the Supreme Court. In 1969 he became a member of the Knesset, representing the right-wing Likud formation, which he left in 1977. He died in 1996.

The prosecutor acting on behalf of the state against Gruenwald was Amnon Tel, Assistant Attorney of the District of Jerusalem. He was inexperienced and ill-prepared for what was to follow. On 1 June 1954 he was joined by Attorney-General Cohn himself, but neither proved a match for the defence counsel, Shmuel Tamir.

Tamir, born in Israel and in his early thirties, was a right-wing radical. He was also a brilliant advocate who did not suffer from an excess of scruples. Coming from a family of Revisionists, he belonged to the violent Irgun group before he helped to found the Herut party, which in turn later became part of the Likud party under Menahem Begin. Tamir was bitterly opposed to Mapai, and its leader, Ben Gurion, was one of his pet hates. By the time of the trial he was a leading political lawyer, having defended various right-wing cases. In Segev's words, 'he was a crafty politician, an attorney with a quick eye and a sharp tongue, with a craving for dramatic intrigues and media attention'.[10] Driven by a fierce political ambition, Tamir hoped to bring down the Mapai government and head a right-wing Greater Israel in the not too distant future. He did not achieve that aim, but his performance in the trial contributed a great deal to the eventual demise of Mapai rule. It also helped his election to the Knesset in 1969 and his appointment as Minister of Justice under Begin in 1977. He died in 1987.

When Gruenwald asked Tamir to defend him, Tamir was not interested either in the case itself or in the stamp collection the impoverished client offered him as a fee. However, he immediately recognised that he could use the trial for his own political ends. He agreed on two conditions: one was that he should be given a completely free hand in his conduct of the defence, the other that he should be allowed to widen the libel issue into an investigation of the conduct of the Yishuv leaders during the Holocaust.

The case for the prosecution

After two postponements the trial opened in earnest on 18 February 1954. For three days Kasztner, calm, confident and proud, delivered yet another detailed account of his achievements from the rescue of the Bergen-Belsen group to the peaceful handover of concentration camps to the Allies, and he listed the privileges he had been granted by the Germans – exemption from the yellow star, permission to use the telephone, right to travel – which made his rescue missions possible. He clearly enjoyed the limelight. The press was full of praise for his heroic deeds. The judge was so impressed that he asked Gruenwald whether he wished to withdraw his accusations. But Tamir's cross-examination turned the tables.

From the outset Tamir treated Kasztner as if he had been the accused, while Kasztner, being a witness, was unable to resort to the legal defences that are normally available to the defendant. Recognising where Kasztner was most vulnerable, Tamir began by attacking him for testifying in favour of Becher. Kasztner explained that between 1945 and 1948 he had worked in London and Nuremberg, giving evidence – or, as he put it rather grandiloquently, acting as 'advisor in matters pertaining to Jewish extermination' – in the War Crime Trials, but he rejected Tamir's accusation:

I gave no testimony in Nuremberg in favour of Becher. I gave it neither to the International Court nor to any of its institutions or officials. Gruenwald's statement in his pamphlet that I went to Nuremberg to save Becher is a total lie. The German court of de-Nazification of Becher invited me to give them a

testimony about Becher when I was in Nuremberg. I refused.
I had no desire to appear before any Germans. I'd had enough
of Germans during the war. I agreed, however, to give them a
sworn affidavit, which I sent them. It is a total lie that I helped
Kurt Becher escape punishment in Nuremberg. I gave no testimony or affidavit in his favour.[11]

On the second day of the cross-examination, Tamir asked whether
the 'sworn affidavit' had been 'in favour of Becher or against him'.
Kasztner's reply was: 'Neither in favour nor against. I tried only to
tell the truth.' When Kasztner affirmed that his testimony had been
'in no way decisive' in securing Becher's release, Tamir retorted: 'I
tell you now that owing to your personal intervention, Kurt Becher
was released from prison at Nuremberg.' Kasztner shouted: 'That's
a dirty lie!'[12] At this point Tamir produced Kasztner's letter of July
1948 to Eliezer Kaplan, in which he had described Becher's release
as 'the result of my personal intervention' with the occupying forces.[13]
After some prevarication Kasztner admitted that he had 'phrased the
letter somewhat boastfully' because at the time in question Becher
had offered to 'hand over certain Jewish money to the state of Israel'
and he wanted Kaplan to take the offer seriously. While accepting
responsibility for 'the incautious wording of a letter',[14] he continued
to deny any intention of helping Becher.

In a technical sense Kasztner was telling the truth, as was proved
in another court case. In July 1955 Tamir lodged a complaint of
perjury against him. This case was heard in the Jerusalem Magistrate's
Court, with Kasztner being represented by a more competent lawyer,
Micha Caspi. Caspi argued that Kasztner had not lied in the District
Court, because the affidavit he had given for Becher was addressed
to a German denazification court and not to the International Military
Tribunal. On 16 March 1956 Judge Moshe Perez acquitted Kasztner
of perjury. Unfortunately, by then Judge Halevi in the District Court
had already announced his own ill-advised verdict.

In the main trial, Kasztner's letter to Kaplan had been disclosed to the court and the defence, but in the heat of the debate Tamir had managed to make it appear as a momentous new discovery. As for Kasztner, the impression created by his failed attempt to hide what he had earlier paraded as a great personal success was devastating: a senior Israeli official had saved a German war criminal from his deserved punishment, and had lied about it under oath. This was the turning point of the trial. From now on Judge Halevi no longer believed anything Kasztner said. And if Kasztner had lied about helping Becher, Halevi concluded, he must be lying about many even graver offences.

As Tamir continued his relentless cross-examination Kasztner lost all his confidence. The stress made him ill, and the judge interrupted the proceedings several times to allow him to recover. Outside the court, the right-wing press was having a field day. The noisiest agitation was carried on by Tamir's greatest ally, Uri Avneri, the editor of the weekly news magazine *HaOlam HaZeh*, which specialised in campaigns against real or alleged abuses by the establishment. Tamir himself had by now openly declared that his true aim was not to ensure Gruenwald's acquittal, but to bring Kasztner, and with him the Jewish Agency and Mapai, to justice. In fact he was now literally calling Kasztner 'the accused'. Kasztner, for his part, was not helped by his own behaviour. He had begun his plea with great self-assurance, expecting at last to receive the recognition that he believed was his due. Now that things were not going his way, as Segev puts it, he 'lost his temper, shouted, became flustered.'[15]

One of the worst mistakes of the prosecution was calling prominent public figures who knew very little about Kasztner's missions to testify against Gruenwald, rather than inviting people who had actually helped Kasztner save lives. With such friends in the witness box, Kasztner needed no enemies. The best-known was Joel Palgi, the only one of the three parachutists to survive the war. Palgi was regarded as a national hero but had never ceased to feel guilty about his failure in Hungary. His attitude to Kasztner was profoundly ambivalent. According to Tamir, Kasztner had delivered Palgi and Goldstein to the Gestapo in order to save his own skin, and Palgi had collaborated with the Gestapo under Kasztner's influence. Palgi did his best to defuse these charges, but Tamir entangled him in a web of contradictions that proved extremely damaging for Kasztner.

The fate of the parachutists touched a particularly raw nerve in Israel. The three young Jews who flew into German-occupied Europe to beard the Nazis had become part of a heroic myth, on a level with the rebels of Masada who chose mass suicide rather than enslavement by the Romans, the inmates of the Warsaw ghetto who died while resisting the Germans, and the militant groups who fought the British in Palestine. All these embattled Jews were seen as the opposite of the submissive millions who had gone meekly into the gas chambers, and also of the alleged wheeler-dealers who tried to make compromises with the Nazis. Hanna Szenes is still venerated as one of the supreme Jewish martyrs, although Goldstein is almost forgotten and Palgi's image has become somewhat tarnished. In any case, Palgi's confused testimony failed to prove that Kasztner had not betrayed them.

Another key witness who turned out to be less than helpful to the prosecution was Joel Brand. Although he had intended to refute Gruenwald's accusations, he undermined Kasztner throughout his testimony. This was probably a reaction to his own predicament, rather than a deliberate attempt to hurt Kasztner. Brand was bitter and disillusioned. Life in Israel had fulfilled none of his hopes. He was haunted by the miscarriage of his Istanbul mission. While he had failed, Kasztner had scored some spectacular successes. While he was imprisoned in the Middle East, Kasztner was having an affair with his wife in Hungary. Rather than giving a balanced statement in support of Kasztner's merits, he attacked his own supposed enemies. In particular he claimed that the leaders of the Jewish Agency had deliberately engineered his capture by the British in Syria in order to endear themselves to the mighty colonial power. Brand's paranoia was no more help to Kasztner's cause than Palgi's equivocation.

Attack the best defence?

After a recess the trial resumed on 1 June 1954. Kasztner had changed a great deal since his first confident statement. As one of the papers reported, 'he was pale, and looked as if he had just gotten out of bed after a long illness. He spoke in a soft, low voice.'[16] But Tamir gave no quarter. Forging ahead along the Becher trail, he charged Kasztner: 'You not only saved Becher from the International court in Nuremberg, but . . . you gave a sworn affidavit to the de-Nazification court of the Germans, and also saved him from their punishment.' Kasztner replied: 'No! That's untrue!' Tamir then set him a trap: 'Dr Kasztner, will you agree with me that to intervene in favour of a high S.S. Nazi officer and to bring about his release is a criminal act from our national point of view?' Kasztner concurred: 'My answer is positive. It is a crime from a national point of view.'[17] During the recess Tamir had unearthed Kasztner's affidavit of 14 August 1947. Having led Kasztner to condemn himself in advance, he now read out the incriminating document to the court. Before Kasztner could recover from this blow he continued his relentless onslaught: 'You have agreed with me that any intervention by a Jewish official on behalf of a high S.S. officer, including Becher, is a national crime. Now that it has been revealed that you did exactly that, do you agree with me that you are a national criminal?' Kasztner's feeble reply was: 'That is your version.'[18] He had lost the contest.

It was bad enough for Kasztner to have helped a Nazi war criminal. Had he not been in court as a witness, he could even have been indicted, and possibly sentenced to death, under the Nazis and Nazi Collaborators (Punishment) Law introduced in Israel in 1950. But there was more. He had committed the further offence of signing the affidavit as the representative of the highest Jewish organisations. It is not entirely clear why he had done so. Weitz, for example, believes that he had 'conferred on himself various titles, including some he had no right to flaunt, in order to inflate his own importance'.[19] Kasztner himself told the court that with the benefit of hindsight he would not have used those titles, but he also claimed that he had acted with the knowledge and agreement of the relevant officials:

> Before going to Nuremberg I sat with the people of the Jewish Agency and with people from the Congress to discuss what to do to bring the Nazis, particularly those who participated in the extermination of the Jews, to trial. There was also a question of what to do about the few cases in which we received help from the Nazis. I mentioned then especially Becher, and the court knows my opinion on him. I asked if in case of a request to give an opinion on this matter I may say, not only in my name, but also on behalf of the Jewish Agency or the Congress, that he deserves consideration for his help in rescuing the Jews. I got a positive answer.[20]

The 'people' in question were Chaim Barlas and Eliahu Dobkin of the Jewish Agency, and Maurice Perlzweig and Gerhart Riegner of the World Jewish Congress. Dobkin actually appeared before the court, but denied ever hearing of Becher.

By the time the Attorney-General began his cross-examination on behalf of the prosecution, Kasztner was totally demoralised. As Hansi Brand recalls, he had 'managed to keep a grip on himself' until he was confronted with his affidavit in favour of Becher, but at that point 'he totally lost his self-confidence'.[21] He tried to backtrack and to stick to his guns simultaneously: 'I don't think I phrased my testimony in the most truthful manner. If under the pressure of demagogic cross-examination I said here and there a few things for which I am truly sorry – it doesn't change my basic attitude in the matter.'[22] But by now, in Halevi's eyes, he was a complete liar and worse. And Tamir, who had reduced him to this condition, began his final assault.

When Kasztner visited Kolozsvár on 3 May 1944, Tamir asserted, he knew all about Auschwitz but deliberately withheld it from the Jewish community in return for Eichmann's promise to release a few VIPs. Kasztner's silence had lulled the Jews there and elsewhere into a false sense of security, so that they willingly boarded the trains to Auschwitz, rather than resisting or trying to escape. Tamir called a large number of witnesses, many of them from Kolozsvár, who had lost their relatives and almost their own lives in the death camps. They all accused Kasztner of keeping them in the dark or actively misleading them about the true purpose of the deportations. Jacob Freifeld, for example, asserted that the Jewish leaders had 'knowingly sent' his family 'to death' in order to 'save themselves'. Yechiel Shmueli affirmed that the Jews had not resisted being put on the train 'because we had all been told that we were being taken to Kenyérmező to work'. David Rozner said that if Kasztner had 'showed himself in the street' after the war 'he would have been killed' because 'he was the man who misled the Jews to believe in the good intentions of the Germans'.[23] In all these testimonies, in Weitz's words, Kasztner was 'depicted as a cynical, opportunistic man, prominent in the community, who instead of protecting the lives of his "flock", had abandoned them to their death for the sake of a handful of privileged friends and family'.[24]

One of Tamir's key witnesses was Moshe Krausz, who used his testimony to settle accounts with Kasztner, the Mapai party and the Jewish Agency. He argued that Kasztner's original intentions might have been good, but his ambition to become the supreme power in the Jewish community had turned him into a Nazi collaborator. The release of the Bergen-Belsen group was a devious German ploy to blind the Jewish population to the truth about Auschwitz and to sow discord among the Jewish leaders. Kasztner suffered from 'megalomania' and had 'no conscience and no consideration for others' when it came to realising his own aims.[25] For his part, Krausz claimed to have found better ways of saving Jews, and it is true that he played an important part in the large-scale rescue operations of Lutz, Wallenberg and other diplomats from neutral countries. However, it must be remembered that Krausz and Kasztner were fierce competitors and that Krausz himself had been heavily criticised for his irregular methods.

Tamir's star witness was Hanna Szenes's mother, Kató, who had emigrated to Israel after the war. She stated that every time she had tried to see Kasztner to beg for his help in freeing Hanna, his secretary had sent her away. Tamir made the most of Hanna's legendary status to blacken Kasztner's character. He glorified her as the true Israeli who was prepared to fight and die, in contrast to the supine Jew from the diaspora, who tried, often in vain, to survive by compromise and appeasement. In Weitz's words, he crudely but effectively played 'Hanna Szenes, symbol of dedication, self-sacrifice and heroism' off against 'Kasztner, the symbol of obsequiousness and collaboration'.[26]

Gruenwald's own testimony was as full of hate and anger as his pamphlet. His general drift corresponded exactly to Tamir's tactic, but his sad mixture of genuine pain and obsessive bombast was all his own. While his lament for fifty-two members of his family gassed in Majdanek and Auschwitz seemed sincere, the hotchpotch of bluster and pedantry in his indictment of Kasztner was typical of his customary rhetoric: 'The man the Nazis used to carry out the vilest historical crime was, based on my investigation, and as I became convinced, Rudolf Kasztner.'[27] In short, Gruenwald's testimony was as confused as one would have expected, but it served Tamir well.

After the witness statements Tamir recited a lengthy summary. He began by outlining 'how an idealistic, Zionist youth like Kasztner, owning a few flaws, but full of talent, deteriorated into a trusted chum of the Nazi leaders'. He placed special emphasis on the group Kasztner had selected in May 1944 from the Kolozsvár ghetto to be rescued, while all the others were deported. Kasztner had sacrificed 'a community of twenty thousand Jews . . . in order to save 380 of his friends and relatives'. The release of this group – and by implication the whole 'VIP train' from Bergen-Belsen – was the price Eichmann had paid Kasztner for keeping the Jewish masses in ignorance of their true destination, so that they would do nothing to save themselves before they were all 'sealed and delivered to the gas chamber'. That was how 'Kasztner's collaboration' had 'accomplished the complete extermination of the people'.[28]

Assuming the posture of the psychologist, Tamir spoke of Kasztner's 'sickly ambition to be considered a big shot, a leader of Jews', which was the cause of 'his blindness, his lies, and his terrible crimes.' He granted that until May 1944, Kasztner had on the whole meant well: 'He was a self-seeking, slippery fellow, but basically his intentions were to save Jews.' When Eichmann offered him the chance of saving the 'prominents', the 'little journalist from Cluj' allowed his ambition to 'confuse his values'. He accepted the offer, even though Eichmann had made it conditional on his help with the destruction of hundreds of thousands. The deportations had begun in mid-May, and from then Kasztner's 'entanglement deepened, his crime grew'. Finally, 'in the last months of the war, Kasztner became the agent for the whole Nazi gang – the most effective Jewish agent in their ranks . . . their trusted ally and apologist'.[29]

Tamir then reinforced this devastating, if far from accurate, charge by homing in again on Kasztner's relationship with Becher. Building on Kasztner's own unfortunate equivocations, he alleged that 'in delivering Kurt Becher, one of the arch-killers, from judgement in Nuremberg', Kasztner had 'brazenly tried to cover up his own crime'. He asked the judge to note that Kasztner had 'perjured himself maliciously' and that 'he and his colleagues' had 'conspired together to conceal from this court and from the whole world the historical truth'. Reflecting on 'the enormity of the collaboration with Nazi killers', he demanded that Kasztner be 'put on trial by the Israeli government in accordance with the law against Nazis and their collaborators'[30] – a law that included the option of the death penalty.

In fact Tamir had bigger fish to fry than either Gruenwald or

Kasztner. He announced quite openly: 'Though I am here to prove the guilt of Kasztner, I say that his responsibility is lesser than that of the leaders of our free Jewish world.'[31] Drawing on all the tactical skills at his disposal, he turned the defence of his small-time client into a sensational attack on the Israeli establishment. By dubious analogies he extended the scope of Gruenwald's charges to the wartime leaders of the Jews in Palestine. He asserted that Kasztner had not acted on his own: 'He participated in a destructive system which was being developed at the time by other Jewish institutions, including the Jewish Agency and the JDC, which suppressed information about the Holocaust, prevented revolt and directly assisted the Germans'. It was an 'inevitable result of the system' that 'Kasztner became an entangled collaborator – a Nazi agent'.[32]

Of course, the 'system' as Tamir called it, also aimed at more than simply clearing Kasztner's name. This is how the jurist Asher Maoz sums up the situation: 'In the same way as Tamir wished to use Kasztner as a means of striking at the leadership of the Yishuv ... the prosecution was also motivated otherwise than by the mere desire to convict Gruenwald. By absolving Kasztner they would also be absolving the Yishuv leadership of the accusations raised against it.'[33] Both sides, then, were using Kasztner for their own purposes, but Tamir was more effective.

During the Holocaust the Jewish community in Palestine had watched events in Europe with mixed feelings. As vague rumours solidified into precise knowledge of the genocide, they felt not only horror and pity but also contempt for their fellow-Jews in the diaspora, who had either tried – and often failed – to survive by lying low or had gone to Auschwitz like 'lambs to the slaughter'. Well into the 1950s they still saw armed resistance, ending in death, as the only acceptable alternative. The most admired models were the inmates of the Warsaw ghetto, who lost their lives but saved their honour by fighting a hopeless battle against overwhelming German forces. It took a long time – and not least the after-effects of the trial itself – for Israelis to realise that there was a valid third way.

Palestine at the time of the Holocaust was administered by Britain under a League of Nations mandate. Jewish attitudes were roughly divided between mainstream centre-left Zionism, represented by the Mapai party and the Jewish Agency, and Revisionism, represented mainly by militant right-wing groups such as Irgun Zvai Leumi (or Etzel) and the Stern gang (or Lehi). Mapai and the Jewish Agency consisted largely of older immigrants from Europe. The Revisionist groups included more young people born in Palestine (*sabras*). During the war Mapai and the Jewish Agency cooperated with the British in the struggle against the Nazis, hoping that compliance and compromise would finally lead to a free Israel within agreed borders. The Revisionists, on the other hand, were dreaming of a Greater Israel, achieved through force against the British, and both Irgun and the Stern gang committed acts of terrorism. After the war Mapai emerged as the dominant party in the Israeli parliament, and the leaders of the Jewish Agency formed the government. Revisionism gave rise to the Herut party, which later became part of Likud. By attacking Kasztner, Tamir was hoping to topple the Mapai government and to bring Herut to power.

Both during and after the war the Revisionists accused the Jewish Agency and Mapai of sharing the cowardly mentality of the Jews of the Galut (or diaspora), while they saw themselves as proud fighters for a new Israel. Accordingly, Tamir set out to discredit the leaders of the Jewish Agency and Mapai by drawing parallels between them and Kasztner. Kasztner's collaboration with the Germans, he said, equalled the collaboration of the Jewish Agency with the British. Both had wilfully suppressed the news of Auschwitz, and just as Kasztner's silence had sent the Jews of Hungary to their deaths, the Jewish Agency's silence resulted in a missed opportunity either to rouse the Jews in Palestine against the British occupation or to force the Allies to take some action to save the Jews of Europe. The officials of the

Jewish Agency in Istanbul and Palestine, particularly Sharett, had conspired against Joel Brand. By having him arrested in Syria, they had sabotaged a mission that might have saved hundreds of thousands, in order to satisfy the British, who wanted to prevent any mass immigration to Palestine. Fuelled by righteous anger and calculating ambition, Tamir fulminated against 'this overt crime done by the great men of the Jewish Agency'.[34] Continuing to follow parallel lines where there were none, he arrived at the alleged common denominator: the desire for power. Just as Kasztner had betrayed the Hungarian Jews because of his ambition, the Yishuv's 'official institutions submitted to the British Government' and abandoned 'European Jewry in the most horrible hour' because of 'their utter refusal to give up the internal rule' they exercised in Palestine.[35]

So much for history, but Tamir was more interested in the present. Given that many of the wartime Yishuv leaders were holding important positions in the Mapai-led establishment of the new state of Israel, by discrediting their behaviour in the 1940s he was trying to destabilise the Mapai-led government of the 1950s. Since the war, he argued, that same establishment had created a 'curtain of deceit and silence'[36] around events during the Holocaust. The silence was intended to cover up Kasztner's misdeeds, but had much wider implications. 'All the powerful government institutions', Tamir explained, were protecting Kasztner 'for fear he would reveal all the facts known to him about another collaboration – the Jewish Agency collaboration with the British – which sabotaged the rescue of Europe's Jews and contributed to their annihilation'.[37] By this last manoeuvre, Tamir succeeded in making the Mapai government of his own time an accessory to the alleged earlier crimes of the Jewish Agency, which in turn were revealed through the alleged crimes of Kasztner. It was the point Tamir had wanted to reach ever since Gruenwald had asked for his help.

Kasztner's closing speech was short and subdued. He had been worn down by Tamir's incessant accusations and Halevi's hostile questions and comments. In addition, the prosecution had handled the case ineptly, the right-wing press was demonising him, and more and more people were beginning to regard him as a criminal. He had weakened his own case by being too complacent in the early stages of the trial and too defensive when the tide turned against him. He had done himself the most serious damage by equivocating about his support for Becher. Replying to the central charge of having kept quiet about Auschwitz, he conceded that, before the German occupation in March 1944, the Vaada had 'failed to prepare the ground for underground actions that would have enabled us to properly warn the Jews of Hungary and perhaps also to carry out acts of resistance'. He did not accept that this amounted to collaboration or betrayal, and insisted on his and his associates' good intentions: 'Within our limited possibilities, we did our best.' But, abandoning his swagger, he admitted that 'compared with the dimensions of the catastrophe, that was very little'.[38]

Outside the court the public followed the proceedings with mounting suspense. While Sharett, Ben Gurion and their Mapai associates kept their heads down, Herut and the press supporting it laid into Kasztner with increasing savagery. Tamir had made the most of the Revisionist stereotype. His encounters with Kasztner had assumed the proportions of a mythical struggle between the young, brave, upstanding *sabra* and the grovelling, conniving and doomed diaspora Jew. When the judge retired to consider his verdict, the suspense gradually died down. When he delivered it several months later, the effect was explosive.

The judgment

On 21 June 1955, nine months after closing the hearings, Judge Halevi returned to the Jerusalem District Court from his seclusion. Kasztner waited nervously on his own in the Moriah boarding house nearby. From 8 am until 10 pm Halevi read out extracts from his 300-page judgment, which proved to be as devastating as it was unfair. Maoz calls it 'one of the most provocative and controversial judgments in the history of the State'; Segev describes it as 'one of the most heartless in the history of Israel, perhaps the most heartless ever'.[39]

Halevi turned Gruenwald's rambling diatribe against Kasztner into four specific charges: '1. Collaboration with the Nazis; 2. "Indirect murder" or "preparing the ground for murder" of Hungary's Jews; 3. Sharing plunder with a Nazi war criminal; 4. Saving that war criminal from punishment after the war.'[40] He echoed Tamir's contentions in almost every respect. He noted that 'the masses of Jews from Hungary's ghettos boarded the deportation trains in total obedience, ignorant of the real destination and trusting the false information that they were being transferred to work camps in Hungary'.[41] These falsehoods had been disseminated by the Jewish councils and in particular by Kasztner. The same Jewish leaders who had 'spread or confirmed the rumours' about relocation within Hungary and 'failed to organise any resistance or sabotage' did not 'accompany their brothers and sisters to Auschwitz', but 'were almost all included in the Bergen-Belsen transport'.[42] If Kasztner had done his duty of warning his fellow-Jews, the Nazis could not have deported them as expeditiously as they had done. By concealing what he knew he had prevented the victims from trying to escape to Romania, going undergound or resisting. Consequently he had 'oiled the wheels of the destruction machine as a whole' and 'made an important contribution to its overall efficiency'.[43] Because he had kept the 'complete information' he possessed to himself, 'about half a million men, women and children boarded the trains that carried them to Auschwitz, unknowingly and as victims of a malicious deception'.[44]

Moving on to motives, Halevi explained that Kasztner had knowingly 'abandoned the large majority of Hungary's Jews to their fate' in order to save a few 'favoured individuals'.[45] He had succumbed to a 'temptation' that he was unable to resist. When Eichmann's cat-

and-mouse game had made him feel most vulnerable he was offered 'the opportunity to save six hundred souls from the impending Holocaust and a chance to somewhat increase their number through further payment or negotiations'. He accepted, even though Eichmann's condition was absolute secrecy, so that the deportations could proceed without encountering panic or resistance. When invited by Eichmann to select those 'people who were most important and deserving of rescue in his eyes',[46] he chose his closest family, his other relatives and friends, and some Jewish community leaders. Therefore, by agreeing to the rescue of 'the privileged' at the price of his silence, Kasztner had not merely 'accepted the extermination of the ordinary people',[47] but actually helped with the deportations and, consequently, the exterminations. Thus, 'the collaboration of the leader of the Jewish rescue committee with the head of the destroyers of the Hungarian Jews in the deportation of these victims to Auschwitz in exchange for the rescue of the privileged' had been 'a criminal collaboration in the full sense of the word'.[48]

Halevi then pronounced what may be regarded as one of the most outrageous judgments ever heard in a court of law in the modern world. Kasztner, he said, may have hoped to save more Jews, but he regarded his own approach as the only one likely to produce results. When Eichmann offered him the opportunity, 'he considered the rescue of the most important Jews as a great personal and Zionist success, a success that would also justify his own conduct'. It was therefore 'no wonder' that he 'accepted the gift without hesitation'. But it was a Greek gift, as Halevi underlined by quoting the Latin tag 'timeo Danaos et dona ferentes'. He then detonated his bomb-shell: 'By accepting this gift, K. sold his soul to Satan.'[49]

Halevi later regretted using such a loaded expression, but the harm was irrevocably done. In the overwrought atmosphere surrounding the trial, with emotions running high and ratcheted even higher by Tamir's oratory inside the court and the agitation of the anti-Mapai press outside it, he had not only supplied an irresistible headline but, far overstepping the mark, inflicted a stigma that still haunts Kasztner's memory.

The next highly sensitive issue addressed by Halevi was that of the three parachutists. He argued that Kasztner had betrayed the parachutists by persuading Goldstein to give himself up to the Gestapo, failing to prevent the deportation of Goldstein and Palgi, and taking no action to save Hanna Szenes from her ordeal. The reason was that 'his most vital interests – the rescue operation, the fate of the rescued, the fate of his relatives, and his own safety – compelled Kasztner to be loyal to the ruler'.[50] It is indeed true that Kasztner had to keep the parachutists at arm's length, but the reason was anything but loyalty to the Nazis.

Halevi continued his demolition job by pronouncing judgment on the Becher affair: 'Kasztner was knowingly lying in his testimony before this court when he denied he had interceded on behalf of Becher. Moreover, he concealed the important fact that he interceded for Becher in the name of the Jewish Agency and the World Jewish Congress.'[51] He dismissed Kasztner's comment in his affidavit on Becher's 'good intentions' as 'a deliberately false statement made in favour of a war criminal to save him from trial and punishment'.[52] Looking for the lowest possible motive, he decided that Kasztner's support had been his payment for Becher's silence about his own misdeeds: 'Just as the Nazi criminals knew they needed an alibi and hoped to achieve it by the rescue of a few Jews at the eleventh hour, so K. as a Nazi collaborator was concerned to procure an alibi for himself.'[53]

In his summary Halevi reiterated that Kasztner had lied when he claimed that he had done all he could for the parachutists, and likewise when he denied his intention to help Becher. As for the cessation of the gassings, the surrender of the concentration camps, the preservation of the Budapest ghetto, even the release of our Bergen-Belsen group, he decided that in each case Himmler's orders had been due to factors other than Becher's influence, and that Kasztner had made these false statements in order to provide both Becher and himself with alibis. On three of the charges he dismissed the case of the prosecution: Gruenwald, he ruled, had proved that Kasztner collaborated with the Nazis, aided the murder of Hungarian Jewry and saved a war criminal from punishment. In respect of the allegation that Kasztner had stolen Jewish property together with Becher, he found Gruenwald guilty of libel and sentenced him to a symbolic fine of one Israeli pound.

The judgment was followed by fierce debates in the Israeli press and parliament. While Mapai kept a low profile, Herut gloated and the journalists supporting Herut tore Kasztner to pieces, inevitably below glaring headlines repeating Halevi's highly quotable soundbite. The Mapai leaders were accused of supporting Kasztner in order to cover up their own misdeeds, and both they and Kasztner were represented as corrupt wheeler-dealers who were prepared to collaborate with the enemy, whether Nazi or British. The long-term repercussions on Israeli politics were even more significant. About a week after the judgment, the General Zionists in the Mapai-led coalition government abstained in two votes of no confidence, which significantly reduced the power base of Prime Minister Sharett. On 29 June he resigned and immediately set up a new government. Elections to the third Knesset took place on 26 July. Naturally, Kasztner was no longer a candidate. Mapai remained the largest party, but lost 5 of the 45 seats it had held before. Herut, led by Menachem Begin, won 15 seats, as opposed to 8 in 1951, and became the second largest party. In 1977 Likud, which had absorbed Herut, won the elections for the first time. The Kasztner affair had played a crucial part in the decline of Mapai and the rise of its opponents.

The effects of the judgment on Kasztner and his family were devastating. Kasztner received the news from Hansi Brand at his Jerusalem lodgings. Although he had long suspected that the trial was not going his way, he was utterly shocked. When he got back to his home in Tel Aviv he told Bogyó that the judge had delivered an 'incredibly harsh verdict', which even Tamir had 'never expected in his wildest dreams'.[54] His 'world was totally shattered', Weitz writes. 'For years, his activity in Budapest had been a source of pride to him', but now he needed 'almost superhuman stores of strength, simply to get up in the morning, go out of the house and walk about the city streets as if nothing had happened'. Deeply hurt by the 'badge of shame' that had been attached to him, he remained 'convinced that he was the victim of an unbearable injustice'. As he gradually withdrew into himself, 'his pride, arrogance and self-confidence were replaced by suspicion and anxiety'.[55]

Kasztner was not the only one to suffer. His wife and daughter were also hounded by the rabble. Their block of flats was daubed with graffiti saying 'Kasztner is a murderer' and worse. Their balcony was bombarded with rubbish. Neighbours called Bogyó a 'Nazi' and shopkeepers refused to serve her. Zsuzsi, from the age of nine, was harassed, bullied and called a 'murderess' at school and in the street.[56] The witchhunt was to continue for many years, and the lasting emotional damage caused to both women is easy to imagine.

The atmosphere surrounding Kasztner was characterised by Hansi Brand as 'one of open hostility from strangers, and cautious forbearance from his friends, which was no less painful'.[57] He was hounded by death threats, which the authorities took seriously enough to assign him two bodyguards, although ironically these were withdrawn shortly before he really needed them. On the other hand, he received many letters of support, particularly from members of the young pioneer groups who had worked with him in Budapest. He was offered sanctuary in two kibbutzim, but refused to hide. He was also advised to leave the country until the storm died down, but was not prepared to flee. He was determined to restore his reputation. He issued a statement, which was printed in most newspapers and in which he announced defiantly: 'History and all those who know what really happened during those woeful times will bear witness for me ... I will do everything in my power to clear my name and regain my honour.'[58]

Two months after Halevi's judgment the Attorney-General submitted an appeal to the Supreme Court of Israel.

A miscarriage of justice

Kasztner was clearly the victim of a disastrous miscarriage of justice. Instead of holding the reins of the trial firmly in his hands, Halevi allowed Tamir to introduce a large amount of inadmissible material and to digress from the case under investigation into politically inspired harangues. He joined Tamir in asking leading questions. Like Tamir, he treated Kasztner as a convicted criminal rather than a witness for the prosecution. The moment Kasztner was caught contradicting himself about his support for Becher he lost his objectivity and one-sidedly adopted Tamir's accusations.

To begin with the charge of silence, it is not entirely true that Kasztner withheld all the information about the deportations. According to his own report, as early as 26 December 1941 he helped organise a meeting of Hungarian and Romanian public figures, to which he reported the 'news of mass executions' in eastern Europe 'in great detail', predicting the 'violent death of more than a million Jews'. His call to set up an unofficial group of 'Jewish representatives with the task of beginning the political struggle against the destruction of Hungarian Jewry' was rejected by the majority of those present.[59] One day before the German occupation of Hungary, on 18 March 1944, Kasztner and the Vaada sent a number of Zionist pioneers to warn people in the provinces, but these were ignored, shouted down, told to go away, and occasionally even assaulted as panic-mongers. When Kasztner visited Kolozsvár on 3 May he warned József Fischer and other Jewish leaders that there was 'a danger of deportation and deportation means extermination',[60] but they took no action. There is some uncertainty about this issue. It has been suggested, by Braham among others, that by then Kasztner had exact knowledge of the extermination because he had been given a copy of Vrba and Wetzler's *Auschwitz Protocols* on a visit to Slovakia 'at the end of April 1944'.[61] Others, including Kasztner's nephew Yitzhak Katsir, believe that he did not receive the document until after the deportations had started. But the date matters less than it might seem. In either case Kasztner had enough information to issue yet another warning if he had wanted to. He chose not to do so for reasons of his own – which were not those attributed to him by his enemies.

Nor were the Jews of Hungary as unaware of the danger as Kasztner's enemies assert. Some were misled by soothing lies. Others did not want to know the truth. They believed, or tried to make themselves believe, that such horrors might happen elsewhere, but not in Hungary: the Hungarians would reward the Jews for their loyalty or realise that by harming the Jews they would be harming their own economy and culture. However, by the time of the German occupation the majority of Hungarian Jews had some idea of the massacres in the east, thanks to reports by refugees or Zionist activists.

Even though as a young child I did not understand what people in Budapest were fretting, speculating, arguing and agonising about, I could tell that it was a matter of life and death. Interviews with three members of the Bergen-Belsen group reflect the range of responses. Vera John-Steiner's recollection is typical of the vague but far from negligible knowledge of many: 'There was one cousin of somebody in my school who had a relative who knew something about Auschwitz. And I can't tell you how much that person knew, but we somehow knew that nothing worse could happen than to be taken to Auschwitz.'[62] Martha Gotthard's memory of how refugees from Poland were treated when they tried to raise the alarm conforms to the common tendency of frightened people to blame bad news on the bearer: 'People were very angry with them, they said this is not possible, this is a lie, it cannot be.'[63] Ben Hersch draws attention to two factors, one the deliberate lies about resettlement to salubrious work camps, circulated on German orders by the Jewish Councils, the other the combination of inertia and fear that made it easier to ignore the danger than trying to escape or resist: 'When it came to remembering the stories that we had heard from former refugees, the temptation was to march and not think about it because it was not pleasant to think about it. And why not, when your leadership tells you that you are going to be alright?'[64]

The charge that Kasztner's silence prevented the masses of Hungarian Jews fighting back or taking refuge in Romania does not stand up to scrutiny. With no access to the media and limited opportunities to travel, under constant observation by German and Hungarian secret police, he could hardly have raised the alarm in an effective way. But even if he had done more to issue warnings, there was very little the Jews in large numbers could have done. Surrounded by enemies, stripped of their rights and possessions, having neither the arms nor the experience, they were unable to organise resistance, and mass escapes were similarly beyond their means and capability. As Ann Pasternak Slater puts it, 'the visible dangers of resistance' seemed greater than 'the unknown risks of obedience', and compliance appeared 'preferable to immediate death and reprisals'.[65] Lying low and waiting for the storm to pass was the hope of most. Sadly, this hope proved illusory, but if Kasztner had put all his efforts into trying to persuade the Jews to escape or resist he would probably have saved fewer than he actually did.

Kasztner was aware of the dangers of keeping silent. In his diary note of 15 July 1944 he recalls telling Becher: 'I have thought many times whether it would not have been more correct to mobilise the Zionist youth and organise the people into active resistance against entering the brickyards and the cattle trucks.' When Becher pragmatically pointed out that this 'wouldn't have achieved anything', Kasztner replied: 'Possibly, but at least our honour would have been saved.' He recognised that his silence had contributed to the catastrophe: 'Our people went to the wagons like cattle, because we were sure of the success of our negotiations and failed to tell them what a terrible fate awaited them.' But this does not confirm Tamir's charge of deliberate betrayal. What Martin Gilbert, one of the outstanding historians of the Holocaust, wrote a quarter of a century ago still seems to me to offer the most likely explanation of the Vaada's conduct: 'Not urgent warnings to the fellow Jews to resist deportation, but secret negotiations with the SS aimed at averting deportation altogether, had become the avenue of hope chosen by the Hungarian Zionist leaders.'[66] If Kasztner was guilty of anything, it was overconfidence and vanity rather than treachery. Rightly or wrongly, he kept quiet about Auschwitz because he believed that he could save more lives through clandestine diplomacy than through a quixotic public gesture.

After the war Rudolf Vrba became one of Kasztner's most hostile critics. Lumping the Jewish Council and the Vaada together, he wrote in the *Daily Herald* in 1961: 'This small group of quislings knew what was happening to their brethren in Hitler's gas chambers and bought their own lives with the price of silence.'[67] Or not only their own lives, because in a later article – in which he insinuates that our very mixed Bergen-Belsen group consisted entirely of VIPs – Vrba describes Eichmann's 'release of those 1,800 relatively rich and/or well-connected Jews to Switzerland as a reward for keeping the atrocities at Auschwitz a secret from the remainder of their fellow Jews'.[68]

By a strange coincidence, Vrba's article appeared one year after the serialisation in *Life* magazine of 'The Confession of Adolf Eichmann'. Here Eichmann explains that one of his main concerns in Hungary had been to make the deportations run smoothly. It was to avoid hitches like the uprising of the Warsaw ghetto that he had entered into negotiations with Kasztner. His description of the deal curiously echoes Tamir's worst charge: 'He agreed to help keep the Jews from resisting deportation and even keep order in the collection camps if I would close my eyes and let a few hundred or a few thousand young Jews emigrate illegally to Palestine. It was a good bargain.'[69]

I hardly need to stress that the testimony of an Eichmann is not the most trustworthy of sources. In fact Kasztner understood precisely how Eichmann was trying to use him, but in a desperate game of double bluff he tried to use Eichmann in his turn. He makes this point unequivocally in one of his 1945 affidavits: 'The Germans entered into discussions with the leaders of the Jewish community for reasons of administrative efficiency. We conducted the discussion in the hope that we might be able to save some human lives.'[70]

Nevertheless, one well-known observer seems to have swallowed Eichmann's story whole. In her book *Eichmann in Jerusalem* Hannah Arendt mounts a furious attack on the Jewish Councils for their alleged complicity in the destruction of their own people. She claims that the Vaada, with its connections abroad, was even more useful to the Nazis and therefore 'received greater privileges'. Its members were 'free to come and go practically as they pleased, they were exempt from wearing the yellow star, they received permits to visit concentration camps' and Kasztner in particular 'could even travel about Nazi Germany without any identification papers showing that he was a Jew'.[71] She alleges that Kasztner paid for these privileges by becoming a willing partner to an agreement whereby Eichmann 'would permit the "illegal" departure of a few thousand Jews to Palestine . . . in exchange for "quiet and order" in the camps from which hundreds and thousands were shipped to Auschwitz'.[72] For good measure, Arendt attributes a fascist cast of mind to Kasztner, who is alleged to share the Nazi view that 'a famous Jew had more right to stay alive than an ordinary one'.[73] If Arendt had studied the facts more carefully instead of indulging her prejudices, she might not have come to the same conclusions as Eichmann.

The charge that Kasztner made up the Bergen-Belsen group entirely of his relatives and his Zionist cronies from Kolozsvár also stands on shaky ground. Given the appalling task of selecting a few hundred from hundreds of thousands, no selection could have been 'right'. Although Kasztner obviously exerted considerable influence, the lists were compiled according to agreed guidelines by small committees set up for the purpose. As for his relatives, only his mother, his brother, his sister-in-law, his wife, his father-in-law, his mother-in-law and his wife's two sisters with one child each were included, making 'a total extended family of ten',[74] by Ann Pasternak Slater's reckoning. Scores of his other relatives – among them his mother's brother and sister and his father's brother with all their children, whom Eichmann had offered to spare for a price – were left to be deported and murdered in Auschwitz. The dominance of Zionists from Kolozsvár is hardly surprising, since Kolozsvár was Hungary's second largest city with the largest and most active Zionist community, and the whole rescue enterprise was founded on Palestine immigration certificates. Nevertheless the group as a whole was far from exclusively Zionist. My father and I were only two of many non-Zionists, and the point is strongly made by Peretz Revesz, a former leading member of the youth movement who carried out many dangerous rescue missions of his own in Slovakia and Hungary with Kasztner's help. In his auto-biography Revesz remarks that the list contained 'a wide range of representatives and public activists of all areas: doctors, artists, scien-tists, economists and so on', most of whom were Zionists, but he adds that 'the other end of this rainbow included a group of very Orthodox Jews', among them 'Joel Teitelbaum who was notorious for being one of the strongest objectors to Zionism'.[75]

It cannot be denied that the group was top-heavy with the elite of Hungarian Jewry, but the selection principles went far beyond Kasztner's own sympathies. Our ages ranged from zero to eighty, practically all occupations were represented, and every shade of political opinion or religious orientation could be found. It was also by no means true that the whole group was made up of rich people. We have already seen that some 150 wealthy individuals provided most of the ransom for everybody. My father and I, again, are good examples of the many who were neither rich nor distinguished, just lucky. Revesz, who observed events at close quarters, stresses the limits of Kasztner's role in the selection and the sincerity of the Vaada's attempts 'to choose an appropriate representation of Hungarian Jewry'. Naturally, in such a horrific situation there could be no question of absolute fairness, but the Vaada was determined to continue its mission beyond our rescue: 'The fact that the present transport was to be the first in a chain of transports provided a certain kind of relief and hope for those who were supposed to make these decisions.'[76] If Kasztner believed that our rescue would be followed by many others, then the charge that he betrayed the rest of Hungary's Jews in order to save us alone loses all conviction.

I do not believe that Kasztner deliberately collaborated with the Nazis, but a number of difficult questions still remain unanswered. Two very awkward ones are why he gave that affidavit for Becher and why he tried to deny it in court.

According to one hypothesis Kasztner, with his usual over-confidence, thought that he could see the opposition off by admitting nothing. According to another, he lied because he had a bad conscience. More convincingly, Kasztner's daughter Zsuzsi has told me that he panicked when he was suddenly exposed as having broken the taboo on helping Nazis. Given the stress of the court proceedings, the inef-fectiveness of his lawyer, the unhelpfulness of the witnesses on his own side, and the battering he was receiving from Tamir, it would be under-standable that he momentarily lost control. A further possibility, suggested to me by Kasztner's nephew Yitzhak Katsir, is that both Kasztner and his lawyer had been instructed by their superiors not to own up to anything that might damage the Mapai government.

Gruenwald's allegation that Kasztner wanted to buy Becher's silence about the crimes they had committed together is far off the mark, even though Tamir and Halevi adopted it. Three other expla-nations put forward by Weitz add some useful pieces to the puzzle. The first is what Weitz calls the 'gentlemanly'.[77] It assumes that Becher had persuaded Kasztner to promise him an alibi if Germany lost the war, and Kasztner had felt duty-bound to keep his word. This is the reason given by Kasztner's daughter Zsuzsi, with both Becher and his colleagues in mind: 'Why did he speak for them? Because he promised them. And for a gentleman of his upbringing, a promise is a promise.'[78] Eva Speter, who is generally happy to point out Kasztner's faults, says roughly the same: 'I think that was correct because he promised him – without the help of Becher, he couldn't have done whatever he had done.'[79] Even without an explicit promise, Kasztner could have felt an obligation to the few among the vast number of enemies who – for whatever motives of their own – had helped him in his desperate uphill struggle. Alex Barzel commends Kasztner for giving Becher credit for saving Jews, regardless of any other considerations: 'He really did what he did. Only because he had been a Nazi earlier, it would not have been right to deny what he had actually done.'[80] Weitz may well strike the correct note by identifying the desire for fairness as one of Kasztner's motives: 'It is possible that Kasztner really believed that Becher had assisted in the rescue of Jews and therefore deserved gratitude and a reward.'[81]

The second explanation, again in Weitz's words, is the 'megalomanic'.[82] For a long time Kasztner had experienced not only a heavy reponsibility, but also the thrill of holding the life and death of thousands in his hand, of dealing with some of the most notorious mass murderers in the world on an apparently even footing, of making history. We have seen how deflated he felt when he no longer needed to summon all his nervous energy to confront the Nazis day by day. It would be understandable that he tried to overcome his sense of anticlimax by engaging in a new rescue attempt, even if the individuals concerned were SS bosses. This was Joel Brand's view: 'In Nuremberg he regained the feeling of power – picking up the phone, a good word, intervention, a written statement – these were enough to save human lives.'[83] Similarly, Weitz suspects that the affidavits may well have given Kasztner the 'opportunity to re-experience at least a fraction of the power he wielded during the occupation: he was back at centre-stage, determining people's fate'.[84]

The third explanation is the 'psychological'. Based on the concept of 'cognitive dissonance', Weitz argues that having to work closely with individuals he feared and hated, Kasztner needed to develop an acceptable idea of them, even if that idea did not correspond to the reality: 'The prolonged proximity, which made him dependent on people he abhorred, made Kasztner want to see them in a different light.' It was self-deception in emotional self-defence. His involvement with such enemies affected Kasztner in two ways: it placed him under an appalling stress and it made him feel guilty. To lighten both the stress and the guilt, he may have convinced himself that the enemies were partners or even friends. He did this unconsciously, 'in order to justify himself in his own eyes and enable him to go on negotiating with them; and more than that, to enable him to live with himself after the war'.[85]

This theory may be too speculative for many, but Kasztner does seem to have developed friendly feelings towards Becher. A letter he wrote to him in 1951 points in that direction. After expressing his condolences on the death of Becher's mistress and reporting briefly about his own life in Israel, he continues: 'I work a lot, am happy and now hope to build up closer contact with you, which would be more appropriate for the two of us who have achieved something singular.'[86] Two things are particularly striking. One is Kasztner's use of 'Du', the familiar form of address, together with Becher's first name Kurt, and the closing words 'With my old friendship'. The other is the hope of 'closer contact'. Kasztner may be thinking of new business relations, but the warm tone suggests a more personal element. Becher may or may not have deserved Kasztner's friendship, but Kasztner's obvious pride in their joint achievement of 'something singular' seems genuine and unlikely to hide any guilty secrets. Completing an important project together in such cataclysmic times may create a bond even between an SS extortionist and a Jew with a mission to save Jews.

Nevertheless, it seems surprising that Kasztner supported a bunch of Nazi thugs who had used him so cynically as an instrument of extortion, even if, for reasons of their own, they had furthered his rescue operations. I believe that the most compelling reason was a pragmatic one. After the war Kasztner was trying to recover Jewish property, hunt down Eichmann, and bring the Mufti of Jerusalem to justice. The support he gave the SS officers was designed to enlist their help in these projects. Nor was he acting merely as a private individual, but with the knowledge and agreement of high Jewish officials. The point is most convincingly made by Shoshana Barri, based on documents that were not generally known when they might literally have saved Kasztner's life. In her words, Kasztner's change 'from his initial description of Becher, Krumey and Wisliceny as war criminals to his naming them as saviours of Jews' was 'coordinated with the Jewish Agency's efforts to capture Eichmann and the Mufti on the one hand and to reclaim the property of Hungarian Jewry on the other'.[87] This interpretation has been confirmed to me by Katsir, who had discussed many important issues with his uncle. Kasztner's remark, also quoted by Katsir, that the affidavits were meant to demonstrate that a Jew could keep his promises, makes most sense in connection with these plans.

One reason why Kasztner wanted to recover the stolen property was personal. The rumours about his malpractices included embezzlement, and some members of the Bergen-Belsen group pressed him to produce precise accounts or even to repay their original contributions to our ransom. At the best of times Kasztner's strengths were not those of a patient administrator or a meticulous bookkeeper. Given the frantic haste with which the ransom had to be collected from terrified Jews and delivered to the insatiable SS behind the backs of suspicious Hungarians, as arrest, torture, deportation and death waited round every corner, it was absurd to expect him to have kept accurate records. In his own words: 'Our primary mission was to save human lives; for that we fought for a whole year, we worked, we took risks . . . In those circumstances, who could undertake technical legal commitments?'[88] Nevertheless, he hoped to put an end to the slurs either by reimbursing claimants or by turning the recovered property over to a Jewish organisation.

It is safe to say that several leading figures in the Jewish Agency were aware of Kasztner's attempts to recover the stolen property. In his memorandum of December 1946, which was probably intended for the Agency, Kasztner recalls that the Vaada had delivered currencies and valuables worth 8,750,000 Swiss francs to Becher for our ransom. He asks how this, and other substantial assets, could be salvaged before the Americans tried to appropriate them: 'Would a simple procedure reach the goal or is a higher political intervention necessary? The matter is extremely urgent because otherwise there is a danger that the deposit is transformed into war booty and lost to the Jewish community.' For the next two or three years extensive discussions took place between a variety of individuals and organisations about the same matter. They involved survivors, the Jewish Agency, the World Jewish Congress, the Joint, the US occupation authorities, the French and Hungarian governments, some Swiss banks and the head of the Palestine office in Geneva, Chaim Posner. Naturally, Kasztner, Schweiger and Becher played key roles. The ransom Becher had been paid for the Bergen-Belsen group and apparently given back to Schweiger eventually reached the Jewish Agency in Palestine, where it turned out to be worth only a fraction of its supposed value. Everything else – including the famous 'gold train' containing far greater treasures stolen from the Jews of Hungary – vanished without a trace and will probably never be found.

Kasztner's ambition to track down Eichmann also remained unfulfilled. In March 1946 he informed Tartakower that a member of the Jewish Agency had 'suceeded in following the tracks of the vanished Eichmann and it doesn't seem impossible that the fellow can still be found'.[89] A year and a half later he wrote to the lawyer Friedrich Steiner: 'I am going to Nuremberg today, where I will also be consulted about the question of E. I hope I'll manage to convince the relevant

Allied authorities of the need to conduct a trial in absentia and a judgment in contumatiam.'[90] Around the same time he sent 100 or 200 Swiss francs to Wisliceny, who was in prison in Slovakia. He made this unexpected gesture in the hope of receiving a lead to Eichmann in return. For the same reason he wanted Wisliceny to be extradited to the US authorities as the 'only available member of Eichmann's staff who can give a complete and thorough picture of the extermination program'.[91] His wish was not granted. Wisliceny was executed by the Slovaks and Kasztner never lived to see Eichmann caught and punished.

His campaign against the Mufti of Jerusalem was equally unsuccessful. The revelations he publicised, with the help of Aryeh Tartakower and Nahum Goldmann of the World Jewish Congress, about the Mufti's collaboration with the Nazis made a splash in the US and Swiss press, but no action was taken by the western powers.

Despite Halevi's fury, Kasztner had good reason to believe that he had the right to sign the Becher affidavit in the name of the supreme Jewish organisations, even though he had not been expressly instructed to do so. It is interesting to recall one particular phrase in his letter of 5 February 1947 to Krumey: 'I don't easily forget those who have shown us understanding at certain moments.' In July 1944, Wenia Pomeranz and Menahem Bader of the Jewish Agency had advised him to promise future assistance to SS officers in return for the release of our Bergen-Belsen group and for their willingness to do more business: 'Try to convince your clients . . . We will never forget those who have helped us.'[92] In August 1944, the Jewish Agency's representatives in Istanbul sent the Vaada in Budapest the same undertaking: 'We will not forget those who stand beside us today, and that is more important than money.'[93] The almost identical formulation in the three letters seems to confirm that Kasztner did in 1947 what the Jewish Agency had already envisaged in 1944.

The substantial body of correspondence between various officials cited by Barri, mainly from 1945 to 1948, reveals that the Jewish

Agency was not averse to negotiating with ex-Nazis and using Kasztner's services for that purpose. The intention was not only to recover stolen Jewish property, but also to establish business connections with post-war Germany. These projects, which became a very hot potato in Israeli politics, go far beyond the scope of this book, but I may mention at least one example: in 1948 Chaim Posner in Switzerland was trying to buy machinery for the manufacture of ammunition from Becher in Germany on behalf of the Jewish Agency in Palestine.

Kasztner, then, had reasonably assumed that his tactic was sanctioned by his superiors. To quote Barri again: 'Whether he had received the explicit prior authorization of the Jewish Agency, or whether such authorization was only partial and retroactive, Kasztner acted in Nuremberg as representative of the Jewish Agency and the World Jewish Congress.'[94] In this context Eliahu Dobkin's behaviour in the witness stand is highly instructive. As we have seen, Kasztner included Dobkin among the officials who had given him a green light to assist Becher in the name of the two supreme organisations, but Dobkin denied ever hearing of a man called Becher. This is contradicted, for example, by Joel Brand, who claims that in 1944 he had been invited by Dobkin 'to go with him to Lisbon to meet Becher'.[95] If what Brand says is true, Dobkin must have been lying. And if he was lying, he may well have done so because, to quote Barri for the last time, Israeli government officials 'could not openly admit' that 'representatives of "our new, pure, idealistic" State had established contact with Nazi officers ... and had permitted testimonies and appeals on their behalf'[96] even in the hope of punishing Nazi criminals and obtaining funds, goods and military equipment for their young country. Kasztner was left in the lurch for the sake of Israeli 'Realpolitik'.

The appeal and after

On 21 August 1955 the Attorney-General lodged his appeal against Halevi's judgement. He listed an impressive array of grounds. The judge had acquitted Gruenwald on false, or no, evidence. He had been influenced by Kasztner's behaviour in the witness stand and by some contradictions in the statements given by Kasztner himself and some others. He had ignored the psychological state of the Jews under Nazi terror. He had not appreciated the limitations of human memory, particularly in relation to terrible times such as those under discussion. There was no justification for accusing Kasztner of criminal collaboration with the Nazis or for concluding that he had willingly and knowingly assisted in the extermination of Jews. To talk about selling souls to Satan was entirely subjective. The assertion that Kasztner's failure to warn the Jews of Kolozsvár about the death camps had facilitated the mass exterminations was baseless, and Kasztner's alleged loyalty to the Nazis in the matter of the parachutists had not been demonstrated. There was no evidence that Kasztner's affidavit on behalf of Becher had been intended to save a war criminal from trial and punishment.

Criminal Appeal 232/55 opened in the Jerusalem Supreme Court on 19 January and closed on 6 February 1957. It was heard by five judges: Chief Justice Yitzhak Olshan, acting Chief Justice Zalman Cheshin, and Justices Shimon Agranat, Moshe Silberg, David Goitein. Kasztner had recovered much of his former energy. He was convinced that his name would be cleared. In the event he did win, but things did not work out quite as he expected.

A circle of Kasztner's friends had instructed the leading legal partnership of Micha Caspi and Chaim Tzadok to represent him. Unlike Tel in the original trial, Caspi was a match for Tamir. His main line of attack was to demonstrate that nothing would have been achieved if Kasztner had warned the Jews of Kolozsvár of the fate hanging over them. He collected a number of testimonies to that effect. One of the most impressive witnesses was Israel Szabo. He explained that 'the ordinary Hungarian in the street knew about Auschwitz', but 'mass flight' was impossible, and believing that the Hungarian Jews could have 'organised any resistance' would have been 'a fatal error'.

They had been methodically worn down by 'the expropriation of their wealth, the loss of their place of work, the yellow patch, the closure inside their homes, in the ghetto under inhuman conditions'. This process had drained them of all confidence and energy. It was not the knowledge that they lacked, but the opportunities and the will to save themselves. Therefore, instead of facing up to a reality that was too dreadful to contemplate, they pretended that it was not there: 'They knew about the danger but didn't want to believe it.'[97] Attempts to rouse them from their apathy were usually met with incomprehension, inertia or hostility. Zvi Goldfarb was one of the young Zionist activists who had escaped from Slovakia to Hungary and tried to warn the local Jewish communities about what they had already experienced in their own country. According to his testimony, this was what happened: 'When we came and told them, they didn't believe us, they didn't want anything to do with us. Even at a later period they didn't want to listen.'[98]

It took the five judges nearly a year to arrive at their decision. On 15 January 1958 they began to read out their judgments, one by one. All five concurred that the proper forum for the original case would have been a commission of inquiry rather than a court of law. All five dismissed the appeal in respect of Becher, agreeing that Kasztner had deliberately helped a Nazi war criminal to escape justice and had lied about it in court. Four against one upheld the appeal in relation to the gravest charges, clearing Kasztner of conscious and willing collaboration with the Nazis and complicity in mass murder. Gruenwald was given a one-year suspended jail sentence for libel and ordered to pay costs to the tune of 500 Israeli pounds. The judges did not dispute Halevi's factual findings, but drew different conclusions from them. Essentially, they said that, given the unique conditions in 1944, Kasztner's actions could not be judged in absolute terms according to the standards of more normal times. What mattered was the intention behind those actions, and the majority accepted that Kasztner's intention was to save lives.

Thus the judgment, taken as a whole, amounted to a slightly grudging rehabilitation.

The first and most substantial judgment was Agranat's. He criticised Halevi for failing to take account of the general background of the times in which Kasztner and his associates had to work. In contrast to Halevi's blunt notion that Kasztner had collaborated with Eichmann on the basis of an evil contract, Agranat pointed out that where Eichmann had all the power and Kasztner none, there could be no question of a contract, which presupposed freedom of choice and equality for both partners. As to the content of the alleged contract, Agranat stressed that 'everything depends on the motives'.[99] He categorically denied that Kasztner had ever intended to bring about the destruction of Hungarian Jewry. Far from selling out the masses for the benefit of a few prominent individuals, 'at all times, Kastner's goal was to save the Jews of Hungary in general, and the implementation of the "Bergen-Belsen plan", which was intended for only a small group of Jews, always remained just a part of this goal and never became for him an exclusive objective'.[100] If Kasztner genuinely believed that his financial negotiations with the SS held out the best prospects of rescuing 'the maximum number which, considering the circumstances of time and place as assessed by him, could have been saved',[101] then it was his moral duty to act accordingly. If he was convinced that by informing the Jewish leaders in Kolozsvár about Auschwitz he would be jeopardising those negotiations, he had the right to keep silent. If, according to the original deal, the Bergen-Belsen group was to go to Palestine, his decision to include a relatively large number of prominent Zionist leaders was perfectly rational. Therefore, Agranat concluded, 'one cannot find moral defects in that behaviour; one cannot find any causation between it and the expediting of the deportation and the extermination and one cannot consider it amounting to the degree of collaboration with the Nazis'.[102]

Chesin concurred with Agranat. He considered that even if Kasztner knew and concealed the 'whole bitter truth' in Kolozsvár, this did not prove 'his wish to help the Germans in their extermination'. He explained that Kasztner did not 'warn Hungarian Jewry of the danger facing it because he did not think it would be useful, and because he thought that any deeds resulting from information given them would damage more than help'. While agreeing with Agranat that the Jews of Hungary 'were not capable, either physically or mentally, of carrying out resistance operations', he did not absolve Kasztner from 'bad leadership both from a moral and public point of view'. Nevertheless, he concluded that Kasztner's silence – 'premeditated and calculated' as it was – could not be considered 'wilful collaboration and assistance in the extermination, because all the signs indicate that Kasztner's efforts were aimed at rescue and rescue on a big scale'.[103] Olshan also concurred with Agranat and added a criticism of Halevi for allowing irrelevant details and hearsay to encumber the proceedings. Goitine initially sat on the fence, but eventually decided to follow Agranat's line.

Only Silberg accepted most of Halevi's rulings. He denied any large-scale rescues by Kasztner and declared that the Nazis had been able to achieve 'an easy and peaceful extermination without special efforts, without casualties to themselves' as a 'direct result of the concealment of the horrifying truth from the victims'. He insisted that 'Kasztner, in order to carry out the rescue plan for the few prominents, fulfilled knowingly and without good faith the said desire of the Nazis, thus expediting the work of exterminating the masses'. To emphasise Kasztner's alleged criminal propensities, he resorted once more to the Becher case: 'He who is capable of rescuing this Becher from hanging proves that the atrocities of this great war criminal were not so horrifying or despicable in his eyes.'[104] But even Silberg objected to Halevi's slur that Kasztner had 'sold his soul to Satan', pointing out that he had not 'willingly assisted in the extermination of 600,000 Jews'.[105]

After the ruling of the Supreme Court the country remained polarised. While Mapai and its supporters were pleased with the result, those on the Herut side – including Uri Avneri and his weekly *HaOlam HaZeh* – insisted that Kasztner had not really been cleared. Tamir demanded a public inquiry and for the rest of his life continued to assert that Kasztner was guilty. Sadly, by the time the Supreme Court had pronounced its judgment, Kasztner was dead.

Once again the fullest account of events is given by Weitz. Kasztner left the editorial offices of *Új Kelet* in Tel Aviv on 3 March 1957 around 11.30 pm and drove to his home at 6 Emanuel Street. When he got out of his car a thin man in khaki walked up to him, lit up his face with a torch and asked: 'Are you Dr Kasztner?' When Kasztner said that he was, the man drew a revolver and holding it at Kasztner's head, pulled the trigger. Nothing happened. Kasztner pushed the man aside and ran towards the house. The man fired two more shots, and the second hit Kasztner, who fell on the pavement, shouting for help. The gunman fled in a jeep. Neighbours called the police and an ambulance. Bogyó tried to make Kasztner comfortable on the ground with a pillow and a blanket, before he was rushed to the Hadassah hospital. All this time their daughter Zsuzsi was asleep in the flat above.

When Kasztner arrived at the hospital it was found that 'the bullet had entered his left side, torn his spleen, penetrated his intestines and damaged internal organs near his chest'. He was able to describe the events to the police before he underwent a three-hour operation. His condition improved somewhat, but the danger to his life remained. He received many telegrams and flowers. Gruenwald cabled: 'Shocked by the inhumane act. Wishing you a complete recovery despite our fundamental disagreements.' Tamir's comment in a newspaper interview was suitably unforgiving: 'There can be no act more repugnant to those who view Kasztner's activity in Hungary in light of what the defence revealed at the trial in Jerusalem.'[106] Eight days after the attack Kasztner's condition began to deteriorate. On 15 March 1957, at 7.20 am, he died of heart failure.

The funeral took place in Tel Aviv on 17 March. As Kasztner lay in his coffin in the square in front of the hospital thousands of mourners came to pay their respects.

The assassination was splashed over all the papers. There were a number of prompt arrests and releases. In April 1957 the trial of three men began in the Tel Aviv District Court. They were Zeev Eckstein, who had actually done the shooting, Dan Shemer, who had driven the jeep, and Joseph Menkes, the head of an underground movement, who had incited the other two. In January 1958 they were found guilty of murder and imprisoned for life. Soon attempts were made to reduce the sentences, in particular for Menkes, who was in a bad physical and emotional condition. In 1963 Prime Minister Ben Gurion personally sought the opinion of Kasztner's widow and daughter. Bogyó remained bitter and implacable. Zsuzsi pitied Menkes's children. She said to Ben Gurion: 'My father will never return. At least their father can return to them.'[107] Later that year all three were released.

The true circumstances of the assassination have never been cleared up. According to one version, based on the discovery by the police of a large cache of arms, the attack was the first symbolic action of a dangerous underground movement. Another version blamed the extreme right-wing groups that had agitated against Kasztner for a long time. Yet another – put forward by Herut circles – pointed the finger at the state security forces, and behind them the government that had supposedly given the order to silence Kasztner because he knew too many guilty secrets of the Mapai leaders. In this context Eckstein was identified as a former member of the security services, who had been dismissed in 1956 after two years' employment. But despite the rumours, the truth remains hidden.

Kasztner's widow and daughter were in desperate straits, both financially and emotionally. Friends tried to obtain help for them, and eventually Bogyó made a modest living running a small business. Five years after Kasztner's death her application for a state pension under the terms of her husband's national insurance was turned down on the ground that the murder was not connected with his job. She died sixteen years later, hard-up and having never got over her grief. Zsuzsi trained as a nurse and works in a hospital in Petach Tikvah near Tel Aviv. She is divorced, with three daughters. Her belief in her father has never faltered.

In due course the affair ceased to make headlines, but was never forgotten. Debate revived in 1961 as a result of the Eichmann trial. When Hannah Arendt regurgitated the allegations of Tamir and Halevi, not to mention Eichmann himself, she was expressing views held by the majority of Israelis. But by the 1980s Israeli society had undergone changes that enabled it to adopt a more balanced attitude. The historian Dov Dinur's volume of 1987, the Hebrew title of which translates as 'Kasztner. Leader or Villain', did a great deal to restore Kasztner's reputation. Other academic books and articles – quoted in this book where appropriate – followed suit. Several film or television documentaries, also aiming at a true representation, have emerged in the past few years: Moti Lerner's *The Kasztner Trial* in Israel (1994), Bill Treharne Jones's *Last Train from Budapest* in Britain (2000), Axel Brandt's *Zug um Zug* in Germany (2005), Gyula Radó's *A Kasztner-vonat* (The Kasztner train) in Hungary (2006). At the moment a documentary, *The Persecution and Assassination of Dr Israel Kasztner*, is being prepared by the American director Gaylen Ross. In 2004 an exhibit was installed in Kasztner's memory in Yad Vashem and in July 2007 a collection of documents was presented to Yad Vashem by Zsuzsi Kasztner and other members of the family. Although campaigns to name a street after Kasztner in Tel Aviv or Haifa have foundered on political manipulations, a small forest near Haifa now bears his name, as does a plaque at the entrance to his old block of flats at 12 Váci Street, Budapest. Travelling to Israel recently, I was asked by a fierce young immigration officer what I was going to do there. When I told her that I intended to do some research on Kasztner she looked blank, but before I could say anything else, her equally young colleague came to the rescue and started to tell her about the trial and the murder as if it had all happened the day before.

Yechiam Weitz best sums up the change that has occurred in the perception of Kasztner's achievement: 'It had been difficult at the time to understand how courageous and daring he had to be' to do what he did, Weitz writes, but 'a generation later' a 'more mature and confident' public could understand that 'there was no shame in negotiations for the purpose of saving lives'.[108]

CHAPTER 14

A Hero of Circumstance

It may seem strange that a Jew who saved the lives of hundreds – possibly thousands – of his fellow-Jews was branded a collaborator with the Jews' worst enemies by a Jewish judge, ostracised by a Jewish public, and murdered by a Jewish gunman. To understand why Kasztner encountered so much hostility in Israel it is important to remember the mood prevailing in the country a decade after the Second World War. For many Jews still reeling from the Holocaust, the accusations levelled against Kasztner in court seemed to confirm all the dark rumours that had been circulating about him and to open wounds that had never completely healed. His apparently friendly relations with Becher were repulsive to former victims of the SS. The concessions he wrested from Eichmann gave rise to suspicions of impropriety. His success, combined with his arrogance, provoked envy. His rescue of our group of 1,670 men, women and children from Bergen-Belsen contrasted sharply with the destruction of hundreds of thousands in Auschwitz. It is understandable that he was hated for saving a tiny minority while the vast majority perished, and it is understandable that our own group was hated for being alive while all the others were dead. Understandable, but not necessarily fair or rational.

Most of the Jews in Israel at the time had suffered irreparable losses. Many also felt guilty about their own impotence during the Holocaust. Such a mixture of helpless grief and guilt was apt to turn into anger, and the anger found an outlet in blame. Since the real culprits, the Nazis, were out of reach, a man with a high profile, who seemed to have flourished in the midst of disaster by means of suspicious deals with the enemy, was an obvious target. A perceptive member of our own group, Naomi Herskovitz, describes it in these words: 'People in pain, torment, grief obviously can't be objective. They look for somebody whose fault it is, and they take it out on him ... People see that we are here and their loved ones are not here, and it's hard, and so they must find a scapegoat.' Kasztner, then, became a scapegoat for the accumulated misery of a whole society. It was irrational and unfair, but it had a sad logic. Herskovitz again: 'Kasztner didn't kill, he saved, he saved lives. But psychology is a difficult matter.'[1]

Kasztner had expected a hero's welcome in Israel and he was treated as a traitor. For the Jews of the Yishuv, a hero was a man who stood up to fight armed battles for his cause. If he died in the process, he became a celebrated martyr. On no account did he hide, grovel or make deals. Kasztner came from the diaspora, where Jews often had to resort to ruse and subterfuge in order to survive. When the Holocaust engulfed Hungary he assumed the burden of saving lives without hesitation and without regard to his own safety. Avoiding theatrical gestures, he raised wheeling and dealing to a high art for a good purpose. If this was not the warlike heroism admired in Israel in the 1950s, it was nevertheless heroism of an equally valid kind. Kasztner himself explained it to Yitzhak Katsir in a few words, which are all the more compelling for being neither boastful nor defensive: 'After the German occupation of Hungary a hopeless situation developed. There was no way out, and there was nobody else who could, would or dared do something. So I did it. So I was a hero. You could say I was a hero, but I was a hero because of the circumstances.'[2]

The circumstances were extraordinary, and so was Kasztner's response. He bluffed, lied and cheated, but he also showed uncommon bravery. The word 'hero' has been debased by thoughtless usage, but two members of our Bergen-Belsen group apply it to Kasztner in what I believe to be a particularly appropriate way. Edit Goldstein reflects that dying in the Warsaw ghetto, while more spectacular, was no more heroic than courting death by forging documents, hiding fugitives and, above all, confronting murderers like Eichmann in order to save lives: 'He entered the lion's den again and again, risking his own life, in order to save others. If he had only saved one it would have been magnificent, but he saved thousands. That makes him a hero in my eyes.'[3] In Ervin Heilper's view, too, Kasztner deserved admiration for standing up to Eichmann and refusing to shirk life-and-death decisions, but what made him a real 'hero' was his determination to return to Germany, when he could have stayed comfortably in Switzerland with his wife and family, because he had 'promised to save more Jews'. While not denying Kasztner's reckless side, Heilper rightly pays tribute to his willingness to sacrifice himself for his cause: 'This goes well beyond a desire for adventure. This is a commitment, a vocation. I can't think of anybody else who could do that.'[4] Finally, among the professional historians, Yehuda Bauer sums up the matter most fairly. He lists Kasztner's faults profusely, but ends by describing him as an 'incredibly heroic person' who accomplished exceptional feats 'without a gun in his hand' thanks to a 'quite incomprehensible civilian courage'.[5]

Kasztner did not act alone. He could not have done what he did without the contribution of people such as Otto Komoly, Joel Brand and Endre Biss, the unfaltering support of Hansi Brand, and the irritating but healthy caution of Saly Mayer. They all had their faults, and relations between them were difficult, but jointly they achieved a great deal against the most daunting odds. To quote Bauer again:

The Jewish individuals who opened the door to negotiation took tremendous risks, personal and communal. In the end, our conclusion must be that they did the right thing, took the only possible way to save lives. Contrary to all logic, some lives were saved . . . Given the circumstances, they could not fully succeed. That they did in part is a wonderment.[6]

Nevertheless, it was still only a drop in the ocean. The faint light shed by them was surrounded by a darkness of unimaginable proportions. Raul Hilberg strikes the right balance by giving the Vaada all the credit that is its due, but closing on a sad note by reminding us how little it was able to do against so much evil: 'Considering the impotence of Hungarian Jewry and the lack of all outside support, its success was remarkable, but weighed against the magnitude of the disaster, its accomplishment was very limited.'[7]

I do not believe that Rezső Kasztner was a collaborator. I do not believe that he betrayed the parachutists. I do not believe that he sold out Hungary's Jewry in exchange for the opportunity to save a few hundred alleged VIPs. I do not believe that he kept silent about Auschwitz with the intention of helping Eichmann carry out the deportations without hiccups. He did try to mislead the court about his support for Becher, but assisting SS officers may seem a less heinous crime to us today than it seemed to Israelis at the time. Moreover, he did so, at least in part, on an understanding with his political masters. The accusation that he was 'playing God' by selecting a few hundred men, women and children to be saved out of hundreds of thousands fails to take into account his practice of leaving the compilation of lists to small committees working to agreed guidelines, rather than imposing his own will on the proceedings. As to the charge of nepotism, the striking thing is not how many members of his own family he included, but how few.

One could argue that in the monstrous situation created by the Nazis no selection could be satisfactory, so that the only logical alternative to saving those people who were saved would have been saving nobody. It might have been logical, but it would not have been human, and it would not have been Kasztner's way. As Arthur Stern, a member of our Bergen-Belsen group, said in an interview, Kasztner 'did the right thing under the circumstances' because 'life for some is better than life for none'.[8]

The brutal truth is that while millions – including most of my own relatives – were killed, I am still alive more than half a century later. At the metaphysical level I do not know why I should have been spared when so many died, and, for the sake of my own sanity, I will not speculate. At the practical, human, level the answer is plain: I am alive because Rezső Kasztner saved my life. Perhaps I should feel guilty for not having died with the others. I can understand that some of those who have suffered more than we did hate us, but I am comforted by the knowledge that when my father and I were admitted to the group we did not knowingly and willingly deprive anybody else of a place. On a larger scale, the same applies to Kasztner himself. The number of those he saved was infinitesimal in comparison to that of the dead, but he too did not deliberately send others to their deaths in order to save us. At times his frustration and anguish must have been almost unbearable as he watched Eichmann dispatching the trains to Auschwitz day after day, but rather than giving in to despair, he saved whom he could.

Those who take the moral high ground may wonder whether it is at all possible to compromise with evil without fatally compromising one's own integrity. Those in search of absolute rules may ask whether it is better to let disaster take its course or to intervene and possibly dirty one's own hand. In my view such questions cannot really be answered in theory, but must be tested by each individual in practice. I do not think that Kasztner spent much time even asking them. As most of his fellow-Jews passively awaited their fate, he acted on their behalf. While others were trembling before Eichmann, he suppressed his own fear, and by determination and cunning extracted unparalleled concessions from the chief organiser of the Holocaust. Faced with a choice between two evils, he chose what he regarded as the lesser one and was cruelly punished for it. He may not have saved as many Jews as he is sometimes said to have done, but there is no doubt that he saved the 1,670 of us and almost certainly thousands more. He deserved better than a miscarriage of justice and an assassin's bullet.

Glossary

Abwehr: Wehrmacht military counter-intelligence service

Aliyah: emigration to Palestine or Israel, literally 'ascent'

Arrow Cross: Hungarian ultra-fascist political party

Balfour Declaration: statement by British Foreign Secretary Arthur Balfour in 1917, promising the 'Jewish people a national home' in Palestine

bar mitzvah: coming of age ceremony for boys of thirteen

Barisia: young Zionist movement

Betar: revisionist Zionist youth movement

chalutz: Jewish pioneer immigrant to Palestine

Chassid: member of a strictly Orthodox Jewish sect

cheder: religious Jewish elementary school

cholent: stew of meat, potatoes and beans, traditionally for Sabbath

chutzpah: nerve

Division IVB4: office directly responsible for Jewish affairs within the RSHA

Etzel: revisionist Zionist terrorist group, also known as Irgun Tzvai Leumi

galut: exile from the Jewish homeland

Gestapo: Nazi secret police, short for Geheime Staatspolizei

Gordonia: non-Marxist Zionist labour movement

gymnasium: Central European high school

Hagana: Zionist military organisation, forerunner of the Israeli army

Hashomer Hatzair: socialist Zionist youth organisation

Herut: right-wing political party in Israel

Ihud: association of socialist Zionist parties

Irgun Zvai Leumi: revisionist Zionist terrorist group, also known as Etzel

Jewish Agency: representative body of the Jewish community under the British mandate in Palestine, forerunner of government of Israel

Joint: American Jewish Joint Distribution Committee, worldwide aid organisation for Jews in need

Judenrat: Jewish Council, body of representatives set up on German orders

Kaddish: prayer for the dead

kapo: concentration camp inmate in charge of other inmates

kibbutz: collective farm in Israel

Knesset: parliament of Israel

kosher: fit for consumption according to Jewish dietary laws

Lehi: right-wing Zionist terrorist group, also known as Stern gang

Likud: right-wing political party in Israel

Mapai: social democratic political party in Israel

Masada: scene of a Jewish tribe's legendary mass suicide in preference to Roman captivity

matzot: unleavened bread, eaten at Passover

mikveh: ritual bath

International Military Tribunal: court set up by the Allies to conduct trials of war criminals in Nuremberg 1945–6

Mizrachi: religious Zionist organisation

Muselmann: concentration camp inmate about to die of his ordeal

Neologue: following modernised religious rules and assimilated to Hungarian culture

Orthodox: strictly observing established religious rules

Palestine Office: Zionist agency designed to assist immigration to Palestine

pengő: Hungarian currency

Reichssicherheitshauptamt: Reich Security Main Office, SS organisation responsible for fighting the enemies of the Nazi state, abbreviated as RSHA

Revisionist: member of right-wing Zionist movement, including terrorist groups

Rosh Hashana: Jewish New Year

sabra: native-born Israeli

Sicherheitsdienst: SS intelligence service, abbreviated as SD

shofar: ram's horn, blown in the synagogue at Rosh Hashana and Yom Kippur

shtetl: small Jewish town in Eastern Europe

Simchat Torah: annual festival celebrating the Torah

Sondereinsatzkommando: special operational unit, charged with the deportation of Jews, also known as Judenkommando

SS: elite military unit designed to carry out atrocities on behalf of the Nazi party

Starkosan: chocolate-flavoured nutrient powder

Stern gang: right-wing terrorist group, also known as Lehi

Talmud: compendium of ancient rabbinic writings

tiyul: excursion, code word for escape from fascist countries

Torah: the body of Jewish religious law and learning, written on a scroll

Vaada: short for Hebrew Vaadat Ezra ve'Hazalah, Relief and Rescue Committee

Völkischer Beobachter: daily paper published by Nazi party

Wannsee conference: meeting of senior Nazis in 1942, leading to the Holocaust

War Refugee Board: US agency set up by President F. D. Roosevelt in 1944 to rescue victims of the Nazis

Warsaw ghetto: one of the rare places where Jews offered armed
  resistance to the Nazis
Wehrmacht: joint armed forces of Germany in the Second World War
World Jewish Congress: international Zionist federation of Jewish
  organisations
yeshiva: rabbinic academy
Yishuv: Jewish population of Palestine
Yom Kippur: Day of Atonement
Zählappell: roll call

Notes

Chapter One

1. For some helpful additions to my own memories I am indebted to Yizkor Books Online: *Margitta*.

Chapter Two

1. The definitive history of the Holocaust in Hungary is Randolph Braham's monumental *The Politics of Genocide: The Holocaust in Hungary* (1994). The quotation is from p 1. Concise studies of the same events are Braham, 1997 and Braham, 1998. In the updated edition of Raul Hilberg's seminal *The Destruction of the European Jews* (2003) the fate of the Hungarian Jews is discussed in Vol. II, pp. 853–919. An important German contribution is Gerlach and Aly, pp. 7–114. A Hungarian view is found in Szita, pp. 19–55.
2. Braham, 1997, p. 39–40.

Chapter Three

1. For a more detailed description of the Kolozsvár ghetto see Löwy, pp. 185–92.
2. Löwy, p. 325.
3. Hatvan éve.

Chapter Four

1. A fairly comprehensive picture of the events can be gained by studying Kasztner's own *Bericht* in conjunction with the reminiscences of other actors, such as Joel Brand, Hansi Brand and Endre Biss, the recollections of survivors, and historical studies, notably by Yehuda Bauer, Randolph Braham, Shlomo Aronson and Szabolcs Szita. For the group's work in this period see Kasztner, *Bericht*, pp. 31–87; Weissberg, pp. 15–82; Brand, Hansi, testimony; Brand, Joel, testimony; Biss, pp. 1–3, 24–39; Braham, 1994, pp. 1069–78; Bauer, 1994, pp. 151–63; Aronson, pp. 88–96, 170–80; Szita, pp. 1–17, 57–63.
2. Quoted in Gerlach and Aly, pp. 7–8.
3. Kasztner, *Bericht*, p. 71.
4. Kasztner, *Bericht*, p. 72.
5. Kasztner, *Bericht*, p. 73.
6. Kasztner, *Bericht*, p. 77.
7. Kasztner, *Bericht*, p. 83.
8. Kasztner, *Bericht*, p. 84.
9. Kasztner, *Bericht*, p. 85.

Chapter Five

1. Brand's recollections were written down by Alex Weissberg and first published in German. My quotations are from the British edition, sometimes amended with reference to the German. For further details on the Brand mission see Weissberg, pp. 83–185; Brand, Joel, 1961; Brand, Hansi, 1961; Kasztner, *Bericht*, pp. 87–96; Biss, pp. 39–43; Braham, 1994, pp. 1078–88; Bauer, 1994, pp. 152–95; Aronson, pp. 227–61; Szita, pp. 76–87; Cesarani, 2005, pp. 173–81.
2. Weissberg, pp. 85–6.
3. Weissberg, pp. 85–6.
4. Weissberg, pp. 86–7.
5. Weissberg, p. 95.

6. Weissberg, pp. 95–6.

7. Kasztner, *Bericht*, p. 93.

8. Weissberg, pp. 107–8.

9. Brand, Hansi, 1961.

10. Quoted in Bauer, 1989, p. 13.

11. Quoted in Hilberg, p. 1225.

12. Quoted in Bauer, 1989, p. 11.

Chapter Six

1. Quoted in Weitz, 1995, pp. 25, 43.

2. Weissberg, p. 27.

3. Quoted in Szita, p. 147.

4. Kasztner, Susi, p. 6.

5. Pasternak Slater, p. 30.

6. Eichmann, p. 146.

7. Barzel, Shoshana, p. 4.

8. Speter, interview.

9. Quoted in Weitz, 1995, p. 302.

10. Weitz, 1995, pp. 428–9. I am grateful to Professor Weitz for giving me a copy of the unpublished English translation of his book.

11. Kasztner, *Bericht*, p. 334.

12. Kasztner, *Bericht*, p. 97.

13. Kasztner, *Bericht*, p. 101.

14. Kasztner, *Bericht*, pp. 101–3.

15. Brand, Hansi, 1961.

16. Brand, Hansi, 1961.

17. Brand, Hansi, 1961.

18. Brand, Hansi, 1961.

19. Kasztner, *Bericht*, pp. 103–4.

20. Kasztner, *Bericht*, p. 105.

21. Kasztner, *Bericht*, p. 105.

22. Kasztner, *Bericht*, p. 106.

23. Kasztner, *Bericht*, p. 107.

24. Kasztner, *Bericht*, p. 108.

25. Kasztner, *Bericht*, p. 107.

26. Kasztner, *Bericht*, p. 122.

27. Kasztner, *Bericht*, p. 111.

28. Kasztner, *Bericht*, p. 113.

29. Quoted in Pasternak Slater, p. 13.

30. Brand, Hansi, 1961.

31. Kasztner, *Bericht*, pp. 130–2.

32. Kasztner, *Bericht*, p. 131.

33. Kasztner, *Bericht*, p. 145. For further details of the parachutist affair see Braham, 1994, pp. 1130–2; Bauer, 1994, pp. 215–16; Pasternak Slater, p. 17; Szita, pp. 77–8.

34. Kasztner, *Bericht*, p. 144; letter to Hillel Danzig, 6 February 1946, supplied by Yitzhak Katzir.

35. Kasztner, *Bericht*, p. 145.

36. Brand, Hansi, 1961.

37. Biss, p. 68.

38. Quoted in Fischer, 'Változatok'.

39. Fischer, 'Változatok'; Karsai and Molnár, 'Kasztner'.

40. Hilberg, p. 906; Bauer, 1994, p. 201.

41. Aronson, pp. 276–7.

42. Kasztner, *Bericht*, pp. 118–19.

43. Kasztner, *Bericht*, p. 119.

Chapter Seven

1. Jacobs, interview.

2. John-Steiner, interview.

3. Herskovitz, p 11.

4. Brief, interview.

5. Hasson, pp. 3–4.

6. Anon., p 5.

7. Buck, p 1.

8. Stern, interview.

9. Unbekannt, p. 2.

10. Jungreis, interview.

11. Revesz, interview.

12. John-Steiner, interview.

13. Herskovitz, pp. 12–13.

14. Devecseri, Szidonia, p. 3.

15. Buck, p. 1.

16. Buck, p. 2.

17. For the history of Bergen-Belsen, see Kolb, Eberhard 2002; Keller, 2002; Wenck, 2000; Reilly, 1997.

18. See e.g. Kolb, Eberhard, pp. 27–86; Keller, pp. 164–5; Reilly, pp. 45–59.

19. Quoted in Philips, pp. 31–2.

20. Quoted in Kemp, pp. 136–7.

21. Anon., p. 9.

22. Jacobs, interview.

23. Jacobs, interview.

24. Unbekannt, p. 2.

25. Goldstein, p. 11.

26. Goldstein, p. 12.

27. Buck, p. 4.

28. See Kasztner, *Bericht*, pp. 133–4; Kolb, Jenő 2–4 August; Wenck, p. 297. Kolb, Eberhard, p. 72 cites 1,683 and Szita, p. 91, between 1,683 and 1,685.

29. Pasternak Slater, pp. 13–14, from *KasztnerMemorial.com* website.

30. Ladány, p. 38.

31. Kolb, Jenő, 10 July. The diary of Jenő Kolb is the most important document of the group actually produced in the camp. Kolb was not only an acute observer but also an active participant in many of the events he records. The immediacy and wealth of detail make his diary an indispensable record of our everyday

lives. Historical studies of the group in Bergen-Belsen in particular are those of Thomas Rahe and Alexandra Wenck.

32. Rahe,1994, pp. 5–6.
33. Pasternak Slater, p. 13.
34. Mayer, *KasztnerMemorial.com*.
35. Pasternak Slater, pp. 13–15.
36. Kolb, Jenő, 2–4 August.
37. Anon., p. 10.
38. Unbekannt, p. 2.
39. Buck, p. 4.
40. Heilper, p. 20.
41. Adler, Tiborné, p. 9.

Chapter Eight
1. Anon., p. 12.
2. Brief, interview.
3. Goldstein, pp. 12–13
4. Kolb, Jenő, 11 and 21 November.
5. Devecseri, Szidonia, p. 37.
6. Ladány, p. 38.
7. Anon., pp. 11-12.
8. Hendell, interview.
9. Hersch, interview.
10. Munk, interview.
11. Goldstein, p 13.
12. Anon., p 23.
13. Kolb, Jenő, 18 July.
14. Gross, interview.
15. Anon., p 21.
16. Stern, interview.
17. Kolb, Jenő, 30–31 October.
18. Mandel, interview.
19. Buck, pp. 10–11.

20. Kolb, Jenő, 10 July, 6; 10–11, 28–30 August; 3–4, 13–20 September.

21. Devecseri, Szidonia, p. 4.

22. Kolb, Jenő, 6 October.

23. Anon., p. 18.

24. Kolb, Jenő, 25 July.

25. Jacobs, interview.

26. Jacobs, interview.

27. Munk, interview.

28. Kohn, p. 6.

29. Three deaths and eight births are recorded by Kasztner, *Bericht*, p. 252.

30. Kolb, Jenő, 12–13 August.

31. Kolb, Jenő, 6 October.

32. See Wiehn, p. 285.

33. Berger, pp. 14–15.

34. Buck, pp. 13–15.

35. Szondi-Radványi, p. 47.

36. Kolb, Jenő, 28 November.

37. Tábori Szervezeti Szabályzat.

38. Kolb, Jenő, 18 November.

39. Anon., p. 11.

40. Kolb, Jenő, 13, 27 November.

41. Kolb, Jenő, 1 December.

42. Adler, Hermann, p. 1.

43. Kolb, Jenő, 2–4 August.

44. Goldstein, p. 25.

45. Bishop, interview.

46. Kolb, Jenő, 8 November.

47. Adler, Hermann, p. 15.

48. Kolb, Jenő, 16–21 October.

49. Goldstein, pp. 14–15.

50. Kolb, Jenő, 28, 30 July.

51. Kolb, Jenő, 7–12 September.

52. Kolb, Jenő, 11 October.

53. Kolb, Jenő, 8 November.

54. Devecseri, Szidonia, p. 8.

55. Kolb, Jenő, 24 July.

56. Szondi-Radványi, pp. 49–50.

57. Kolb, Jenő, 8–9 November.

58. Hendell, interview.

59. Gross, interview.

60. Kolb, Jenő, 31 July.

61. Adler, Hermann, p. 15.

62. John-Steiner, interview.

63. Kolb, Jenő, 17–20 September.

64. Anon., p. 24.

65. Jungreis, Ester, interview.

66. Kolb, Jenő, 15, 19–21.

67. Kolb, Jenő, 2–4 August.

68. Kolb, Jenő, 8–10 October.

69. Kolb, Jenő, 12 October, 14–15 November.

70. Blum, 1997, p. 18.

71. Kolb, Jenő, 20 August.

72. Blum, 1997, p. 20.

73. Gross, interview.

74. Kolb, Jenő, 8–10 October.

75. Kolb, Jenő, 23 July.

76. Kolb, Jenő, 2–4 August.

77. Kolb, Jenő, 6 October.

78. Kolb, Jenő, 14–15 October.

79. Gador, p. 7.

80. Devecseri, Szidonia, testimony, p. 6.

81. Jacobs, interview.

82. Gross, interview.

83. Buck, p. 13.

84. Jacobs, interview.

85. Buck, p. 5.

86. Kolb, Jenö, 3 November.

87. Cohen, Eliezer, interview.

88. Goldstein, p. 27.

89. Unbekannt, p. 3.

90. Kolb, Jenö, 13–20 September.

91. Kolb, Jenö, 23–25 October.

92. Hendell, interview.

93. Blum, 1997, p. 16.

94. Kasztner, *Bericht*, pp 162–3.

95. Anon., p. 15.

96. Blum, 'Erinnerungen', p. 13.

97. Buck, p. 8.

98. Kohn, p. 6.

99. Devecseri, Szidonia, p. 4.

100. Both letters were supplied by Kasztner's daughter Zsuzsi. On 22 July 2007 all the documents in Zsuzsi Kasztner 's possession were handed over to Yad Vashem.

Chapter Nine

1. Quoted in Braham, 1994, pp. 914–15.

2. Kasztner, *Bericht*, pp. 176–7.

3. For further details of the negotiations described in this chapter see Kasztner, *Bericht*, pp. 146–246; Biss, pp. 71–103; McClelland, 1982; Bauer, 1994, pp. 196–238; Bauer, 1977; Bauer, 1997; Braham, 1994, pp. 1088–101.

4. Kasztner, *Bericht*, p. 149.

5. Biss, p. 91.

6. Quoted in Bauer, 1994, p. 196.

7. Kasztner, diary notes.

8. Lulay, Nyilatkozat.

9. Kasztner, *Bericht*, p. 154–5.

10. Kasztner, *Bericht*, p. 157.

11. Kasztner, *Bericht*, p. 157.

12. Brand, Hansi, Testimony.

13. Kasztner, *Bericht*, pp. 151–2.

14. McClelland, 'Report', p. 46.

15. Bauer, 1994, p. 195.

16. Quoted in Bauer, 1994, p. 217.

17. Kasztner, *Bericht*, p. 170.

18. Kasztner, 'Diary notes'.

19. Kasztner, *Bericht*, p. 173.

20. Kasztner, *Bericht*, p. 175.

21. Quoted in Dinur, pp. 58–60.

22. Quoted in Dinur, p. 62.

23. Emmenegger, part 13.

24. Quoted in Dinur, p. 60.

25. Bauer, 1994, p. 221.

26. Kasztner, *Bericht*, p. 193.

27. Kasztner, *Bericht*, p. 178.

28. Kasztner, *Bericht*, p. 179.

29. Kasztner, *Bericht*, p. 187.

30. Supplied by Zsuzsi Kasztner.

31. Kasztner, *Bericht*, p. 205.

32. Kasztner, *Bericht*, p. 208.

33. Bauer, 1994, p. 226.

34. Kasztner, *Bericht*, p. 209.

35. Kasztner, *Bericht*, p. 210.

36. Quoted in Braham, 1994, p. 1098.

37. Kasztner, *Bericht*, p. 211.

38. Kasztner, *Bericht*, p. 211.

39. Kasztner, *Bericht*, p. 217.

40. Kasztner, *Bericht*, pp. 236–7.

41. Kasztner, *Bericht*, p. 234.

42. Kasztner, *Bericht*, p. 235.

43. Bauer, 1994, p. 228.
44. Kasztner, *Bericht*, p. 243.
45. Kasztner, *Bericht*, p. 244.
46. Kasztner, *Bericht*, p. 245.
47. Kasztner, *Bericht*, p. 241.
48. Kasztner, *Bericht*, p. 243.
49. Kasztner, *Bericht*, p. 250.
50. Kasztner, *Bericht*, p. 251.
51. Letter supplied by Zsuzsi Kasztner.
52. Letter supplied by Zsuzsi Kasztner.
53. Kasztner, *Bericht*, pp. 252–3.
54. 27 December 1944, supplied by Zsuzsi Kasztner.

Chapter Ten

1. Buck, p. 15. For further details of our last months in Bergen-Belsen and our journey to Switzerland see mainly Kolb, Jenő, November–December; Anon., pp. 27–32; Blum, 1997, pp. 21–3; Blum, 2003, pp. 15–18; Buck, pp. 15–18; Hasson, pp. 6–7; Kohn, pp. 6–7; Zsolt, pp. 381–400; Rahe, 'Kasztner-Gruppe', p. 21; Wenck, pp. 333–5.
2. Anon., p. 28.
3. Kolb, Jenő, 13 November.
4. Kolb, Jenő, 18 November.
5. Kolb, Jenő, 22 November.
6. Letters supplied by Zsuzsi Kasztner.
7. Kolb, Jenő, 24 November.
8. Kolb, Jenő, 26 November.
9. Kolb, Jenő, 27 November.
10. Kolb, Jenő, 28 November.
11. Kolb, Jenő, 1 December.
12. Hasson, p. 6.
13. Kasztner, *Bericht*, pp. 133–4.
14. See, for example, Kolb, Jenő, 10 July, 2–4 August. One list,

probably prepared in Bergen-Belsen soon after our arrival contains 1680 names on 42 pages, and ends with Tova Wullkan. In the absence of names beginning with Z, I suspect that a page 43, which probably contained four names, is missing.

15. Kasztner, *Bericht*, pp. 172, 252–3.
16. Kolb, Jenő, 3 December.
17. Kohn, Jenő, pp. 6–7.
18. Kolb, 4 December.
19. Buck, p. 17.
20. Zsolt, pp. 391, 394. The second part was too incomplete to be included in my English translation of this book.
21. Zsolt, p. 394.
22. Zsolt, pp. 382–3.
23. Kolb, Jenő, 6 December.
24. Buck, pp. 17–18.
25. Kolb, Jenő, 7 December.
26. Bielik, interview.
27. Buck, quoted in Rahe, 'Kasztner-Gruppe', p. 22.

Chapter Eleven
1. For further details see Kasztner, *Bericht* pp. 262–329; Biss, pp. 150–214; Bauer, 1994, pp. 222–51; Wenck, pp. 361–82; Braham, 1994, pp. 943–1018, 1143–8; Breitman.
2. Kasztner, *Bericht*, p. 266; Biss, p. 174.
3. Kasztner, *Bericht*, p. 230.
4. Kasztner, *Bericht*, p. 256.
5. Kasztner, *Bericht*, pp. 258.
6. Kasztner, *Bericht*, pp. 279–80.
7. Kasztner, *Bericht*, p. 290.
8. Kasztner, *Bericht*, p. 292.
9. Supplied by Zsuzsi Kasztner.
10. Kasztner, *Bericht*, pp. 304–5.
11. Kasztner, *Bericht*, pp. 309–10.

12. Kasztner, *Bericht*, p. 313.
13. Kasztner, *Bericht*, p. 316.
14. Kasztner, *Bericht*, p. 319.
15. Quoted in Dinur, p. 92.
16. Kasztner, *Bericht*, p. 320.
17. Supplied by Zsuzsi Kasztner.

Chapter Twelve
1. October 1946, supplied by Zsuzsi Kasztner.
2. April 1946, supplied by Zsuzsi Kasztner.
3. Weitz, 1995, p. 45. For my discussion of Kasztner's life after the war I am greatly indebted to Professor Weitz's account.
4. Quoted in Weitz, 1995, p. 75.
5. 22 December 1945, quoted in Barri, p. 148.
6. 3 April 1946, supplied by Zsuzsi Kasztner.
7. 17 April 1946, supplied by Zsuzsi Kasztner.
8. In Central Archives, Yad Vashem.
9. 17 April 1946, supplied by Zsuzsi Kasztner.
10. February 1946, supplied by Zsuzsi Kasztner.
11. Letter of 7 December 1946, supplied by Zsuzsi Kasztner.
12. 7 December 1946, supplied by Zsuzsi Kasztner.
13. See Weitz, 1995, pp. 66–8; Bilsky, p. 119; pp. 65–8; Segev, p. 258; Szita, p. 206.
14. Szita, p. 206.
15. McClelland, 'Report,' pp. 46–7.
16. McClelland, 'Report', pp. 47–8.
17. Letter of 18 July 1946, copy in Museum of Hungarian-Speaking Jewry, Zefat.
18. 6 February 1946, copy supplied by Zsuzsi Kasztner.
19. Kasztner, affidavit, 13 September 1945, pp. 3–4.
20. 5 May 1948, quoted in Weitz, 1995, p. 87.
21. 30 April 1948, kindly supplied by Professor Victor Harnik.

22. 6 October 1946, supplied by Zsuzsi Kasztner.

23. 5 February 1947, supplied by Zsuzsi Kasztner.

24. 5 May 1948, quoted in Weitz, 1995, p. 86.

25. Kasztner, affidavit, 13 September 1945, pp. 3–4.

26. Quoted in Hecht, p. 78; amended with reference to Segev, pp. 269–70 and German translation at http://www.kokhaviv publications.com/kuckuck/feature/biss_bericht/.

27. Kasztner, Susi, pp. 10–11.

28. Biss, p. 202.

29. Emmenegger, part 13.

30. Emmenegger, part 18.

31. Quoted in Emmenegger, part 5.

32. Kasztner, *Bericht*, p. 132.

33. Bauer, 1994, p. 211.

34. Emmenegger, part 18.

35. Emmenegger, part 3.

36. Emmenegger, part 3.

37. Quoted in Mayer, 'Whose Booty', p. 11.

38. Zweig, p. 231.

39. Quoted in Emmenegger, part 2.

40. Quoted in Mendelsohn, p. 22.

41. Quoted in Hecht, p. 81.

42. Letter of 28 July 1948, supplied by Zsuzsi Kasztner.

43. Becher, testimony, part 4.

44. Emmenegger, part 5.

Chapter Thirteen

1. Letter to Chaim Posner, 11 January 1948, supplied by Zsuzi Kasztner.

2. Weitz, 1995, p. 349. The most thorough study of Kasztner's fate after the war is Weitz, 1995. Other important discussions of the trial are found in: Weitz, 'Changing conceptions'; Weitz, 'Herut Movement'; Maoz; Bilsky; Barri; Segev, Part V. Hecht's *Perfidy*

is an undisguised polemic against Kasztner and the Mapai establishment.

3. Segev, p. 256.

4. Quoted in Yablonka, p. 13.

5. Quoted in Segev, pp. 257–8.

6. Given in March 1967, quoted in Segev, p. 263.

7. Quoted in Weitz, 1995, p. 117.

8. Quoted in Weitz, 1995, p. 118.

9. Quoted in Weitz, 1995, p. 120.

10. Segev, p. 267.

11. Quoted in Hecht, p. 64.

12. Quoted in Hecht, pp. 71–2.

13. 28 July 1948.

14. Quoted in Hecht, p. 74.

15. Segev, p. 271.

16. Quoted in Weitz, 1995, p. 196.

17. Quoted in Hecht, pp. 74–5.

18. Quoted in Hecht, p. 79.

19. Weitz, 1995, p. 201.

20. Quoted in Orr, p. 103.

21. Quoted in Weitz, 1995, p. 241.

22. Quoted in Hecht, p. 82.

23. Quoted in Hecht, pp. 106–8.

24. Weitz, 1995, p. 220.

25. Quoted in Weitz 1995, p. 227.

26. Weitz 1995, p. 215.

27. Quoted in Weitz 1995, p. 208

28. Quoted in Hecht, pp. 168–73.

29. Quoted in Hecht, pp. 172–4.

30. Quoted in Hecht, p. 176.

31. Quoted in Hecht, p. 148.

32. Quoted in Weitz, 'Herut Movement', pp. 354–5.

33. Maoz, p. 584.

34. Quoted in Hecht, p. 226.

35. Quoted in Hecht, p. 144.

36. Quoted in Weitz, 1995, p. 265.

37. Quoted in Hecht, p. 170.

38. Quoted in Weitz, 1995, p. 251.

39. Maoz, p. 591; Segev, p. 282.

40. Halevi, p. 1. I quote Halevi's judgment from a 316-page German typescript, supplied by Zsuzsi Kasztner.

41. Halevi, p. 26.

42. Halevi, p. 28.

43. Halevi, p. 153.

44. Halevi, p. 89.

45. Halevi, p. 89.

46. Halevi, p. 63.

47. Halevi, p. 150.

48. Halevi, p. 140.

49. Halevi, p. 63.

50. Halevi, p. 241.

51. Halevi, p. 310.

52. Halevi, p. 313.

53. Halevi, p. 297.

54. Quoted in Weitz, 1995, p. 314.

55. Weitz, 1995, pp. 314–15.

56. Quoted in Weitz, 1995, pp. 315–17.

57. Quoted in Weitz, 1995, p. 314.

58. Quoted in Weitz, 1995, p. 320.

59. Kasztner, *Bericht*, p. 37.

60. Quoted in Weitz, 1995, p. 243.

61. Braham, 1994, p. 827.

62. John-Steiner, interview.

63. Gotthard, interview.

64. Hersch, interview.

65. Pasternak Slater, p. 24.

66. Gilbert, p. 205.

67. Quoted in Hecht, p. 261.

68. Vrba, p. 93.

69. Eichmann, p. 146.

70. 13 September 1945.

71. Arendt, p. 199.

72. Arendt, p. 42.

73. Arendt, p. 132. A similar line is adopted in a play entitled *Perdition* by Jim Allen. The first performance, scheduled in London in 1987, was prevented by Jewish protests, but there have been occasional productions in obscure small theatres since. Based on the Kasztner trial, the play repeats the old charge that the Zionists collaborated with the Nazis because they wanted to use the Holocaust as a bargaining counter in the creation of Israel. Regardless of the merits or otherwise of this thesis, the play does nothing to illuminate the story of the real Kasztner. With its gross misrepresentations of historical facts it provides welcome ammunition to anti-Semitic agitators. At the time of writing a thorough study of *Perdition* and its context was being written by Michael Ezra in London.

74. Pasternak Slater, p. 16.

75. Revesz, p. 207.

76. Revesz, p. 207.

77. Weitz, 1995, p. 82.

78. Kasztner, Zsuzsi, p. 19.

79. Speter, interview.

80. Barzel, Alexander, interview.

81. Weitz, 1995, p. 82.

82. Weitz, 1995, p. 82.

83. Quoted in Weitz, 1995, p. 81.

84. Weitz, 1995, p. 81.

85. Weitz, 1995, p. 84.

86. 26 June 1951, supplied by Zsuzsi Kasztner.

87. Barri, p. 159.

88. Quoted in Weitz, 1995, pp. 95–6.

89. 18 March 1946, supplied by Zsuzsi Kasztner.

90. 30 July 1947, supplied by Zsuzsi Kasztner.

91. Affidavit of 22 July 1947, quoted in Barri, p. 156.

92. 22 July 1944, supplied by Zsuzsi Kasztner.

93. 31 August 1944, quoted in Barri, p. 162.

94. Barri, p. 164.

95. Quoted in Orr, p. 104.

96. Barri, p. 165.

97. Quoted in Weitz, 1995, pp. 371–2.

98. Quoted in Weitz, 1995, p. 373.

99. Quoted in Maoz, p. 595.

100. Quoted in Maoz, p. 596.

101. Quoted in Hecht, p. 275.

102. Quoted in Hecht, p. 275.

103. Quoted in Hecht, pp. 270–1.

104. Quoted in Hecht, pp. 272, 275.

105. Quoted in Weitz, 1995, p. 411.

106. Quoted in Weitz, 1995, pp. 386–7.

107. Quoted in Weitz, 1995, p. 405.

108. Weitz, 1995, p. 425.

Chapter Fourteen

1. Herskovitz, interview, p. 22.

2. Katsir, p. 5.

3. Goldstein, pp. 28–9.

4. Heilper, p. 24.

5. Bauer, interview, p. 11.

6. Bauer, 1994, pp. 259–60.

7. Hilberg, p. 906.

8. Stern, interview.

Bibliography

Books and articles

Arendt, Hannah: *Eichmann in Jerusalem: A Report on the Banality of Evil*, Harmondsworth: Penguin (1964).

Aronson, Shlomo: *Hitler, the Allies, and the Jews*. Cambridge: Cambridge University Press (2004).

Barri (Ishoni), Shoshana: 'The Question of Kastner's Testimonies on Behalf of Nazi War Criminals', in: *The Journal of Israeli History*, Vol. 18, nos 2 and 3 (1997), pp. 139–65.

Bauer, Yehuda: 'The Negotiations between Saly Mayer and the Representatives of the S.S. in 1944–45', in Marrus, Michael (ed.): *The Nazi Holocaust: Historical Articles on the Destruction of European Jews*, 9. Westport, London: Meckler (1989), pp 156–96.

Bauer, Yehuda: *Jews for Sale? Nazi–Jewish Negotiations, 1933–1945*, New Haven and London: Yale University Press (1994).

Bauer, Yehuda: 'The Holocaust in Hungary: Was Rescue Possible?', in: David Cesarani (ed.): *Genocide and Rescue: The Holocaust in Hungary 1944*, Oxford: Berg (1997), pp. 193–209.

Becher, Kurt: Testimony to the Trial of Adolf Eichmann. Testimony taken abroad, 1961. www.nizkor.org/hweb/people/e/eichmann-adolf/transcripts/Testimony-Abroad/Kurt_Becher-01.html.

Bilsky, Leora: 'Judging Evil in the Trial of Kastner', in: *Law and History Review,* Spring 2001, Vol. 19, no. 1, pp. 117–60.

Biss, André: *A Million Jews to Save.* London: New English Library (1975).

Braham, Randolph L.: *The Politics of Genocide: The Holocaust in Hungary,* revised and enlarged edn, New York: Columbia University Press (1994), 2 vols.

Braham, Randolph L.: 'The Holocaust in Hungary: A Retrospective Analysis', in: David Cesarani (ed.): *Genocide and Rescue. The Holocaust in Hungary 1944,* Oxford: Berg (1997), pp. 29–46.

Braham, Randolph L.: 'The Holocaust in Hungary', in: Randolph L Braham with Scott Miller (eds): *The Nazis' Last Victims: The Holocaust in Hungary,* Detroit: Wayne State UP (1998), pp. 27–43.

Brand, Hansi: Testimony to Trial of Adolf Eichmann, session 58–9. Record of Proceedings in the District Court of Jerusalem, 1961. www.nizkor.org/hweb/people/e/eichmann-adolf/transcripts/.

Brand, Joel: Testimony to Trial of Adolf Eichmann, session 56. Record of Proceedings in the District Court of Jerusalem, 1961. www.nizkor.org/hweb/people/e/eichmann-adolf/transcripts/.

Breitman, Richard: 'Himmler and Bergen-Belsen', in: Reilly, Jo et al. (eds): *Belsen in History and Memory,* London: Frank Cass (1997), pp. 72–84.

Cesarani, David: *Eichmann. His Life and Crimes,* London: Vintage (2005).

Dinur, Dov: *Kasztner: Leader or Villain.* Haifa: Gestlit (1987). In Hebrew.

Eichmann, Adolf: 'The Confession of Adolf Eichmann', in: *Life,* Vol. 49, No. 22–3, 28 November – 5 December 1960, pp. 21–161.

Fischer, István: 'Változatok pár ezer zsidóra' [Variations on a few thousand Jews], in: *Élet és irodalom,* 48/18, www.es.hu/pd/display.asp?channel=AGORA0418.

Fischer, István: 'Legendák és történelem' [Legends and history], in: *Élet és irodalom,* 48/28, www.es.hu/up/printable.asp?channel=AGORA0428&article=2004-0712-0951-28BKCG.

Fischer, István: 'Ki volt a gyilkos?' [Who was the assassin?], in: *Élet és irodalom*, 51/46, http://www.es.hu/pd/display.asp?channel=AGORA0646&article=2006-1119-2021-36THEP.

Emmenegger, Kurt: 'Reichsführers gehorsamster Becher. Vom SS-Mann zum Multimillionär – und was alles dahinter steckt' [Reichsführer's most obedient Becher. From SS soldier to multimillionnaire – and whatever is behind it], in: *Sie + Er*, Zofingen: Ringier, December 1962 – April 1963.

Gerlach, Christian and Aly, Götz: *Das letzte Kapitel. Realpolitik, Ideologie und der Mord an den ungarischen Juden 1944/1945* [The last chapter. Realpolitik, Ideology and the murder of Hungarian Jews 1944/1945], Stuttgart and Munich: Deutsche Verlags-Anstalt (2002).

Gilbert, Martin: *Auschwitz and the Allies*, London: Michael Joseph (1981).

'Hatvan éve. Légitámadás Kolozsvár ellen.' [Sixty years ago. Air raid on Kolozsvár], in: *Szabadság. Kolozsvári Közéleti Napilap*. http://www.hhrf.org/szabadsag/archivum/2004/06/4jun-02.htm#E13E74.

Hegyi, Ágnes: 'Információáramlás az információkorlatozás idején a holokauszt erdélyi dokumentumai alapján' [Flow of information at the time of restrictions on information, based on documents of the Holocaust in Transylvania] Erdélyi magyar adatbank. http://adatbank.transindex.ro/inchtm.php?kod=310.

Hecht, Ben: *Perfidy*, Jerusalem: Gefen (1999).

Hilberg, Raul: *The Destruction of the European Jews*, 3rd edn, New Haven and London: Yale University Press. (2003), 3 vols.

Kádár, Gábor and Vági, Zoltán: *Aranyvonat:Fejezetek a zsidó vagyon történetéből*. Budapest: Osiris (2001). English edition *Self-financing Genocide: The Gold Train*. Budapest: Central European University Press (2004).

Kádár, Gábor and Vági, Zoltán: *Hullarablás: A magyar zsidók gazdasági megsemmisítése* [Robbing dead bodies: the economic annihilation of Hungarian Jewry]. Budapest: Hannah Arendt Egyesület (2005).

Karsai, László and Molnár, Judit: 'Kasztner Rezső – hős vagy áruló?' [Rezső Kasztner – hero or traitor?], in: *Élet és irodalom*, 48/20, www.es.hu/pd/display.asp?channel=AGORA0420&article=2004-0517-1027-41IUJY.

Kasztner, Rezső: *Der Kastner-Bericht über Eichmanns Menschenhandel in Ungarn*. Munich: Kindler (1961).

Keller, Rolf *et al.* (eds): *Konzentrationslager Bergen-Belsen. Berichte und Dokumente* [Concentration camp Bergen-Belsen. Reports and Documents], 2nd edn. Göttingen: Vandenhoeck & Ruprecht (2002).

Kemp, Paul: 'The British Army and the Liberation of Bergen-Belsen, April 1945', in: Reilly, Jo *et al.* (eds): *Belsen in History and Memory*, London: Frank Cass (1997), pp. 134–48.

Kolb, Eberhard: *Bergen-Belsen. Vom 'Aufenthaltslager' zum 'Konzentrationslager', 1943–1945*. [Bergen-Belsen. From 'detention camp' to 'concentration camp'], 6th edn. Göttingen: Vandenhoeck & Ruprecht (2002).

Komoly, Ottó: *The Diary of Ottó Komoly: August 21 – September 16, 1944*, in: Randolph L Braham (ed.): *Hungarian-Jewish Studies*, vol, III. New York: World Federation of Hungarian Jews (1973).

Last Train from Budapest, in: Secret History series, broadcast on Channel 4 television, 24 August 2000.

Löwy, Daniel: *A Kálváriától a tragédiáig. Kolozsvár zsidó lakosságának története.* [From calvary to tragedy. The history of the Jewish population of Kolozsvár], Kolozsvár: Koinónia (2005).

Maoz, Asher: 'Historical Adjudication: Courts of Law, Commissions of Inquiry, and "Historical Truth"', in: *Law and History Review*, Vol. 18, no. 3 (2000), pp. 559–606.

Mayer, Egon: *KasztnerMemorial.Com*. Website http://www.kasztner-memorial.com/.

McClelland, Roswell: 'Report on the activities of the World Refugee Board', in: Mendelsohn, John and Detwiler, Donald S. (eds): *The Holocaust*, New York: Garland (1982), Vol. 16, pp. 37–53.

Mendelsohn, John and Detwiler, Donald S. (eds): *The Holocaust*, New York: Garland (1982), Vol. 16.

Müller-Tupath, Karla: *Reichsführers gehorsamster Becher. Eine deutsche Karriere* [Reichsführer's most obedient Becher. A German career], Hamburg: Konkret (1982).

Nagy, Sz Péter: A Kasztner Akció 1944 [The Kasztner enterprise], Budapest: Rejtjel (1995).

Orr, Akiva: 'The Kastner Case, Jerusalem 1955', in: Allen, Jim: *Perdition*, London: Ithaca Press (1987), pp. 81–105.

Pasternak Slater, Ann: 'Kasztner's Ark', in: *Areté* 15 (Autumn 2004), pp. 5–40.

Philips, Raymond (ed): *Trial of Josef Kramer and Forty-Four Others (The Belsen Trial)*, London: William Hodge (1949).

Porat, Dina: *The Blue and the Yellow Stars of David, The Zionist Leadership and the Holocaust, 1939–1945*. Cambridge, Mass: Harvard University Press (1990).

Porter, Anna: *Kasztner's Train. The True Story of Rezső Kasztner, Unknown Hero of the Holocaust*. Vancouver/Toronto: Douglas & McIntyre (2007).

Rahe, Thomas: 'Kultur im KZ. Musik, Literatur und Kunst in Bergen-Belsen' [Culture in the concentration camp. Musik, literature and art in Bergen-Belsen], in: Füllberg-Stolberg, Claus *et al.* (eds): *Frauen in Konzentrationslagern* [Women in concentration camps], Bremen: Temmen (1994), pp. 193–206.

Rahe, Thomas: 'Die "Kasztner-Gruppe" im Konzentrationslager Bergen-Belsen: soziale Struktur, Lebensbedingungen und Verhaltensformen' [The 'Kasztner group' in the concentration camp of Bergen-Belsen: social structure, living conditions and forms of behaviour], (unpublished manuscript).

Reilly, Jo *et al.* (eds): *Belsen in History and Memory*, London: Frank Cass, (1997).

Schiller, József: *A strasshofi mentőakció és előzményei* [The Strasshof rescue mission and its antecedents]. Budapest: Cserépfalvi (1996).

Segev, Tom: *The Seventh Million: The Israelis and the Holocaust*, New York: Holt (1991).

Szita, Szabolcs: *Trading in Lives? Operations of the Jewish Relief and Rescue Committee in Budapest, 1944–1945*. Budapest and New York: Central European University Press (2005). Hungarian edition: *Aki egy embert megment, a világot menti meg: Mentőbizottság, Kasztner Rezső, SS-embervásár, 1944–1945*. Budapest: Corvina (2005).

Szondi-Radványi, Lili: 'Ein Tag in Bergen-Belsen' [A day in Bergen-Belsen], in: *Leopold Szondi. Zum 100. Geburtstag*. Szondiana Sonderheft 2/1993, pp. 43–60.

Vrba, Rudolf: 'Preparations for the Holocaust in Hungary. An Eyewitness Account', in: Braham, Randolph L (ed): *The Nazis' Last Victims. The Holocaust in Hungary*, Detroit: Wayne State University Press (1998), pp 55–101.

Wasserstein, Bernard: *Britain and the Jews of Europe. 1939–1945*, 2nd edn, London and New York: Leicester University Press, (1999).

Weissberg, Alex: *Advocate for the Dead. The Story of Joel Brand*. Translated by Constantine Fitzgibbon and Andrew Foster-Melliar. London: André Deutsch (1958). German edition: *Die Geschichte von Joel Brand*, Berlin: Kiepenheuer & Witsch (1956).

Weitz, Yechiam: 'Changing Conceptions of the Holocaust', in: *Studies in Contemporary Jewry* (1994), pp. 211–30.

Weitz, Yechiam: 'The Herut Movement and the Kasztner Trial', in: *Holocaust and Genocide Studies*, Vol. 8, no. 3 (1994), pp. 349–71.

Weitz, Yechiam: *The Man who Was Murdered Twice. The Life, Trial and Death of Dr Israel Kastner*. Hebrew original Jerusalem: Kettner (1995). Translated by Chaya Naor, unpublished manuscript.

Wenck, Alexandra-Eileen: *Zwischen Menschenhandel und 'Endlösung': Das Konzentrationslager Bergen-Belsen* [Between trade in humans and the 'final solution': the concentration camp of Bergen-Belsen], Paderborn: Schöningh (2000).

Wiehn, Erhard and Wiehn, Heide: 'Gespräche mit Alexander Barzel' [Conversations with Alexander Barzel], in: *Dajenu. Tagebuch einer Israelreise* [Dajenu. Diary of a journey to Israel], Konstanz: Hartung-Gorre (1987), pp. 214–37, 284–91.

Yablonka, Hana: 'The Development of Holocaust Consciousness in Israel: The Nuremberg, Kapos, Kastner and Eichmann Trials', in: *Israel Studies* Vol. 8, no. 3 (2003), pp. 1–24.

Yizkor Books Online: *Margitta,* http://yizkor.nypl.org/index.php?id =2419.

Yizkor Books Online: *Kolozsvár,* http://yizkor.nypl.org/index.php?id =1880.

Zweig, Ronald: *The Gold Train. The Destruction of the Jews and the Second World War's Most Terrible Robbery,* Harmondsworth: Penguin (2003).

Zsolt, Béla: *Kilenc koffer,* Budapest: Magvető (1980). English translation by Ladislaus Löb: *Nine Suitcases,* London and New York: Jonathan Cape, Schocken Books (2004).

Unpublished memoirs, interviews and testimonies

Adler, Hermann: Interview with Alexandra Wenck, 26. 3. 1992, Bergen-Belsen Memorial.

Adler, Tiborné: No title, January–August 1945, Memorial Museum of Hungarian Speaking Jewry, Zefat, and Bergen-Belsen Memorial.

Anon.: 'Die Deportation nach Bergen-Belsen' [Deportation to Bergen-Belsen], Archives of the YIVO Institute for Jewish Research (New York), and Bergen-Belsen Memorial.

Barzel, Alexander: Testimony, 1994, Bergen-Belsen Memorial.

Barzel, Alexander: Interview with Bertram von Boxberg, Bergen-Belsen Memorial.

Barzel, Shoshana: Testimony, 3. 8. 1993, Yad Vashem and Bergen-Belsen Memorial.

Bauer, Yehuda: Interview with Bertram von Boxberg, Bergen-Belsen Memorial.

Berger, Joseph: Interview with Dana L. Kline, 20 August 1981, Center for Oral History, University of Connecticut, and Bergen-Belsen Memorial.

Bielik, Tibor: Interview with Rosemary Block, 10 March 1995, Shoah Foundation.

Bishop, George: Interview with Dana Schwartz, 25 October 2000, Shoah Foundation.

Blum, Yehuda: Interview with Thomas Rahe, 1. 6. 1997, Bergen-Belsen Memorial.

Blum, Yehuda: 'Erinnerungen an das Konzentrationslager Bergen-Belsen' [Memories of the concentration camp of Bergen-Belsen]. Talk given on 22 June 2003 at the Bergen-Belsen Memorial.

Brief, George: Interview with Kenneth Aran, 2 November 1997, Shoah Foundation.

Buck, Miriam: 'Aufzeichnungen' [Notes], 1945, Yad Vashem, and Bergen-Belsen Memorial.

Cohen, Eliezer: Interview with Hans-Jürgen Hermel, 5 December 2002, Bergen-Belsen Memorial.

Devecseri, Szidonia: 'Unser Schicksal. Tagebuch' [Our destiny. Diary], Yad Vashem, and Bergen-Belsen Memorial.

Devecseri, Emil and Szidonia: Testimony, Yad Vashem 25 July 1960, Yad Vashem, and Bergen-Belsen Memorial.

Gador, Blanka: Manuscript, Bergen-Belsen Memorial.

Goldstein, Edit: Interview with Bertram von Boxberg, Bergen-Belsen Memorial.

Gotthard, Martha: Interview with Doris Stecklow, 20 March 1997, Shoah Foundation.

Gross, Jack: Interview with David Brotsky, 9 November 1997, Shoah Foundation.

Hasson, Shoshana: Testimony, 6. 2. 1966, Yad Vashem and Bergen-Belsen Memorial.

Heilper, Ervin: Interview with Bertram von Boxberg, Bergen-Belsen Memorial.

Hendell, Ági: Interview with Elisabeth Pozzithanner, 5 May 1996, Shoah Foundation.

Hersch, Ben: Interview with Margaret Holding, 8 July 1997, Shoah Foundation.

Herskovitz, Naomi: Interview with Bertram von Boxberg, Bergen-Belsen Memorial.

Jacobs, Judy: Interview, 1 April 1966, Shoah Foundation.

John-Steiner, Vera: Interview with Hilary Helstein, 18 November 1988, Shoah Foundation.

Jungreis, Esther: Interview with Rachel Reis-Gruenwald, 9 January 1995, Shoah Foundation.

Kasztner, Rezső: Diary notes, Memorial Museum of Hungarian Speaking Jewry, Zefat.

Kasztner, Susi: Interview with Bertram von Boxberg, Bergen-Belsen Memorial.

Katsir, Yitzhak: Interview with Bertram von Boxberg, Bergen-Belsen Memorial.

Kohn, Georg: 'Életem története' [The story of my life], unpublished manuscript, supplied by the writer.

Kolb, Jenő (Eugen): 'Tagebuch' [Diary]. Kindly supplied by Shoshana Hasson, the diarist's daughter.

Ladany, Shaul P: The King of the Road, manuscript, Bergen-Belsen Memorial.

List of inmates, prepared in Bergen-Belsen on arrival of Kasztner group, Yad Vashem and Bergen-Belsen Memorial.

List of inmates released to Switzerland in December 1944, Yad Vashem and Bergen-Belsen Memorial.

Lulay, Leo: 'Nyilatkozat' [Statement], 1961, Yad Vashem.

Mandel, Emanuel: Interview with Esther Funder, 20 June 1997, Shoah Foundation.

Mayer, Egon: 'Last Chance: The Tragedy of the Kasztner Rescue of Hungarian Jewry', unfinished manuscript.

Mayer, Egon: 'Whose Booty Did German Plunder Become?', unfinished manuscript.

Mayer, Egon: 'A Tale of Two Lists. Reflections on the Ethical Dilemmas of Group Rescue', unfinished manuscript.

Mayer, Eugene: Interview with Judy Offen, 19 December 1976, Shoah Foundation.

Munk, Olga: Interview with Judy Breuer, 31 July 1996, Shoah Foundation.

Revesz, George: Interview with Len Getz, 30 December 1996, Shoah Foundation.

Revesz, Peretz: Autobiographical fragment, Bergen-Belsen Memorial.

Speter, Eva: Interview with Shelly Roberts, 26 July 1996. Shoah Foundation.

Stern, William: Interview with Israel Abelis, 23 July 1997, Shoah Foundation.

Széder Hamachane /Táborrend/ [Camp rules], Yad Vashem and Memorial Museum of Hungarian Speaking Jewry, Zefat.

Tábori Szervezeti Szábályzat [Camp Organisation], Yad Vashem and Memorial Museum of Hungarian Speaking Jewry, Zefat.

Unbekannt (unknown): Letter signed Willy, 1954, Yad Vashem and Bergen-Belsen Memorial.

Utasitás [Instructions], Yad Vashem and Memorial Museum of Hungarian Speaking Jewry, Zefat.

Index